ORGANIZATIONAL COMMUNICATION 1977:
ABSTRACTS, ANALYSIS, AND OVERVIEW

Howard H. Greenbaum
Hofstra University

Raymond L. Falcione
University of Maryland

Research Assistant

Joseph Walter, Hofstra University

Contributors

Robert Carter, General Motors Institute
John Daly, University of Texas
Cal Downs, University of Kansas
Mark Hickson III, Mississippi State University
Charles Tardy, University of Iowa

Special acknowledgement and thanks to the following University of Maryland graduate students: Paula Alicandro, Sharon Cefaly, Gary Hattal, Joan Marzitelli, Paul Noga, Inge Orendt, Liz Shirai.

A Joint Publication of the
American Business Communication Association, Champaign, Illinois
International Communication Association, Austin, Texas

April 1979

First Printing, April 1979
Printed in the United States of America
ISSN 0149-1644
ISBN 0-931874-08-4

Table of Contents

APPENDICES:

Foreword

The objectives of this volume are threefold: (1) to provide a general structure for students, scholars, and practitioners to obtain comprehensive information on recently published and unpublished literature in and related to the field of organizational communication, (2) to continue to develop a classification system for the literature of interest to the field of organizational communication, and (3) to provide abstracts of that literature for the year 1977 in the form of classified and annotated bibliographies.

In addition to the abstracts, the presentation includes an overview chapter that comments on the nature of the literature written in the year 1977, furnishing a considerable subclassification system for each of the nine major categories of organizational communication in this volume. Following the main body of the book, consisting of the abstracts, will be found an appendix concerned with research methods and limitations, and three indexes: (1) author, (2) type of organizations involved in the field studies, and (3) data collection instruments utilized in field studies.

The abstracts are divided into nine classifications and each classification is further divided into two subclassifications: (1) books and dissertations, and (2) articles, papers, and U.S. Government publications. The major classification, Texts, Anthologies, Reviews, and Bibliographies, is an exception to this treatment; as this classification combines books and articles when presenting Reviews and Bibliographies.

As in last year's book, this volume is intended to enable the reader to obtain more information and to minimize the time investment in doing so:

1. The depth of the literature search has been increased by adding the doctoral dissertations written in the field of industrial and social psychology, and by screening the book review sections of leading periodicals to a much greater extent than in earlier volumes.

2. The coding for research characteristics of each writing, included in *Organizational Communication Abstracts 1974*, but omitted in *Organizational Communication Abstracts 1975*, has been restored. It was decided that the coding

of FS (field study), PD (prescriptive/descriptive writing), TC (Theoretical/Conceptual writing), and LS (laboratory study) did have utility, especially in view of the new indexes relating to field studies.

3. Cross-referencing has been provided in those cases where one piece of literature related to more than one of the nine major classifications.

4. Two recent indexes have been included that are intended to allow the reader fuller understanding of field studies. One index groups the field studies in terms of the organization-type in which the research was conducted; and the other index indentifies the data collection instruments employed in the field studies.

5. We have again undertaken the challenging job of furnishing an annual overview of the literature as presented by the abstracts.

This project has been supported by the officers and directors of the American Business Communication Association and the International Communication Association, and we sincerely thank them.

In particular, we would like to dedicate this volume to the late Robert J. Kibler, past president of ICA. Dr. Kibler was an inspiration to all who knew him. He was an outstanding scholar and a true gentleman. We will miss him.

Howard H. Greenbaum
Raymond L. Falcione

chapter 1

Introduction

NEED FOR AN ORGANIZED KNOWLEDGE BASE

Gieselman (1977) has indicated that, on the one hand, communication research has a jungle of unrelated concepts, and on the other hand, a mass of undigested, often sterile, empirical data; that researchers need shared paradigms to help channel and coordinate efforts; and that analyzing, classifying, and reclassifying may be a procedural direction to achieve some order, some understanding of the state of the art so as to know better how to channel our research activity.[1]

This recent comment by Gieselman, in respect to organizational communication is somewhat similar to the reasoning given by McGrath and Altman (1966) relative to the field of small-group research,—viz., that we already had accumulated an enormous pool of facts about small group behavior and that the time had come to organize this knowledge so that we could see what we did know and what we did not know about small groups. Their volume summarized a classification system for organizing and synthesizing small-group research information, applied that classification system to small-group studies, and presented insights and impressions gained about small-group research, small-group researchers, and the small-group research culture.[2]

Downs (1969) was supportive of this analogy between small-group research and organizational communication research, when he stated that "organizational communication today is in a position comparable to that of group dynamics several years ago, with many short research studies, limited in scope, and no one to synthesize the results."[3] Since 1969, the most noteworthy development for the synthesis of organizational communication knowledge has been the production of textbooks, which is but a partial answer to the need for the establishment of related concepts, shared paradigms, and the construction of an organized and dynamic knowledge base.

Apparently, this kind of dissatisfaction with the state of organization of the knowledge base has occurred in many, if not all of the social sciences, physical sciences, and biological sciences. In

1967, Guetzkow commented on the state of affairs in the field of sociology, when he wrote a piece titled "Now is the Time to Consolidate"—i.e., to consolidate our knowledge about organizations —and he included the following statements, among others:[4]

   —there is a feeling that our efforts in the study of organizations are redundant and inefficient.

   —scholars accidentally repeat studies which already have been done, because of their carelessness in searching the literature.

   —consolidation will permit scholars to build more cumulatively, so that their researches are less fragmental and ephemeral.

Cullinan (1964) notes the following limitations of educational administration as a body of knowledge: 1) a heterogeneity of facts; 2) lack of common definitions and agreement upon classification; 3) lack of a consistent set of principles; and 4) both lack of interest in theory and understanding of its purpose on one hand, and anxiety and impatience to build a comprehensive and full-blown theory on the other. He notes the nature of the growth and refinement of every organized body of knowledge as proceeding from a none-too-ordered description to a system of classifications and generalizations useful in predicting future events, and taking the form of analytical models of the behavior of the elements being studied.[5] Classification is considered as a tool for theory building by organizing and integrating what is known about the area in which the theorizing activity is being conducted; and by demonstrating the voids in a body of knowlege and indicating research needed to fill the gaps.

Laufer (1968) has indicated the need for an organized framework to hold the elements in a theory of management, calling for a taxonomy of management that would ameliorate the semantic difficulties and foster a systematic grouping of interrelated principles. Laufer's taxonomy, similar to that found in the biological sciences, provides for 1) classification; 2) nomenclature; and 3) identification.[6]

Blackwelder (1967), in his definitive work on the subject of taxonomy, quotes many scientists as to the value of taxonomy as a foundation for biological science. For example, he quotes G. G. Simpson, a paleontologist, evolutionist, and systematist, as stating "it is impossible to speak of the objects of any study, or to think lucidly about them, unless they are named; and it is impossible to examine their relationships, to treat them scientifically, without putting them into some sort of formal arrangement."[7]

This need for an organized knowledge base, so evident in other disciplines, is also true of organizational communication; and this book represents a beginning approach to a gigantic project in basic research. In this field we are barely past the starting-line, and our present efforts must be considered exploratory. Refinement can come later, both from the present authors and other students who may hopefully be attracted to this area of work. We are in no position to supply an authoritative work relative to organizational communication in terms of a taxonomy, i.e., an arrangement of phenomena into classes which are hierarchically ordered, but we believe we are taking a step in that direction by our concern with classification (group-making based on relationships), nomenclature (the assignment of a distinguishing name to each group or class), and identification (the process through which the individual unit is placed in a group as a result of the recognition that it is similar to others in that group).[8]

The balance of this chapter gives attention to the following subjects: 1) Classification systems for organizational communication literature, including definitions of research method nomenclature; and 2) Identification of writings in terms of classification system groups.

CLASSIFICATION SYSTEMS

Four general types of classification systems have been employed in this volume: 1) Major literature classifications, 2) Subclassifications of each major literature group, 3) Publication format classifications, and 4) Classification by research characteristics of the written work. All of these classification systems are found in the OVERVIEW chapter immediately following; but the ABSTRACTS section employs only three of the four systems, excluding subclassifications. Each of the classification systems is described below, followed by a brief statement as to failings and shortcomings of the classification techniques employed.[9]

Classification by Major Literature Groups

The literature of organizational communication has been classified in terms of the following nine major groups: 1) Interpersonal Communication in Organizations; 2) Intragroup Communication in Organizations; 3) Intergroup Communication in Organizations; 4) Communication Factors and Organization Goals; 5) Skill Improvement and Training in Organizational

Communication; 6) Communication Media in Organizations: Software and Hardware; 7) Communication System Analysis in Organizations; 8) Research Methodology in Organizational Communication; 9) Texts, Anthologies, Reviews, and General Bibliographies Relative to Organizational Communication.

Table 1 contains a detailed definition of each of the classification titles.

Table 1

Organizational Communication Literature Definitions Of Classifications

Interpersonal Communication in Organizations

Literature analyzing factors relative to the interpersonal situation in the organization, originating in the dyadic relationship, the workgroup, or in conferences.

Factors analyzed may include credibility, trust, status, nonverbalization, knowledge, cognitive similarity, roles, redundancy, feedback, listening, semantics, etc.

Topics in this classification include superior-subordinate relationships, transactional analysis, counseling, conflict, behavior, perception, human relations, managerial style, personal characteristics of managers, and certain works relative to management by objectives.

Intragroup Communication in Organizations

Literature including the above-indicated dimensions of interpersonal communication but distinguished by the fact that the interacting parties are members of the same group.

Groups analyzed include specific functional departments, line, staff, labor, management, consumers, government bodies, etc.

Topics in this classification include participation, conflict, group-size, individual behavior in groups, and group productivity.

Intergroup Communication in Organizations

Literature including the above-indicated dimensions of interpersonal communication but the distinguishing element is that the interacting parties are representatives of different groups.

Groups involved may be different departments in the same organization, -line-staff, labor-management, organization-customers, government-taxpayers, etc.

Topics in this classification include coordination, collaboration, interorganizational conflict, negotiation, effects of hierarchical organization, influence of interest groups, and external communication.

Communication Factors and Organization Goals

Literature analyzing the influence of causal communication factors on the intervening and end-results organization variables.

Causal communication factors include communication attitudes, communication satisfaction, and communication planning, including motivation via communication.

Intervening and end-result variables include organizational performance, morale, conformity to plans, adaptability including organization change, and productivity.

Contains all studies primarily concerned with the influence of communication on organizational effectiveness.

Topics in this classification include organizational climate, job satisfaction, decision-making, problem-solving, management by objectives, participation, leadership, motivation, innovation, change, adaptability, and productivity.

Skill Improvement and Training in Organizational Communication

Literature concerned with communication skill improvement; verbal; written; and nonverbal, including public speaking, meetings, group process; writing skills; listening; and interpersonal skills as in selling, interviewing; and counseling.

Includes training programs, training needs, training materials, training techniques, learning principles, training course syllabi and descriptions.

Topics in this classification include training laboratories, games, role playing, programmed instruction, discussion techniques, and the use of film and videotape.

Communication Media in Organizations: Software and Hardware

Literature concerned with one or more phases of the media as the primary element of study in relation to the fundamental communication variables and their effectiveness.

Communication media relates to both software and hardware including oral, written, telephonic, audiovisual, electronic, and nonverbal media.

Topics in this classification include document retrieval systems, information systems, computer capabilities, and management by objectives as a technique.

Communication System Analysis in Organizations

Literature concerned with case studies of the overall organization or with subunits thereof: communication evaluation, audit or examination of effectiveness; communication networks; communication direction, upward, downward, horizontal; communication diffusion, as in grapevine studies, or ecco analysis studies; and other forms of organization communication analysis including organization development studies.

Topics in this classification include communication network structures, information requirement analyses, data base models, management analysis of communication, change-agent topics, general systems theory, cybernetics, and certain organizational climate studies.

Research Methodology in Organizational Communication

Literature concerned with research instruments, scales, tests, needs, and validation reports.

Includes field research strategies, problems, techniques, and specialized bibliographies restricted to this class.

Texts, Anthologies, Reviews, and General Bibliographies Relative to Organizational Communication

Literature that may be regarded as a text, collection of outstanding writings, or general bibliography.

Includes interpretative literature reviews relevant to the areas for research, shortcomings of research, etc.

Excludes texts, anthologies, reviews, and bibliographies devoted to only one of the other classifications. Such specialized works are classified under the particular area concerned.

Subclassifications of Each Major Literature Group

In the preparation of the 1977 OVERVIEW, we have continued a practice first attempted in the 1976 OVERVIEW, whereby communication factors are related to organizational outcomes as Morale, Performance, and Adaptiveness, and to major determinants of organizational outcomes as Leadership, Motivation, and Communication; and that wherever possible that a writing be subclassified within that group representing the dependent variable. For example, in a work studying the effect of participation on morale, the dependent variable being morale, the particular writing would be placed in the subclass of Morale, under the appropriate major literature classification that might be Interpersonal Communication, or Intra-Group Communication.

As a result of this policy, three of the nine major literature groups (Interpersonal Communication, Intra-Group Communication, and Communication Factors and Organization Goals) each have the following seven subclasses: Morale Studies; Performance-Effectiveness Studies; Adaptiveness-Innovation Studies; Leadership Studies; Communication Studies; Motivation Studies; Specialized Texts, Anthologies, Reviews, and Bibliographies.

Within the time constraints applicable to the production of this annual volume, as yet, it has not been practical to apply this causational or correlational approach to the definition of subclasses to the other six major literature classifications. Therefore, in the balance of the major literature groups, the subject matter was divided into meaningful topical categories relevant to each major class. The subclasses selected follow:

Intergroup Communication in Organizations:

—Group to Group Interface within the Organization (Vertical; Horizontal; Other: Age, Race, Sex).

—Organization to Organization Interface (Management-Union; Industry-Government; Government-Government; Other).

—Organization to Community Interface (General Public; Clients/Customers).

—Specialized Texts, Anthologies, Reviews, and Bibliographies.

Skill Improvement and Training in Organizational Communication:

—Training Feedback and Evaluation.

—Training Techniques.

—Training Media.

—Training and Instruction Programs.

—Training Needs.

—Training Resources & Administration.

—Specialized Texts, Anthologies, Reviews, and Bibliographies.

Communication Media in Organizations:

—Oral Media.

—Written Media.

—Nonverbal Media.

—Telephonic Media.

—Audiovisual Media.

—Electronic Media.

—Information Systems.

—Communication Programs.

—Media Organization & Administration.

—Specialized Texts, Anthologies, Reviews, and Bibliographies.

Communication System Analysis in Organizations:

—Empirical Case Studies Testing Specific Hypotheses.

—Communication Evaluation and Feedback Studies.

—Communication Network and Direction Studies.

—Models.

—The Systems Approach.

—The Organizational Development Approach.

—Information Processing and Requirement Studies.

—Specialized Texts, Anthologies, Reviews, and Bibliographies.

Research Methodology in Organizational Communication:

—Data Collection Instruments.

—Analytical and Processing Methods.

—Models and Theories.

—Experimental Design.
—Research Strategies and Special Techniques.
—Specialized Texts, Anthologies, Reviews, and Bibliographies.

Texts, Athologies, Reviews, and General Bibliographies:
—Textbooks (Management oriented; Communication oriented; Organizational Communication).
—Tradebooks.
—Anthologies.
—Reviews.
—General Bibliographies.

Each of the major literature groups has been divided into subclasses so as to convey a better understanding of the content therein. The number of subclasses average eight per major class, and range from six in Research Methodology to ten in Intergroup Communication, and in Communication Media. In all, there are 69 subclasses of the literature of organizational communication. As indicated above, the logic in establishing the subclasses is not consistent, with three of the major classes being analyzed from the viewpoint of independent and dependent variables; and six of the major classes being subdivided on the basis of topical content. This inconsistency is intended to be the subject of future work related to the construction of more meaningful classification tables, and directed to the construction of a knowledge inventory tool that can serve to consolidate organizational communication research findings.

Classification by Publication Format

Two standard subclassifications have been used to segregate the larger works of books and dissertations from the briefer writings found in articles, papers, and government publications. This classification by publication format has been applied to each of the major literature classifications except for the class relative to Texts, Anthologies, Reviews, and General Bibliographies, where it did not appear to be applicable. Therefore, both in the OVERVIEW and the ABSTRACTS, books and dissertations are listed or discussed first under each major literature class, followed by articles, papers, and reports related to that same literature class.

Classification by Research Characteristics
of the Written Work

Each of the writings is coded as to research characteristics—i.e., field study (FS), laboratory study (LS), theoretical-conceptual study (T/C), prescriptive or descriptive study (P/D). For the reason that there are no generally accepted standards as to meanings for these research methods, it is important to clarify the guidelines used by the authors in designating a writing as a field study, laboratory study, theoretical-conceptual study, or a prescriptive/descriptive study. The following definitions are intended to serve that purpose:

Field Study (FS): a research study in a realistic situation, in industry, government, education, health-care, or other kind of organization, wherein there is no ability to control the many variables present, although the researcher may introduce or influence variables.

Laboratory Study (LS): a research study under special physical conditions that permit the manipulation of one or more independent variables while other variables are controlled.

Theoretical/Conceptual Study (T/C): a writing that gives evidence of a thorough search of the literature and previous research in the subject area, but cannot be classed as a field study due to nonenvolvement of the writer in an ongoing organization, nor as a laboratory study because no variables are being manipulated.

Prescriptive/Descriptive Study (P/D): a writing that is not based on a thorough research of the literature and previous research, but is descriptive of a particular condition or idea, and often is prescriptive as to what should be done. In general, such writings do not employ footnotes or references, or where they do there is no evidence of a considerable review of previous writings in the same field.

Classification System Aspirations

It is our hope that organizational communication research will increasingly contribute to the understanding of the larger field of organizational behavior. We believe this can be facilitated by developing classification systems that permit the organized storage and retrieval of the findings of organizational communication research. The organization of such knowledge base should provide for relating communication factors to major elements in the organizational communication system, to determinants of end-result variables, and to the end-result variables. These goals for a classification system approach to theory development have not been accomplished in this volume, which is basically a multi-classified annotated bibliography.

In the future, we are looking for the development of a conceptual model linking determinants and end-results, so that cumulative research findings may strengthen our understanding of the complex relationships between organizational communication and organizational effectiveness.

IDENTIFICATION OF CLASSIFICATION
SYSTEM COMPONENTS

The several classification systems described above represent a strategy for the logical grouping of writings in the field of organizational communication. The implementation of that strategy involves identifying the writings that may be properly placed in each of the classes or groups. This process of identification requires a literature search, decisions to include or exclude a writing as pertinent to the field or organizational communication, judgments as to the proper major class and subclass, together with note of publication format and research method.

Our skills relative to identification are just as rudimentary as our present abilities to formulate satisfactory classification systems. Each year of work brings to light new inadequacies of old methods. This section will briefly consider the process and problems of identification by noting 1) the widescope of the literature search due to the interdisciplinary nature of the source-field, 2) the lack of an international literature search, 3) the handling of writings that fit into more than one major classification, 4) possible inadequacies of literature search, and 5) other identification problems.

Interdisciplinary Nature of the Selected Writings

The organizational communication abstracts herein represent writings selected on the basis of a broad view of the disciplines of communication, organizational behavior, management, information systems, psychology, sociology, social-psychology, education, and other social sciences. Rather than thinking of this work as consisting of literature *in* the field of organizational communication, it is more accurate to consider it as a representation of literature from the various disciplines within or *related to* organizational communication.

We have tried to bring together the 1977 literature that would be of interest to the student, teacher, researcher, and practitioner of organizational communication. As a consequence, some of the writings included will appear to be out of the central communication area, but will have been admitted on the basis of "related and relevant materials." This type of approach has resulted in a considerable overlap on the "organization-side" of organizational communication with the disciplines of management, organizational behavior, sociology, and information systems, and on the "communication-side" of organizational communication with the disciplines of speech communication, business communication, psychology, and social-psychology.

International Writings not Adequately Represented

International writings relevant to organizational communicaion have not been adequately covered in the present volume of ABSTRACTS. One exception is the work by Osmo Wiio of Finland who has been very active at United States professional conventions and whose work was therefore available to the authors. Undoubtedly, many more European and other-country writings would be of interest to domestic researchers, and it is planned that future annual publications of ABSTRACTS will provide coverage for these areas. We are presently seeking a scholar who would search for and contribute abstracts of such writings to this publication.

Cross-Classification of Writings

The job of classifying a writing into one of the major literature classifications frequently results in the judgment that the writing properly relates to more than one major classification. In such cases, the full bibliography and abstract has been placed under one classification only, but a notation is placed in the SEE-ALSO section of the other major classification to which it relates. Each of the major literature classes has a

SEE-ALSO section after the last abstract in that class. The function of the SEE-ALSO section is to direct the reader to writings annotated under one major class that are relevant to other major classes. Thus, a work that involves both intergroup communication and intragroup communication may be annotated in the intragroup class, but the SEE-ALSO section of the intergroup class will refer to the fact that there is an annotation in the intragroup class that concerns intergroup communication.

Possible Inadequacies of Literature Search

A work of this type cannot guarantee the inclusion of all relevant writings. At best, it is hoped that the writings selected represent a very, very large sample, to the point of being close to a census of the actual literature. Under these conditions, and barring a particular bias in the selection process, generalizations based on the findings will have validity. Appendix I, "Research Methods and Limitations", indicates several areas where omissions are possible.

In the OVERVIEW chapter that follows, the reader will note instances where a given subclass contains books/dissertations but not articles/papers, or vice versa. This condition draws attention to categories enjoying no research effort in one of the publication formats, as perceived by the contributors to this volume. In one or two instances, the subclass may show no publications either for books or articles, and the question properly arises as to whether the contributors sufficiently combed the literature, and properly classified the writings.

The reader should keep in mind the possible inadequacies of our search for relevant literature; and possible errors in our classification and subclassification of the literature actually selected.

Other Identification Problems

Sources utilized, as book reviews and special abstract journals, did not always indicate findings and conclusions, a most essential part of a well-prepared abstract. As a result, many such writings were difficult to class and subclass, and provided a poor basis for a meaningful overview statement.

The identification problem resulting in the cross-classification of an abstract has been noted above. This occurs when a writing relates to more than one major class. The same kind of problem can occur within one major class as it pertains to the various sub-classes. A writing may be applicable to more than one subclass. No provisions has been made to alert the reader to this condition.

Textbooks represented a special problem in the area of identification, and one that will require more attention in future years. The following guidelines have been employed to classify books:

—A book that is concerned with more than one of the eight major classifications (excluding the major class for Texts) is classed as either a Text, Tradebook, Anthology, Review, or General Bibliography, depending on its nature.

—A book that is concerned with one major class only is placed in that major class but the designation of a subclass depends on the following: 1) If that book relates to one subclass only, it is included under that subclass, and not as a Specialized Text in that major class. 2) If that book relates to more than one subclass in that major class, it is placed in the subclass for Specialized Texts, Anthologies, Reviews, and Bibliographies in that major class.

PLAN OF BOOK

This chapter has indicated the need for an organized knowledge base to serve the field of organizational communication, and inventory the findings of communication research. This need has been recognized by communication scholars; and recognition of the same need is found in the early development of other social sciences, as well as in the biological and physical sciences. Systems for classification and identification of the organizational communication literature have been explained in terms of the 1977 state-of-the-art, with the thought that future years should bring considerable modification to present classification, nomenclature, and identification concepts.

In the remainder of this book, Chapter II presents an OVERVIEW of the literature for 1977, and Chapter III provides CLASSIFIED ABSTRACTS of the same literature. This is followed by four appendices containing details as to Research Methods and Limitations (Appendix I), an Index of Authors (Appendix II), an Index of Organizational-Types in Field Studies of Organizations (Appendix III), and an Index of Data Collection Instruments in Field Studies (Appendix IV).

✵✵✵

NOTES AND REFERENCES

1. Robert D. Gieselman, Guest Editor, *The Journal of Business Communication*, Vol. 14, No. 3, Spring, 1977, p. 3.

2. Joseph E. McGrath and Irwin Altman, *Small Group Research: A Synthesis and Critique of the Field*, New York: Holt, Rinehart and Winston, Inc. 1966.

3. Cal W. Downs, "Research Methods in Organizational Communication," a paper presented at the Speech Communication Association Convention, December 1969.

4. Harold Guetzkow in Foreword to James L. Price, *Organizational Effectiveness: An Inventory of Propositions*, Homewood, IL: Richard D. Irwin, Inc., 1968, pp. vii-ix.

5. Paul A. Cullinan, *A Taxonomic Mode of Inquiry and its Application to Educational Administration*, Ph.D. Dissertation, The Ohio State University, 1964, pp. 3, 13.

6. Arthur C. Laufer, "A Taxonomy of Management Theory: A Preliminary Framework," *Academy of Management Journal*, Vol. 11, No. 4, December 1968, pp. 435-442.

7. Richard E. Blackwelder, *Taxonomy*, New York, John Wiley & Sons, Inc. 1967, p. 22.

8. ————; Laufer, op. cit. pp. 437-438.

9. In addition to the four major classification systems noted above, which appear throughout this volume, two other specialized classification systems have been applied to field studies (FS) only. See Appendix III, "Index of Organizational Types of Field Studies of Organizational Communication", and Appendix IV, "Index of Data Collection Methods in Field Studies of Organizational Communication."

chapter 2

Overview of organizational communication literature 1977

This overview's objective is to provide an insight into organizational communication writings in the year 1977. To accomplish this general objective involved the classification, subclassification, and cross-referencing of subject matter relating to each of the major categories noted in Table 1 above, supplemented by writing frequency statistics, and analyses indicating publication formats, characteristics of research methodology, and authors with common interest areas. Much of this information is contained in the immediate pages that follow, but important details have been placed in the appendices at the rear of this volume.

The overview should aid the reader to cut through the extreme detail found in the abstracts, while not taking the place of the abstracts which contain complete bibliographical references and additional information not found in the overview. Furthermore, it should be realized that a considerable number of prescriptive-descriptive writings included in the ABSTRACTS CHAPTER are not included in this overview since such works are not considered to be as relevant to research knowledge as field studies, laboratory studies, and theoretical-conceptual writings.

References in this overview to multi-authored writings have been limited to mention of the senior author only, with few exceptions. The rationale for this decision was based on space conservation and ease of reading. However, all authors of multi-authored writings are independently listed in the AUTHOR INDEX (Appendix II), and in the bibliographical reference in the ABSTRACTS. The reader interested in locating more information as to works mentioned in the commentary below should first refer to the AUTHOR INDEX for the page containing the abstract and full bibliographical reference. In addition, for field studies (FS), Appendix III provides an Index of Organizational Types relative to 343 field studies, and Appendix IV provides an Index of Data Collection Methods pertaining to the same field studies. Data collection instruments are not listed for many field studies due to the fact that secondary sources of information, as book reviews and abstract journals, did not always identify the specific research methodology employed by the researcher.

The following specific purposes are intended to be served by this kind of overview:

—Permit researchers to be exposed to the literature of others working the same field, and in related fields, so as to encourage researcher interaction.

—Provide detail for the major literature classes that will allow a more specific choice of subjects for research.

—Allow readers more direct access to works in their particular field of interest.

—Provide research directors and advisors with an improved means of determining the prevalence of research in given areas, and those areas needing attention.

—Promote interdisciplinary intelligence by incorporating all work in the social sciences relative to organizational communication.

—Provide a convenient reference for the graduate student, researcher, and practitioner to survey the field of organizational communication.

—Allow instructors of organizational communication to keep abreast of the empirical, theoretical, and descriptive writings in the field.

—Provide tentative parameters for the field of organizational communication.

—Provide a synthesis of the voluminous number of abstracts in this volume in order to make this work more coherent.

In order to fulfill the above-stated purposes, we will first present an overall summary and analysis of all organizational communication writings in 1977 in terms of the nine major classifications. Then, each of the major classifications will be discussed, in turn, utilizing subsclassifications to identify commonalities among the writings in a given major classification.

OVERALL SUMMARY:
NINE MAJOR LITERATURE CLASSIFICATIONS

The 1977 literature search for writings within or related to the field of organizational communication uncovered 469 books and dissertations, and 478 articles, papers, and reports, for a total of

947 works. Abstracts of these writings can be found in the later sections of this volume, classified in respect to nine major literature subdivisions and 69 subclasses.

This overview of the 1977 literature does not include all of the 947 writings, mainly due to the exclusion of a great many prescriptive-descriptive works. The overview covers 768 works, consisting of 463 books and dissertations, and 305 articles, papers, and government reports. The frequency of writings in each of the nine major classifications is shown below:

Major Literature Classification	Books/Dissertations		Articles/Papers	
	Quantity	Percent	Quantity	Percent
Interpersonal Communication	39	8	35	12
Intragroup Communication	34	7	19	6
Intergroup Communication	58	12	11	4
Communication Factors and Organization Goals	109	24	105	34
Skill Improvement and Training	45	10	25	8
Communication Media	50	11	24	8
Communication System Analysis	41	9	36	12
Research Methodology	33	7	38	12
Texts, Anthologies, Reviews, and General Bibliographies	54	12	12	4
TOTALS	463	100	305	100

A comparison of the frequency rank order of articles/papers to books/dissertations follows:

	Books/Dissertations	Articles/Papers
Communication Factors and Organization Goals	1	1
Intergroup Communication	2	9
Texts, Anthologies, Reviews, and General Bibliographies	3	8
Communication Media	4	6
Skill Improvement and Training	5	5
Communication System Analysis	6	3
Interpersonal Communication	7	4
Intragroup Communication	8	7
Research Methodology	9	2

In the publication format of books and dissertations, the most popular category was Communication Factors and Organization Goals (24%), credited with twice the volume of books of any other class; followed by Intergroup Communication (12%), Texts, Anthologies, Reviews, and Bibliographies (12%), and Communication Media (11%). All other classes ranged between 7 and 10 percent of all books in the overview, with Research Methodology (7%), and Intragroup Communication (7%) tied for the lowest level of representation.

In the publication format of articles, papers, and government reports, the most popular category was again Communication Factors and Organization Goals (34%), credited with almost three times the volume of articles/papers of any other class; followed by Research Methodology (12%), Interpersonal Communication (12%), and Communication System Analysis (12%). All other classes ranged between 4 and 8 percent of all articles/papers in the overview, with Intergroup Communication (4%) and Texts, Anthologies, Reviews, and Bibliographies (4%) tied for the lowest level of representation.

Interpersonal Communication
In Organizations

Thirty-nine books and thirty-five articles/papers relate to Interpersonal Communication in Organizations. Books accounted for 8 percent of all books and dissertations, and articles/papers were 12 percent of all articles, papers, and reports. The frequency of specific subclasses is shown below:

Subclasses	Books		Articles/Papers	
	Quantity	Percent	Quantity	Percent
Morale Studies	3	7	2	6
Performance-Effectiveness Studies	8	21	6	17
Adaptiveness-Innovation Studies	2	5	1	3
Leadership Studies	9	23	8	23
Communication Studies	8	21	15	43
Motivation Studies	1	2	3	8
Texts, Anthologies, Reviews	8	21	-	-
TOTALS	39	100	35	100

A comparison of the frequency rank order of articles/papers to books/dissertations follows:

	Books	Articles
Leadership Studies	1	2
Performance-Effectiveness Studies	2-3-4	3
Communication Studies	2-3-4	1
Texts, Anthologies, Reviews	2-3-4	7
Morale Studies	5	5
Adaptiveness-Innovation Studies	6	6
Motivation Studies	7	4

For the classification Interpersonal Communication in Organizations, studies of Leadership, Performance-Effectiveness, and Communication were the most popular writing subjects; and Motivation Studies, Adaptiveness-Innovation Studies and Morale Studies were lowest in subject frequency.

Table 2 (page 20) presents the names of authors relevant to each of the subclasses of Interpersonal Communication in Organizations; and the commentary below furnishes a guide and overview as to the contents and findings of selected works.

Morale Studies:

Books and Dissertations: *Cibotti* (FS) indicates that conceptual level is a determinant of student teacher productivity, but has little relationship to the quality of student teacher and cooperating teacher interpersonal relations; *Cohn* (FS) notes that unemployed individuals evidence greater dissatisfaction with self, lower self-confidence, and greater discounting of the importance of others' evaluations; and *Streker* (FS) reports on a method emphasizing employee participation in job redesign that has positive effects on employee satisfaction.

Articles, Papers, and Reports: *Bodden* (LS) evaluates the effects of occupational information giving on subjects' cognitive complexity level, finding that information giving reduces cognitive complexity; and *Kreck* (FS) reports that semantic distances between superiors and subordinates were unrelated to job satisfaction.

Performance-Effectiveness Studies:

Books and Dissertations: *Alessandra* (FS) concludes that buyer-seller demographic similarity (height, weight, sex, hairlength,

Table 2

Interpersonal Communication in Organizations—1977
Classification of Authors
by Subclass, Publication Format, and Nature of Research

Subclasses	Books & Dissertations	Articles, Papers, Reports
Morale Studies:	Cibotti . . . . FS	Bodden. . . . . LS
	Cohn . . . . FS	Kreck. . . . . FS
	Streker . . . . FS	
Performance-Effectiveness Studies:		
—Performance Evaluation	Blue. . . . . FS	Landy . . . . FS
	King . . . . FS	London. . . . . FS
	McGovern . . . . . LS	Schmitt. . . . . FS
	Stano . . . . FS	Shaffer . . . . LS
	Sterrett. . . . . . . LS	Stumpff . . . . FS
—Effectiveness & Coordination	Alessandra . . . . . FS	Bernardin . . . . FS
	Feingold . . . . . . LS	
	Larson . . . . FS	
Adaptiveness-Innovation Studies:		
—Decision Making	Ezell . . . . FS	Becker . . . . LS
—Other	Kasperson . . . . . FS	
Leadership Studies:		
—Managerial Style & Power	Caine . . . . FS	Burlem . . . . FS
	Charlier. . . . . . . FS	Kavanagh. . . . . . . FS
	Farrow . . . . FS	Shapira. . . . . FS
	Gaymon . . . . . . FS	
	Hall. . . . . FS	
	Wortman. . . . . . FS	
—Superior-Subordinate Relations	Arams . . . . PD	Bartol. . . . . LS
	Brittingham . . . . LS	Dansereau . . . . FS
	Fujii . . . . LS	Hester . . . . LS
		Matteson . . . . FS
		Weigand . . . . TC
Communication Studies:	Beebe. . . . . LS	Cahn . . . . TC
	Dodge . . . . FS	Chapanis . . . . TC
	Fahs . . . . LS	Civikly . . . . FS
	Minder . . . . FS	Constantin . . . . . . LS
	O'Reilly . . . . . . LS	Dolgoff. . . . . PD
	Ryan . . . . FS	Herold . . . . FS
	Stetler . . . . LS	Housel . . . . LS
	VanHoeven . . . . LS	Jones. . . . . FS
		Knight . . . . LS
		Norton. . . . . FS
		Rocky Mountain . . . TC
		Rosen. . . . . LS
		Siegman . . . . FS
		Sykes (2). . . . . TC
Motivation Studies:	Ferraro . . . . FS	Dipboye . . . . TC
		Oldham. . . . . FS
		Schneider . . . . FS

Table 2, Continued

Subclasses	Books & Dissertations	Articles, Papers, Reports
Texts & Tradebooks:	Bard	
	Gellerman	
	Lefton	
	Metzler	
	Morrison	
	Nirenberg	
	Rogers	
	Royal	

beard similarities) has a positive effect on sales success; *Feingold* (LS) presents a paradigm of effective communication in which the effective communicator is perceived as "other-oriented," able to adapt communication to the respondent, committed to the message, and recognized as an empathetic listener; and *Larson* (FS) finds that the most effective school principals exhibited a greater desire to initiate interaction than did the least effective principals.

In the area of performance evaluation, *Blue* (FS) studies attitudes and ratings of students and teachers, finding that brief weekly evaluative discussions were more influential on the participants than more intensive evaluations; *King* (FS) indicates that the best rating of employee performance by supervisors is obtained through the combined efforts of direct and indirect supervisors, noting the deficiencies of rating by either source alone; *McGovern* (LS) reports that interviewees high in nonverbal behavior are evaluated more positively than applicants low in nonverbal behavior during an interview; *Stano* (FS) explores area of productive and unproductive performance appraisal interviews, providing explicit guidelines for interview behavior geared to the interviewee; and *Sterrett* (FS) examines the relationship between nonverbal communication during interviews and effectiveness qualities as observed in the insurance industry, noting differences in reactions by male and female interviewers.

Articles, Papers, and Reports: *Bernardin* (FS) studies the Managerial Grid as a predictor of conflict resolution method and managerial effectiveness, concluding that grid placement is a poor predictor.

In the area of performance evaluation, *Landy* (FS) concludes that on-the-street performance of policemen can be successfully predicted from averaged interview factor scores derived from trait ratings made by interviewers; *London* (FS) notes the effects of information on stereotype development in performance appraisal and interview contexts; *Schmitt* (FS) studies applicant decisions in the employment interview, finding that the interviewees likelihood of job acceptance depended on perceived interviewer personality, manner of interviewer delivery, and adequacy of job information offered; *Shaffer* (LS) finds that individuals with confidential placement files were judged more attractive as prospective employees than individuals with open files; and *Stumpff* (FS) proposes a revision of the Coast Guard performance evaluation system so as to better differentiate individual performance and promote individual career development.

Adaptiveness-Innovation Studies:

Books and Dissertations: *Ezell* (FS) examines the use of power, via Machiavellianism, in educational decision-making, finding no significant difference in the level of interpersonal manipulative orientations of registered lobbyists, boards of education, and educational administrators; and *Kasperson* (FS) concludes that scientists are information processors and that creativity can be explained by the information-seeking behavior of the innovative scientist.

Articles, Papers, and Reports: *Becker* (LS) reports experiments conducted to observe the decision-making process of natural dyadic groups, testing various hypotheses as to search for alternatives, selection of acceptable alternative, and importance of decision to the decision-makers.

Leadership Studies:

Books and Dissertations: In the area of managerial style, *Caine* (FS) studies leadership orientation and self-presentation, reporting that low LPC (Least Preferred Co-Worker) leaders described themselves more positively than high LPC leaders; *Charlier* (FS) studies relationships between personal and interpersonal dimensions and leadership behavior of school principals; *Farrow* (FS) states that tight subordinate-boss structure, clear task objectives, and an assertive attitude of the manager promotes a directive leader style, and that a short-term objective perspective with unplanned activities influences a more negotiative leader style; *Gaymon* (FS) explores personal values in an organizational context, recommending that organizations encourage managers to be aware of the values and ethical factors involved in organizational decisions; *Hall* (FS) finds that task-oriented principals are perceived by teachers to vary leadership behavior more from situation to situation than relationship-oriented principals; and *Wortman* (FS) indicates a difference in the perception of real and ideal leader behaviors of assistant principals, suggesting that this is due to inadequate leadership training.

In the area of superior-subordinate relations, *Arams* (PD) focuses on five dilemmas faced by managers, including satisfying individual needs while promoting efficiency; *Brittingham* (LS) reports that negative personal support was the only variable that influenced change in superordinate behavior, noting that positive personal support, negative task assistance, and positive personal support, negative task assistance, and positive task assistance had no significant effect; and *Fujii* (LS) indicates the influence of leader-member compatibility as being positive in respect to follower performance, satisfaction, and interpersonally-oriented leader behavior.

Articles, Papers, and Reports: In the area of leadership style, *Burlem* (FS) compares executives with recognized performance to other executives, finding differences in perception of management function, leadership style, and motivational needs; *Kavanagh* (FS) finds that the popular hypothesis arguing for higher preferences for freedom and self-actualization opportunities in the work role was not completely supported by leadership preference results; and *Shapira* (FS) identifies five leadership styles (direction, negotiation, consultation, participation, and delegation) by a facet analysis of the leader's behavior, the lack of power, and the lack of information within the management-subordinate system.

In the area of superior-subordinate relations, *Bartol* (LS) studies sex effects in evaluating leaders, finding that female managers were seen as more positive on consideration style than male managers, and initiating structure behavior was valued more highly when engaged in by male managers; *Dansereau* (FS) presents a vertical dyad linkage approach to leadership, hypothesizing that the degree of latitude a superior grants a member to negotiate his/her role is predictive of subsequent behavior on the part of both superior and member; *Hester* (LS) investigates the effects of two variables on perceived supervisor attraction, 1) attitudes toward supervisor skill, and 2) similarity between supervisor and supervisee; *Matteson* (FS) examines attitudes toward women as managers, concluding that females have a

more favorable attitude towards women managers than males;
and *Weigand* (TC) indicates that decentralized authority, and
responsibility to subordinates, improves the upward flow of
communications within an organization.

Communication Studies:

Books and Dissertations: *Beebe* (LS) maintains that eye contact is a determinant of enhanced credibility and increased comprehension, and that speaker posture and vocal inflection has
little effect on either credibility or comprehension; *Dodge* (FS)
reports no significant differences between juvenile recidivists
and nonrecidivists in communication patterns between delinquent youths and their counselors; *Fahs* (LS) indicates that
self-disclosure and attitude similarity are effective factors in reducing and controlling interpersonal conflict; *Minder* (FS) finds
that openness of elementary school teachers differs significantly
according to race, with black teachers more closed to experience
than white teachers, regardless of the predominant race in the
school building; and *O'Reilly* (LS) concludes that low trust in
the message receiver leads to suppression of information that reflects unfavorably on the sender's performance, and that a measure of information distortion is inversely associated with job
satisfaction and both individual and group performance.

Ryan (FS) studies the relationships between supervisory conflict management behaviors and personal influence, finding a
negative relationship between supervisory adherence to chain
of command and supervisory personal influence; *Stetler* (LS)
reports that neither verbal nor vocal communicative behavior
plays a major role in the perception of empathetic understanding among registered nurses; and *Van Hoeven* (LS) determines
that sex of person sending message has no effect on trust variable between sender and receiver, but the content or type of
message communicated does increase or decrease trust.

Articles, Papers, and Reports: *Cahn* (TC) applies a development theory of interpersonal communication to the initial job
interview; *Chapanis* (TC) provides reports on eleven laboratory
experiments relative to interactive human communication, including face to face, voice alone, and redundancy; *Civikly* (FS)
studies the pattern of verbal and nonverbal behaviors in social
service interviews between providers and low-income clients,
finding that results suggest the validity of Gibbs' (1961) supportive-defensive paradigm; and *Constantin* (LS) conducts an

investigation of the influence of information favorability and unfavorability in the employment interview, giving consideration to the relevancy and irrelevancy of the information.

Dolgoff (PD) discusses how work determines one's self-concept, self-esteem, and identity; *Herold* (FS) reports five types of feedback, viz., positive feedback from superiors, positive feedback from nonhierarchical others, negative feedback, internal criteria, and workflow feedback; *Housel* (LS) indicates that a source's initial credibility is not affected by source's gender; *Jones* (FS) discusses spatial proximity in relation to friendship formation and interpersonal conflict in nursing homes, indicating that closeness produced conflict while patients living at greater distance sustained positive interaction; and *Knight* (LS) explores degree of comfort relative to different dyadic interaction distances between counselor and client, finding highest comfort at 30 inches, lowest at 18 inches, and intermediate comfort at 48 inches.

Norton (FS) investigates whether differences exist in student perceptions of teacher nonverbal behavior, giving specific attention to race, sex, and age; *Rocky Mountain Gerontology Center* (TC) documents a series of 14 workshops for personnel involved in volunteer programs for elderly persons, including techniques for interviewing volunteers; *Rosen* (LS) concludes that stereotypes regarding older employees' physical, cognitive, and emotional characteristics lead to discrimination against them; *Siegman* (FS) investigates the hypothesis that noncontingent interviewer "mm-hmms" facilitate interviewee verbal productivity; and *Sykes* (TC) suggests a new explanation of the relationship between proximity and attraction based on the variable of territoriality and likelihood of common occupancy.

Motivation Studies:

Books and Dissertations: *Ferraro* (FS) reports that school principals perceived punishment and rewards as preferable techniques for eliciting desired behavior, and did not perceive withholding or substitution of information or postponed decisonmaking as preferred techniques for elicting such behavior.

Articles, Papers, and Reports: *Dipboye* (TC) reviews research on Korman's self-consistency theory of work motivation and occupational choice, noting that chronic self-esteem and situational self-esteem appear to be important determinants of performance, choice, and satisfaction; *Oldham* (FS) studies the conditions under which employees respond positively to enriched work, reporting that employees with strong growth needs and satisfaction with the work context (i.e., pay, job security, co-workers, and supervisors) responded more positively to enriched jobs than other employees; and *Schneider* (FS) indicates that the attraction of the current work context was correlated significantly with organizational participation/withdrawal intentions.

Specialized Texts, Anthologies, Bibliographies, and Reviews:

Books: *Bard* (Text) studies the police as a source of knowledge on interpersonal conflict, concentrating on third party intervention strategies employed by police officers; *Gellerman* (Text) reviews the relationships of managers and subordinates, indicating that the manager must learn communication skills rather than adhering to "cookbook" approaches to motivation; *Lefton* (Text) presents a step-by-step method for doing effective appraisals, and shows how the method can be individualized for each subordinate; *Metzler* (Text) provides a practical guide for the college journalism student in respect to question formulation, use of recording media, and other elements of creative interviewing; and *Morrison* (Text) contributes a simple approach to transactional analysis, believing it to be a way for managers to understand and improve their human relations.

Nirenberg (Text) illustrates, through the use of typical conversations, how to use persuasive communication in organizational settings; *Rogers* (Text) discusses fair employment interviewing techniques, analysis of application information, personnel correspondence, and recruitment sources; and *Royal* (Text) analyzes the art of interviewing and interrogation, furnishing a professional manual and guide.

Intragroup Communication in Organizations

Thirty-four books and nineteen articles/papers relate to Intragroup Communication in Organizations. Books accounted for seven percent of all books and dissertations, and articles/papers were six percent of all articles, papers, and reports.

The frequency of specific subclasses is shown below:

Subclasses	Books		Articles/Papers	
	Quantity	Percent	Quantity	Percent
Morale Studies	3	9	-	-
Performance-Effectiveness Studies	6	18	3	16
Adaptiveness-Innovation Studies	9	26	4	21
Leadership Studies	3	9	2	10
Communication Studies	4	12	10	53
Texts, Anthologies, Bibliographies, Reviews	9	26	-	-
Motivation Studies	-	-	-	-
TOTALS	34	100	19	100

A comparison of the frequency rank order of articles/papers to books/dissertations follows:

	Books	Articles
Adaptiveness-Innovation Studies	1-2	2
Texts, Anthologies, Bibliographies	1-2	5-6-7
Performance-Effectiveness Studies	3	3
Communication Studies	4	1
Morale Studies	5-6	5-6-7
Leadership Studies	5-6	4
Motivation Studies	7	5-6-7

For the classification Intragroup Communication in Organizations, the two most popular writing topics were Adaptiveness-Innovation Studies and Communication Studies, followed by Performance-Effectiveness Studies, Leadership Studies, and Morale Studies. No Motivation Studies were found in this classification of the literature.

Table 3 presents the names of authors relevant to each of the subclasses of Intragroup Communication in Organizations; and the commentary below furnishes a guide and overview as to the contents and findings of selected works:

Morale Studies:

Books and Dissertations: *Absher* (FS) studies teacher involvement in decision-making and morale, concluding that moderate involvement yielded higher levels of morale than underinvolvement or overinvolvement; *Reinheimer* (LS) determines that attitudinal attractiveness in a task-oriented group was directly related to a person's ability to influence the group; and *Shulman* (FS) investigates communication climate of university

Table 3

Intragroup Communication in Organizations—1977
Classification of Authors
by Subclass, Publication Format, and Nature of Research

Subclasses	Books & Dissertations	Articles, Papers, Reports
Morale Studies:	Absher . . . . FS Reinheimer . . . . LS Shulman . . . . . . FS	
Performance-Effectiveness Studies:	Barbanell. . . . . . FS Brill. . . . . TC Eldridge . . . . . . LS Forys. . . . . LS Merton . . . . FS Pendell . . . . LS	Eckloff. . . . . LS Hackman. . . . . . . TC Vallacher. . . . . . . FS
Adaptiveness-Innovation Studies:	Courtright . . . . . LS Drake. . . . . LS Harvey . . . . LS Hoffman . . . . . . FS Marshak . . . . . . FS Mills . . . . LS Miner. . . . . LS Richman . . . . . . FS Stead . . . . FS	Brownlee. . . . . FS Hill . . . . FS Richards . . . . FS Whitmore . . . . TC
Leadership Studies:	Griffin . . . . FS Kozan . . . . FS Tucker . . . . LS	Parker . . . . FS Spreitzer . . . . FS
Communication Studies:	Penley . . . . FS Warnemunde. . . . FS Nykodym . . . . . FS Wilkinson . . . . . TC	Allen . . . . LS Elkins. . . . . FS Greene . . . . LS Hall . . . . FS Kruger . . . . LS Schlenker . . . . FS Schlenker/Miller(2). . LS Sykes. . . . . FS Taylor . . . . FS
Texts and Tradebooks:	Baird Cooper Gulley Harnack Hills Leth Mackenzie Schindler-Rainman	
Reviews:	Hare	Seaver

departments, concluding that the size of department significantly affects faculty perception of influence, and that communication climate is composed of perceptions of downward
communication, familiarity, and influence.

Performance-Effectiveness Studies:

Books and Dissertations: *Barbanell* (FS) reports that teams that do discuss and resolve conflict are more effective than teams that do not recognize conflict; *Brill* (TC) indicates that group work is becoming more important as technology continues to advance and that groups are characterized by a developmental pattern that can be understood and controlled; *Eldridge* (LS) examines the effects of nominal and brainstorm decision-making procedures on group productivity, finding that groups provided with structures generated more ideas than control groups and had high quality decisions; *Forys* (LS) shows that group leaders maintaining minimum or better levels of facilitative conditions led more productive groups; *Merton* (FS) obtains low reliability results from peer reviews among professsionals based on six problem-solving criteria; and *Pendell* (LS) concludes that room design (shape of room and interior decoration) had no effect on communication behavior of small groups.

Articles, Papers, and Reports: *Eckloff* (LS) investigates the effects of cognitive abstractness, interpersonal perception and task type on group performance, as measured by time used and quality of solutions; *Hackman* (TC) proposes a model for the design and maintenance of self-managing workgroups in organizations, noting the advantages of management by interacting groups rather than by individuals; and *Vallacher* (FS) studies small groups at U.S. Antarctic research stations, reporting that conflict was related to supervisor performance, but cohesiveness was not found to be related to performance.

Adaptiveness and Innovation Studies:

Books and Dissertations: *Courtright* (LS) reports no significant differences in the number and quality of solutions for groups of different cohesiveness, noting that cohesive groups tended to have a higher degree of error in judgment; *Drake* (LS) finds that increases in horizontal power within groups resulted in higher commitment by group members while increases of vertical power resulted in less commitment; *Harvey* (LS) studies communication change in group process seminars using the sequential analysis of verbal interaction, finding that T-Group sessions produced no significant change in communication processes; *Hoffman* (FS) concludes that highly structured work units have less influence over work decisions than less structured units; and *Marshak* (FS) indicates that committee outcomes were a function of the decision rule of majority consent and the size of the committee, finding no support for the theory that informal conflict resolution processes as seniority, prestige, and position are influential in committee decisions.

Mills (LS) reports that regulation of dyadic conflict was achieved by means of unilateral peaceable behavior, prior intention by participants to agree, a commitment to a common group, and civility; *Miner* (LS) analyzes small groups conducted as interacting groups, nominal groups, and groups subject to the Delphi Process, concluding that the quality of decision-making is highest where the leader follows a structured decision-making approach placing emphasis on the expression of feelings prior to attempting to solve the problems; *Richman* (FS) examines the influence of a facilitator in problem-solving groups, finding that groups with a facilitator present were more confrontative, less easy-going, exhibiting more active member participation and less teacher domination; and *Stead* (FS) compares nominal grouping and sequenced brainstorming techniques of creative idea generation, finding that sequenced brainstorming groups were more effective, and both methods produced high quality ideas.

Articles, Papers, and Reports: *Brownlee* (FS) investigates the Supreme Court as a small-group in respect to group interaction, decision-making techniques, type and degree of dissent, coalition formations, and value systems; *Hill* (FS) identifies personality conflict as the most common type of conflict for project teams in various phases of project life cycles; *Richards* (FS) examines the effectiveness of brainstorming techniques in real managerial situations, noting that "low-level speculations" were generally produced, and feeling that longer-term belief systems may influence the group in the brainstorming process; and *Whitmore* (TC) discusses methods of analyzing human relations problem situations through group processes.

Leadership Studies:

Books and Dissertations: *Griffin* (FS) finds that the team management approach to the school superintendency is an effective means of administering a school district; *Kozan* (FS) indicates that high flexibility workgroups had higher autonomy and higher supervisory leadership but low peer leadership and a lack of compromise when faced with internal conflict; and *Tucker* (LS) explores leadership in autonomous group environments, concluding that leadership relates to both task and person-oriented behaviors, and that task and people concerns are not opposite poles of a single leadership dimension.

Articles, Papers, and Reports: *Spreitzer* (FS) finds that informal leaders among the clients of an inpatient rehabilitation center had a positive influence that facilitated the rehabilitation process; and *Parker* (FS) studies black-white differences in leader behavior, noting that the behavior of supervisors toward their subordinates is a complex function of a) the supervisor's own race, b) the race of the subordinate, and c) the majority or minority position of racial groups within the group supervised.

Communication Studies:

Books and Dissertations: *Penley* (FS) investigates the relationship between communication and the structure of organizational workgroups, concluding that the relationship between these variables is strong and workgroups can be classified on the basis of their explanatory structure and comparable communication; *Warnemunde* (FS) studies the communication behavior of university department chairmen, indicating that the primary communication flow is informational and upward from subordinates to the chairman, as opposed to the decisional and downward flow in other formal organizations; *Nykodym* (FS) evaluates Transactional Analysis training in workgroups, noting that it improves information flow and organization climate; and *Wilkinson* (TC) synthesizes previous research on triads and the stability of structure, presenting models to predict coalition formation and outcomes of three-party interaction.

Articles, Papers, and Reports: *Allen* (LS) finds no significant differences in verbal patterns by leaders of biracial groups varying in racial composition; *Elkins* (FS) concludes that there is a relationship between group members' percepts of tasks and their individual tendencies to communicate within the group; *Greene* (FS) assesses the effects of body image boundaries on preferred and avoided seating choices in small groups; *Hall* (FS) studies the influence of male versus female deviants on the small discussion group, finding that female deviant behavior affected goals less negatively; *Kruger* (LS) investigates the relationship of group size to performance and communication activity under three problem-solving modes, finding that an increase in group size resulted in an increase in communication as measured by messages and other factors; and *Schlenker* (FS) explores various aspects of egocentrism on group behavior, indicating that it affects leadership patterns, interpersonal agreement and group performance.

Schlenker and Miller, in one laboratory study, look at determinants of egocentric perception, hypothesizing that during group face to face interaction, egocentrism decreases, and group identification increases; and in a second laboratory study, examine the effects of group performance and evaluative feedback from other group members on retrospective perceptions of responsibility for group activities, finding that peer evaluations were directly related to amount of responsibility perceived by successful group members but not so in failing groups; *Sykes* (FS) concentrates on a theory of informal group formation, relating similarity, proximity, and social structure variables to interpersonal attraction; and *Taylor* (FS) indicates that members of informal groups feel less inclined than formal group members to trust workteam members, less willing to rate highly the performance of their group, and less likely to see selves as important to team's productivity.

Specialized Texts, Anthologies, Bibliographies and Reviews:

Books: *Baird* (Text) studies group communication in respect to norms, roles, leadership, decision-making, motivation, group development, and verbal and nonverbal communication; *Cooper* (text) analyzes the development of social skills in managers, evaluating the methods based on participation and group experiences; *Gulley* (Text) adopts a systems theory perspective, emphasizing techniques for improving the quality of small-group communication; *Harnack* (Text) presents group discussion theory and technique, including chapters on group dynamics, communication principles, leadership, and group effectiveness; and *Hills* (Text) furnishes a legal and procedural guide for the managing of corporate meetings.

Leth (Text) reviews small group communication in terms of problem-solving interaction, listening, conflict, leadership, and group evaluation; *MacKenzie* (Text) furnishes a two-volume work in which volume one discusses the basic theory of group structure and volume two provides empirical tests of the theory, group preferences for type of structure, and a model for interperson hostility; *Schindler-Rainman* (Text) concentrates on problems of group meetings, including recommendations for goal setting and stimulating creativity; and *Hare* (Review) summarizes the major trends and findings in group theory and research from 1898 to 1974 including 6,000 references.

Articles, Papers, and Reports: *Seaver* (Review) presents a summary of the literature concerned with group preferences, group uncertainty, and the relative merits of individual versus group judgments.

Intergroup Communication in Organizations

Fifty-eight books and eleven articles/papers relate to Intergroup Communication in Organizations. Books accounted for twelve percent of all books and dissertations, and articles/papers were four percent of all articles, papers, and reports. The frequency of specific subclasses is shown below:

Subclasses	Books Quantity	Percent	Articles/Papers Quantity	Percent
Group to Group Interface Within The Organization:				
—Vertical	14	24	-	-
—Horizontal	-	-	1	9
—Other: Age, Race, Sex	9	16	-	-
SUBTOTAL	23	40	1	9
Organization to Organization Interface:				
—Management-Union	9	16	1	9
—Industry-Government	2	3	-	-
—Government-Government	5	9	1	9
—Other:	-	-	-	-
SUBTOTAL	16	28	2	18
Organization to Community Interface:				
—General Public	12	20	4	37
—Clients-Customers	6	10	1	9
SUBTOTAL	18	30	5	46
Texts, Anthologies, Reviews	1	2	3	27
TOTALS	58	100	11	100

For the classification Intergroup Communication in Organizations, each of the three major subgroups, Group to Group, Organization to Organization, and Organization to Community have a substantial proportion of the total writings. Within these

subgroups, Vertical Group to Group Interface is the most popular subject in the books/dissertation format, but Organization
to General Public Interface has the greatest number of writings
when considering both books and articles. Other popular areas
include Management-Union Organization to Organization Interface, Organization to Clients Interface, and Age/Race/Sex Group
to Group Interface within the organization.

Table 4 presents the names of authors relevant to each of the
subclasses of Intergroup Communication in Organizations; and
the commentary below furnishes a guide and overview as to the
contents and findings of selected works:

Group to Group Interface within the Organization:

Books and Dissertations: In the area of vertical group-to-
group communication, *Acton* (FS) finds that school principals
who rate high on the Consideration Scale of the Organization
Climate Description Questionnaire communicate better with
their faculty, show more concern for staff, and have greater insight as to teachers' needs; *Buroker* (TC) reports on college
presidents' perceptions of student participation in the administrative decision-making of two year colleges; *Capie* (FS) concludes that school board members believed in significantly less
decision-making involvement of teachers, parents, and students
than did school adminstrators; *Hale* (FS) compares Delaware
State Cabinet adaptation to two executive leadership styles,
finding that the agencies tended to run counter to gubernatorial
budgetary decisions; and *Heiting* (FS) indicates significant differences between secondary teachers' perceptions of their interpersonal classroom behavior and students' perceptions of that
behavior.

Jorgenson (FS) examines the influence of participation on
teacher satisfaction, noting that teachers' satisfaction was affected by involvement in school district policy development,
and lack of decision implementation caused dissatisfaction;
Leonard (FS) studies prison-guard communication in a State
Penitentiary, noting that group interaction is infrequent, institutional, brief, and generally hostile; *McCamey* (FS) finds a
positive relationship between principals' perception of leader
behavior and teacher self-concept and a negative relationship
between teachers' perception of leader behavior and teacher self-
concept; *McFillen* (LS) explores the relationship of successful

Table 4

Intergroup Communication in Organizations—1977
Classification of Authors
by Subclass, Publication Format, and Nature of Research

Subclasses	Books & Dissertations	Articles, Papers, Reports
Group to Group Interface	Acton. . . . . FS	
Within the Organization:	Buroker . . . . . . TC	
—Vertical	Capie . . . . FS	
	Hale. . . . . FS	
	Heiting . . . . FS	
	Jorgenson . . . . . FS	
	Leonard . . . . . . FS	
	McCamey . . . . . FS	
	McFillen . . . . . . LS	
	Perry . . . . FS	
	Rosenthal . . . . . FS	
	Sherman . . . . . . FS	
	Tannenbaum. . . . FS	
	Wood . . . . FS	
—Horizontal		Schermerhorn . . . . . FS
—Demographics:		
—Race	Bouch . . . . FS	
	Noel . . . . FS	
—Sex	Davenport . . . . . FS	
	Keener . . . . FS	
	Leenhouts . . . . . FS	
	Tharpe . . . . FS	
—Other	Hall . . . . TC	
	Peitchinis. . . . . . TC	
	Stewart. . . . . . . FS	
Organization to Organization	Brant . . . . TC	Nat'l School Public
Interface:	Childress . . . . . . FS	Relations Assoc.. . . . PD
—Management-Union	Mikrut . . . . FS	
	Moller . . . . FS	
	Muller . . . . FS	
	Pavy . . . . FS	
	Piazza. . . . . FS	
	Tepper . . . . FS	
	Trotta . . . . TC	
—Industry-Government	Heim . . . . FS	
	Owen . . . . FS	
—Government-Government	Boyle. . . . . TC	Akinbode . . . . FS
	Gauldfeldt . . . . . FS	
	Howe. . . . . TC	
	Thompson . . . . . FS	
	Wegner . . . . FS	
Organization to Community	Archer . . . . TC	Bagin . . . . TC
Interface:	Barnett. . . . . . . FS	Bailey. . . . . TC
—General Public	Broom . . . . FS	Grunig . . . . FS
	Crosby . . . . FS	Maloney . . . . TC
	Ehrman. . . . . . . FS	
	Ford . . . . FS	
	Lamoreaux. . . . . FS	

Table 4, Continued

Subclasses	Books & Dissertations	Articles, Papers, Reports
Organization to Community Interface: —General Public (continued)	Locander. . . . . . TC Newsom . . . . . . TC O'Connell . . . . . FS Pollak. . . . . . . FS	Steinberg. . . . . . . FS
—Clients/Customers	Burke. . . . . LS Clark . . . . FS Cook . . . . TC Forrer . . . . FS Lambert . . . . . . FS Orr . . . . FS	Corwin . . . . FS
Texts	Ross	
Reviews		Alderfer Roessler
Bibliographies		Young

and unsuccessful subordinates to supervisors, finding that successful subordinates are perceived to be more trustworthy, more favorable toward superiors, and more internally motivated; and *Perry* (FS) investigates leader behavior, comparing the perceptions of high and low status teachers and reports no significant differences.

Rosenthal (FS) considers relationship and task skills, finding that teacher coordinators of vocational skills tend to view vocational administrators in a negative manner while the supervisors of vocational administrators tend to be neutral; *Sherman* (FS) concludes that teacher perception of ability to participate in the supervisory process positively affects interpersonal relationships between teachers and supervisory personnel; *Tannenbaum* (FS) reports that supervisors were uncertain as to the usefulness of transactional analysis skills in supervising student teachers; and *Wood* (FS) notes that the use of informal faculty groups was only of liminted value in the improvement of teacher-student relationships.

In the area of race group-to-group communication, *Bouch* (FS) finds significant differences in perception of supervisory techniques by black and white supervisors and black and white teachers; and *Noel* (FS) studies communication between black and white high school students and reports that systematic training in experiencing is effective for improving communication.

In the area of sex group-to-group communication, *Davenport* (FS) finds no significant differences between the overall leader behavior of male and female school principals, noting that male super-ordinates favored male principals over female principals; *Keener* (FS) reports little differences in the leadership behavior of male and female college administrators, but some differences in career orientation, career development, and career aspirations; *Leenhouts* (FS) studies communication similarities and differences of female and male legislators in the 1975 Michigan House of Representatives; and *Tharpe* (FS) indicates that female teachers exhibited higher morale levels than male teachers.

In other studies of group-to-group communication, *Peitchinis* (TC) analyzes staff-patient communication in the health services field including approaches that may be taken to improve; *Stewart* (FS) examines the role of a university ombudsman, finding that it is a useful model for evaluating the conflict management process; and *Hall* (TC) discusses cultural influences on behavior, emphasizing the problems of working in cross-cultural contexts.

Articles, Papers, and Reports: *Schermerhorn* (FS) finds a positive relationship between information sharing activity and perceived level of task accomplishment, and a negative relationship between information sharing activity and adminstrator tenure.

Organization to Organization Interface:

Books and Dissertations: In the area of management-union interface, *Brant* (TC) concludes that collective bargaining is the only viable alternative to unilateral policy-making by Boards of Education; *Childress* (FS) studies impasse in collective bargaining negotiations and suggests that there is a direct relationship between the degree of impasse and principal's dissatisfaction with teachers; *Mikrut* (FS) indicates that morale is a significant factor in attitudes towards collective bargaining, noting that personality is not significantly related to negotiation attitudes; *Moller* (FS) presents an empirical study of 18 Danish industries finding that steward effectiveness is related to union strength, worker perceptions of union and steward-management relations; and *Muller* (FS) emphasizes the need to develop a management team model to coordinate all aspects of the management side of collective bargaining in public schools.

Pavy (FS) identifies a set of guidelines to be used by fact finders in impasse negotiations in collective bargaining, noting seven general categories of information needed for fact finders; *Piazza* (FS) examines role of principals in collective bargaining process, concluding that principals' participation should be on the management negotiating team in an advisory role; *Tepper* (FS) analyzes behavior of school principals and teacher-leaders during negotiations and stresses need for teacher-principal communication; and *Trotta* (TC) reviews the causes of grievances in the workplace, indicating how to avoid and how to settle such conflict.

In the area of industry-government interface, *Heim* (FS) investigates the communications between the Wisconsin Governor, State Legislature, and interest groups in respect to the merger of the University of Wisconsin and the Wisconsin State University Systems; and *Owen* (FS) studies the influence of business managers in the process of government policy formulation, concluding that it is not effective in bringing about outcomes desired by managers.

In the area of government-government interface, *Boyle* (TC) analyzes the need for coordination of municipal government field services, noting that agencies have overlapping responsibilities and inter-service conflicts due to environmental pressures to change faster than organizational structure permits; *Gauldfeldt* (FS) reports little communication between U.S. government agencies overseas and host countries; *Howe* (TC) examines relationships between New York City and New York State in the areas of urban reform legislation, noting that communications between the city and interest groups influenced legislation; *Thompson* (FS) concludes that organizational cooperation among four governmental agencies was directly related to a high degree of informational congruence; and *Wegner* (FS) investigates interorganizational relationships between governmental health boards and health delivery agencies, noting that the groups, as a whole, deny conflict, yet individual members perceive conflict.

Articles, Papers, and Reports: In the area of management-union interface, the *National School Public Relations Association* (PD) provides guidelines for the educational administrative team to develop an effective communication plan in a strike or work stoppage crisis.

In the area of government-government interface, *Akinbode* (FS) identifies four types of interagency relationships (cooperation, conflict, competition, and merger), noting that cooperation is facilitated by dynamic and democratic leadership, while competition and conflicts are attributed to change in leadership style and centralized administrative practices.

Organization to Community Interface:

Books and Dissertations: In the area of organization interface with the general public, *Archer* (TC) examines three citizen participation styles in Federal Grant Administration in the Model Cities Programs 1966-1974; *Barnett* (FS) concludes that the investors' understanding of the auditor's report is insufficient and proposes a revised format; *Broom* (FS) reports that a communication experiment in two rural communities involving the use of feedback increased awareness of community problems among community leaders, elected officials, and citizens; *Crosby* (FS) notes that school principals held positive attitudes toward community involvement, but expressed negative attitudes for parent membership on school committees and parent evaluation and selection of teachers; *Ehrman* (FS) studies the problems of disseminating information about schools to the community, noting that barriers to the introduction of new techniques include lack of time and qualified staff; and *Ford* (FS) describes and analyzes the Community Involvement Committee, recommending that all community elements be involved early in the initial planning, and chairperson selection be handled very carefully.

Lamoreaux (FS) reviews the Iranian government program for family planning, concluding that messages to small subaudiences may be more effective than messages to influentials, when subaudiences are selected on basis of age, sex, urbanization, media exposure, and community involvement; *Locander* (TC) examines the methods used by seven Presidents of the United States to communicate with the public, concluding that the President is head of a communications team, interacting with the press and the public; *Newsom* (TC) covers guidelines for successful public relations, including communication theory, public relations theory, and interpersonal relations with media people; *O'Connell* (FS) analyzes efforts of a school superintendent to reconcile the goals of teachers, community, and board of education by the adoption of a more open and collaborative system of communication; *Pollak* (FS) indicates that citizen planning committees will not influence political decision-making unless citizen input is accepted as a valid and valuable contribution; and *Steinberg* (FS) finds that consumer participation in a health-care organization was achieved as a result of internal tension, and not as a result of consumer efforts.

In the area of organization interface with clients and customers, *Burke* (LS) analyzes verbal exchanges between college advisors and students, finding that variations in verbal patterns had no relationship on student outcomes; *Clark* (FS) looks at citizen participation in health organizations, noting the need for open and consistent communication between local community boards and the central government agency; *Cook* (TC) examines citizen participation in public programs, discusses the role of practice theory, and provides fifteen specific agency goals, including transmission of information; *Forrer* (FS) compares the effects of two methods of university parent orientation (oral and written on-campus vs. written off-campus) finding that on-campus communication is more effective; *Lambert* (FS) finds that the parental view of a school is related to both the principal's membership in community organizations and the time spent in community activities; and *Orr* (FS) investigates undergraduate recruitment, finding twenty communication variables significantly related to effective recruitment and retention.

Articles, Papers, and Reports: In the area of organization interface with the general public, *Bagin* (TC) concludes that key communicators (community members who contact many people) can be used by schools as sources of feedback from the community and as information disseminators; *Bailey* (TC) presents a model for evaluating an educational organization in terms of community needs and ability to generate new solutions; *Grunig* (FS) tests a theory of individual communication behavior relative to public relations practitioners; and *Maloney* (TC) suggests means to facilitate communication and cooperation between vocational training institutions and the business-industrial sectors of the community.

In the area of organization interface with clients and customers, *Corwin* (FS) studies the interactions of teachers and parents in a conflict situation.

Specialized Texts, Anthologies, Bibliographies, and Reviews:

Books: *Ross* (Text) writes on the management of public relations, stressing environmental factors as negative attitudes toward business, public affairs, and the elements making for change.

Articles, Papers, and Reports: *Alderfer* (Review) examines classical studies of group behavior and outlines propositions explaining intergroup conflict; *Roessler* (Review) discusses the literature on strategies for interagency linkages in the delivery of human rehabilitation services; and *Young* (bibliography) presents an updated bibliography with abstracts relative to labor-management relationships.

Communication Factors and Organization Goals

One hundred and nine books and one hundred and five articles/papers relate to Communication Factors and Organization Goals. Books accounted for 24 percent of all books and dissertations, and articles/papers were 34 percent of all articles, papers, and reports.

The frequency of specific subclasses is shown below:

Subclasses	Books		Articles/Papers	
	Quantity	Percent	Quantity	Percent
Morale Studies	44	40	22	21
Performance-Effectiveness Studies	15	14	32	30
Adaptiveness-Innovation Studies	18	16	17	16
Leadership Studies	21	19	11	11
Communication Studies	2	2	3	3
Motivation Studies	3	3	15	14
Texts, Anthologies, Reviews	6	6	5	5
TOTALS	**109**	**100**	**105**	**100**

A comparison of the frequency rank order of articles/papers to books/dissertations follows:

	Books	Articles
Morale Studies	1	2
Leadership Studies	2	5
Adaptiveness-Innovation Studies	3	3
Performance-Effectiveness Studies	4	1
Texts, Anthologies, Reviews	5	6
Motivation Studies	6	4
Communication Studies	7	7

For the classification Communication Factors and Organization Goals, the most popular writing area was related to job satisfaction and organizational climate under the subclass of Morale Studies. This was followed by a substantial number of publications relating to Performance-Effectiveness Studies, Adaptiveness-Innovation Studies, and Leadership Studies. Motivation Studies ranked sixth in books and fourth in articles, while studies in technical communication ranked last in both formats.

Table 5 presents the names of authors relevant to each of the subclasses of Communication Factors and Organization Goals; and the commentary below furnishes a guide and overview as to the contents and findings of selected works.

Morale Studies:

Books and Dissertations: In the area of job satisfaction, *Bailey* (TC) finds no relationship between type of school calendar (full year vs. nine month) and job satisfaction of principals; *Behrman* (FS) concludes that perceived interpersonal relations with students, peers, and administrators were all significantly related with teacher job satisfaction; *Buxton* (FS) reports no significant differences in job satisfaction between teachers in open-space schools and teachers in traditional schools; *Carrell* (FS) studies employee perceptions of equitable treatment as an indicator of job satisfaction, concluding that pay increases did not substantially increase job satisfaction; and *Emery* (FS) reviews four studies of Norwegian organizations that attempt to increase worker satisfaction by increasing participation in management.

Faris (FS) analyzes the determinants of job satisfaction, indicating that job satisfaction is highly correlated with perceived success and life satisfaction; *Fatehi-Sedeh* (FS) notes an inverse relationship between intrinsic job satisfaction and extrinsic job satisfaction, suggesting the possibility of trade-offs between intrinsic and extrinsic rewards; *Henderson* (FS) reports that teachers perceiving high participation in school decision-making have higher morale and more positive attitudes towards principals than teachers perceiving low participation; *Herbst* (TC) discusses ways of decentralizing decision-making in organizations and their effects on worker satisfaction; and *Hsieh* (FS) finds that leadership dimensions are positively correlated with teacher job satisfaction in both Chinese and American schools, with Chinese teachers less satisfied than American teachers.

Table 5

Communication Factors and Organization Goals—1977
Classification of Authors
by Sublass, Publication Format, and Nature of Research

Subclasses	Books & Dissertations	Articles, Papers, Reports
Morale Studies:	Bailey. . . . . TC	Ashbaugh . . . . FS
—Job Satisfaction	Behrman . . . . . . FS	Branson . . . . FS
	Buxton . . . . FS	Falcione . . . . FS
	Carrell . . . . FS	Gould. . . . . FS
	Emery . . . . FS	Hackman. . . . . FS
	Faris . . . . FS	Hackman. . . . . TC
	Fatehi-Sedeh. . . . FS	Kavanagh. . . . . . . FS
	Henderson . . . . . FS	Koch . . . . FS
	Herbst . . . . TC	Merryman . . . . FS
	Hsieh . . . . FS	Reeley . . . . FS
	Katzell . . . . TC	Reinkober . . . . FS
	Keffer . . . . FS	Seyboh. . . . . FS
	Meyers . . . . FS	Steers. . . . . FS
	Powers . . . . FS	Strauss . . . . TC
	Reely. . . . . FS	Vrooman. . . . . FS
	Rogers . . . . FS	
	Smith, S. . . . . . . FS	
	Streker . . . . LS	
	Sumrall. . . . . . . FS	
	Wells . . . . FS	
	Zibilich. . . . . . . FS	
—Organizational Climate	Apter. . . . . FS	Bluestone . . . . PD
	Chaplain . . . . . . FS	Franklin . . . . FS
	Czander . . . . . . FS	Gordon. . . . . PD
	Dachanuluknukul. FS	Katerberg . . . . FS
	Dunagan . . . . . . FS	Krivonos. . . . . FS
	Gibbon. . . . . . . FS	Payne. . . . . TC
	Glickman. . . . . . FS	
	Johnson . . . . . . FS	
	Lake . . . . FS	
	Leszczynska . . . . FS	
	Lewis. . . . . FS	
	Manuie . . . . FS	
	Marco. . . . . FS	
	McCalla. . . . . . . FS	
	Ozigbo . . . . FS	
	Powell, G. . . . . . FS	
	Powell, L. . . . . . FS	
	Raspa. . . . . FS	
	Rohr . . . . FS	
	Smith, G.. . . . . . FS	
	Vick . . . . FS	
—Leadership Behavior	Burgett. . . . . . . FS	
	Folkins. . . . . . . FS	
Performance-Effectiveness Studies:	Keadle . . . . FS	Elsasser. . . . . TC
—Leadership Behavior	Jenks. . . . . FS	Marcus . . . . FS
	Mullinix . . . . . . FS	Schriesheim . . . . . FS
	Loehr. . . . . FS	
	Perry . . . . FS	
	Smith, R.. . . . . . FS	
	Stanfield . . . . . . FS	

Table 5, Continued

Subclasses	Books & Dissertations	Articles, Papers, Reports
—Coordination, Consensus, Conformity, Conflict	Dobbins . . . . . . FS Mermoud. . . . . . FS Nicholson . . . . . FS Perkins . . . . FS Perry . . . . FS	Baird . . . . FS Carrel. . . . . FS Gunderson. . . . . . . FS Longest. . . . . FS Miles . . . . FS Morse. . . . . FS Retondi . . . . FS Zagoria. . . . . FS Zenger . . . . TC
—Rewards		Hamner. . . . . PD Ivancevich . . . . . . FS Karmel . . . . LS Lawler . . . . LS Lawler . . . . TC Mainstone . . . . FS Mansperger. . . . . . FS Silverman . . . . FS Steers. . . . . FS
—Job Characteristics:		Cummings, L.L.. . . . TC Forber . . . . LS O'Reilly . . . . FS Powers . . . . FS Umstot. . . . . FS Umstot. . . . . TC
—Innovation	Heirs . . . . TC	
—Communication	Balk. . . . . TC Kilpatrick . . . . . FS	Badawy. . . . . TC Pennings . . . . TC Schuler(2) . . . . FS Stone. . . . . LS
Adaptiveness-Innovation Studies: —Participation and Decision-Making	Cerullo . . . . FS Curtis. . . . . FS Henry. . . . . TC Lambright . . . . . TC March. . . . . FS Mitchell . . . . . . FS Neveaux . . . . . . FS Randolph . . . . . FS Schoppert . . . . . TC Sheldon . . . . . . FS Steiner . . . . TC Weinberg. . . . . . FS	Berman. . . . . TC Hespe. . . . . TC Hilgendorf . . . . FS Jago. . . . . FS Knoop . . . . FS National Institute . . . TC Owens . . . . TC Rubinstein. . . . . . . PD Sakkal . . . . PD Schuler. . . . . FS Seeborg. . . . . LS Singhal . . . . FS
—Innovation and Change	Burke. . . . . TC Page. . . . . FS Steinhauer . . . . . FS Zerla . . . . FS	Acker. . . . . TC
—Organization Structure and Job Design		Gyllenhammar. . . . . PD Moch . . . . FS
—Communication		Stahl . . . . FS Vogt . . . . TC
—Morale	Struzziery . . . . . FS Vegso. . . . . FS	

Table 5, Continued

Subclasses	Books & Dissertations	Articles, Papers, Reports
Leadership Studies: —Leadership Roles and Role Perceptions	Bennis . . . . TC Finley . . . . FS Hedrick. . . . . . . FS Jackson. . . . . . . FS Kirchoff . . . . . . FS Lichtenfeld . . . . FS Nontasak. . . . . . FS Rings . . . . FS Rundle . . . . FS Whiting. . . . . . . FS	Bennis . . . . PD Downey . . . . FS Hazelwood. . . . . . . TC
—Leadership Style	Bandy . . . . FS Bartley . . . . FS Blumstein . . . . . FS Bonen . . . . FS Cox . . . . FS Mead . . . . FS Milburn. . . . . . . FS Perkins . . . . FS Quinn. . . . . FS Schou. . . . . FS Stevens . . . . FS	Adams . . . . FS Gleason. . . . . LS Kaufman. . . . . FS Mowday . . . . FS Paterson . . . . FS Schou. . . . . FS Schriesheim . . . . . . FS Sinha . . . . TC
Communication Studies:	Lagios . . . . FS Waters . . . . TC	Kennedy . . . . FS Lawler . . . . LS Rogers, D. L. . . . . . LS
Motivation Studies:	Remmert. . . . . . FS Manning . . . . . FS Roberts. . . . . . . FS	Brief/Aldag . . . . . . FS Brief/Wallden . . . . . FS Cummings, T.G. . . . . FS Faunce . . . . TC Gemmill . . . . FS Greenberg . . . . LS Hamner. . . . . PD Lawler . . . . PD McAlindon. . . . . . . PD Pinder . . . . LS Scott . . . . TC Singhal . . . . FS Srivastava . . . . . . TC Stewart. . . . . TC Thompson . . . . FS
Texts and Tradebooks:	Caplow Rothman Steele Steers Sutermeister Trotta	
Reviews:		Goodman McKillip Motowidlo Slovic Umstot

Katzell (TC) discusses how work affects the productivity and job satisfaction of workers, exploring whether job satisfaction and productivity combined may be promoted by changing variables as controls, job enrichment, and compensation; *Keffer* (FS) reports significant relationships between overall job satisfaction and both job satisfiers (motivator factors) and job dissatisfiers (hygiene factors), finding that motivator factors were more strongly related to job satisfaction than hygiene factors; *Meyers* (FS) finds that teachers in parochial schools have higher degree of selflessness and morale than their public school counterparts; *Powers* (FS) concludes that congruence of superintendents' and principals' leadership styles resulted in greater teacher loyalty and job satisfaction; and *Reely* (FS) studies U.S. Air Force education faculty, noting that intrinsic job satisfaction contributes more to overall job satisfaction than extrinsic job satisfaction.

Rogers (FS) finds differences in teacher job satisfaction between school districts with labor strife and school districts with labor harmony; *Smith, S.* (FS) states that "bureau climate," the work atmosphere within the organizational subunit, had a greater influence upon job satisfaction than "agency climate," the overall organizational climate; *Streker* (LS) compares the effects of job redesign, with and without employee participation, on job satisfaction; *Sumrall* (FS) studies the relationship between leadership behavior and teacher job satisfaction, suggesting that Texas schools create open organizational climates conducive to the establishment of supportive relationships; *Wells* (FS) concludes that faculty morale varies directly with perceptions of faculty involvement in university policy formulation; and *Zibilich* (FS) reports that morale improved after principals took part in a classroom observation improvement course.

In the area of organizational climate, *Apter* (FS) studies open climate and closed climate schools, finding no significant differences when compared on variables of teacher age, teacher sex, teacher length of service, and principals' self-acceptance; *Chaplain* (FS) notes that open climate schools tend to have older, more experienced principals who have positive attitudes towards self and others, positive self-acceptance, and are self-confident; *Czander* (FS) concludes that size is related to bureaucracy and that increases in bureaucracy cause organizations to move from an open climate to a closed climate; *Dachanuluknukul* (FS) examines the organizational climate of schools in Thailand, reporting a direct relationship between size of organization and closed climate, and noting that principals perceive open climates more frequently than teachers; and *Dunagan* (FS) reports a significant relationship between administrative climate and nursing teacher morale, as judged by perceptions of salary and occupational status, among other variables.

Gibbon (FS) notes significant relationships between leadership style and organizational climate in South African secondary schools; *Glickman* (FS) studies the relationship of teachers' perception of organizational climate and students' perception of classroom climate; *Johnson* (FS) attempts to change school climate and productivity through the use of FIRO-B, concluding that self-awareness and knowledge of interpersonal needs must be supplemented by facilitators trained in human relations and communication skills; *Lake* (FS) reports that effective school climate indicators include teacher sex and principal educational level and do not include principal's age, experience, and self-acceptance, or teacher age and experience; and *Leszczynska* (FS) investigates the influence of organization structure on the organizational climate of children-care organizations, concluding that size and staffing are significantly related to organizational climate.

Lewis (FS) reports that perceived organizational climate for rewards and promotions was lower for clerks and secretaries than for supervisors and technical specialists; *Manuie* (FS) surveys teacher-principal perceptions of the organizational climate in Saudi-Arabian schools and finds weak leadership and poor morale; *Marco* (FS) finds no significant differences in principal and teacher characteristics in open and closed organizational climates; *McCalla* (FS) examines the relationship of teacher morale to the racial composition of high school student bodies, finding higher morale in schools where the racial balance was approximately equal; and *Ozigbo* (FS) studies secondary school teachers attending a university graduate course, reporting significant relationships among teacher dogmatism, pupil control ideology, and teacher perception of school climate.

Powell, G. (FS) maintains that there is no significant relationship between attitude toward work-related change and each dimension of organizational climate as tested by the Margulies (1965) revision of the Organizational Climate Description Questionnaire, concluding that this revision is inappropriate for the measurement of organizational climate in health-care organizations; *Powell, L.* (FS) studies selected characteristics of principals, teachers and schools within two dimensions of organizational climate, finding little difference between more-open schools and less-open schools; *Raspa* (FS) finds no significant relationship between type of climate and personal characteristics of principals or teachers, though younger, less-experienced principals tended to be in open-climate schools; *Smith, G.* (FS) compares perceptions of school climate among students, teachers, and administrators, finding that the greater the hierarchical distance between respondents and the administrator, the less positive the perception of school climate, but the higher the socio-economic level, the more positive the perception; and *Vick* (FS) determines that school principals with teacher-centered management styles tended to have schools with more open climates, but finds no correlation between innovativeness and climate.

In the area of leadership behavior influence on morale, *Burgett* (FS) predicts teacher morale by the use of the Purdue Teacher Opinionnaire, finding that a high level of agreement between school boards and superintendents results in lower teacher morale; and *Folkins* (FS) finds that teacher morale is directly influenced by monetary rewards and personal, frequent contact between administrators and staff.

Articles, Papers, and Reports: In the area of job satisfaction, *Ashbaugh* (FS) analyzes the effect of a special program to increase job satisfaction so as to improve Air Force volunteer and retention rates; *Branson* (FS) concludes that major determinants of job satisfaction for Air Force civilian employees are job related factors as job challenge, freedom, personal growth, and preparation for greater responsibility; *Falcione* (FS) indicates that subordinate satisfaction with immediate supervision is closely associated with perceptions of supervisor communication behavior, credibility, attractiveness, and attitude similiarity, and to a lesser extent with oral communication apprehension and self-esteem; *Gould* (FS) reports as to the status of a long-term Air Force research project in fifth year of studying job satisfaction so as to obtain fuller utilization of personnel; *Hackman, et al.* (FS) study effects of changes in job characteristics on work attitudes and behavior, finding that such changes influenced growth satisfaction, internal motivation, and general satisfaction but did not affect satisfaction with work context; *Hackman* (TC) presents a job characteristics model of work motivation to explain how job redesign can increase productivity and employee satisfaction; and *Kavanagh* (FS) finds that job and life satisfaction are positively related for both males and females regardless of job level.

Koch (FS) examines effect of various aspects of feedback on work behavior and job attitudes of sewing machine operators, noting that increased feedback improved group cohesion and goal commitment; *Merryman* (FS) studies the relationship of organization growth and job satisfaction, finding that increases in size, efficiency, and profits are negatively related to employees' job satisfaction and effective interpersonal communication; *Reeley* (FS) analyzes the relationships between job satisfaction-enrichment factors and demographic variables for U.S. Air Force Military Education faculty; and *Reinkober* (FS) discusses the effects of technology on the employee, reporting that the impact has been one of alienation.

Seyboh (FS) concludes that a greater variety of organizational inducements (pay, job variety, task complexity) are required to satisfy better-educated employees; *Steers* (FS) finds no direct relationships between personality characteristics and turnover when considering high- and low-scope jobs, but did find significant differences in correlations between turnover and needs for achievement and affiliation among employees with different job scopes; *Strauss* (TC) concentrates on participation as a way of improving the quality of work life by increasing the employee's control over the job; and *Vrooman* (FS) analyzes the variables related to job satisfaction and career intent, noting the major factors to be personal growth, personnel standing, job challenge, and preparation for higher positions.

In the area of organizational climate, *Bluestone* (PD) indicates that both management and employees will benefit from sincere organization efforts to create a climate of satisfaction and opportunity for human development; *Franklin* (FS) studies causal relations among four social-psychological aspects of organizations, finding major links to exist between organizational climate and managerial leadership, managerial leadership and peer leadership, and peer leadership and group process; *Gordon* (PD) discusses climate in successful companies, noting that managers in these companies communicate expectations clearly, and provide that employees' compensation is competitive and performance related; *Katerberg* (FS) explores organizational climate and job attitudes, concluding that climate is more predictable than job attitudes, and that climate is a set of shared perceptions at a group level above that of the individual; *Krivonos*

(FS) examines the relationship of intrinsic and extrinsic motivation to the communication climate in organizations, finding partial support for the hypothesis that those who are intrinsically motivated perceive communication climate as being more ideal than those who are extrinsically motivated; and *Payne* (TC) summarizes eight conceptual types of climate and satisfaction.

Performance-Effectiveness Studies:

Books and Dissertations: In the area of leadership influence on performance, *Keadle* (FS) studies the relationships between organizational climate perceptions and selected variables, finding no significant relationship between type of climate and student achievement, student self-perception, classroom behavior, and students' perception of teachers' feelings toward them; *Jenks* (FS) compares perception of overall organizational effectiveness on part of first and second level supervisors, noting that supervisors emphasized productivity of the individual work unit, while higher managers stressed organizational stability; *Mullinix* (FS) determines that the nursing home administrator had a key-role in organizational effectiveness, and employee perception of the administrator's ability to plan, communicate, and solve problems resulted in a more effective organization; *Loehr* (FS) finds no correlation among district size, years of experience, and superintendent success ratings, and no significant relationship between success ratings of superintendents and the quality of decision-making; *Perry* (FS) examines attitudes of physician assistants, indicating that the strongest correlates of both job satisfaction and job performance was the degree of physician supervisory support and the amount of responsibility for patient care; *Smith, R.* (FS) concludes that perceptions about the expected performance of school superintendents, on the part of superintendents, teachers, and school board members, vary according to role, group membership, and school district size; and *Stanfield* (FS) analyzes the characteristics of successful school principals, concluding that communication within the school, and between the school and community are strongly related to success.

In the area of the influence of morale, coordination, consensus, and conflict on performance and effectiveness, *Dobbins* (FS) suggests that there is no relationship between school organizational climate and teacher behavior in managing classrooms; *Mermoud* (FS) indicates no significant relationship among organizational climate, self-concept, and teacher effectiveness; *Nicholson* (FS) studies the relationships among organizational goals, role conflict between commissioners and staff members, and organizational effectiveness; *Perkins* (FS) reports a positive relationship between teachers' perceptions of school environment and educationally-related performance of elementary students; and *Perry* (FS) finds that teacher morale and rapport with principal are positively correlated with the principal's effectiveness in the improvement of teacher performance.

In other books and dissertations wherein performance is treated as a dependent variable, *Heirs* (TC) emphasizes creative thinking as a way of improving organizational productivity; *Balk* (TC) discusses the theoretical aspects of productivity including motivation, measurement, and information systems; and *Kilpatrick* (FS) finds that the effectiveness of two naval ships was directly related to communication climate, indicating that the more effective ship had the better climate.

Articles, Papers, and Reports: In the area of leadership influence on performance, *Elsasser* (TC) discusses the functions of executives and the qualities that distinguish successful leaders from mediocre managers; *Marcus* (FS) examines the relationship between administrative leadership and performance, finding that schools showed achievement gains where principals emphasized the importance of selecting instructional materials and made more decisions in the instructional area; and *Schriesheim* (FS) studies the relationships between leader behavior and subordinate satisfaction and performance, concluding that high leader structure has dysfunctional effects only when accompanied by low consideration.

In the area of the influence of morale, coordination, consensus, and conflict on performance and effectiveness, *Baird* (FS) concludes that work satisfaction is correlated with job performance only when job is not stimulating; *Carrell* (FS) notes the positive relationship between employee perceptions of fair treatment and the outcome variables of longevity and effectiveness; *Gunderson* (FS) examines the importance of environment factors, organizational stress, and individual characteristics on job satisfaction and organizational effectiveness; *Longest* (FS) discusses the role of job satisfaction in relation to the productivity of nurses, concluding that a ranking of job satisfaction factors would assist nursing administrators to deal with problems of absenteeism, turnover, and productivity; and *Miles* (FS) constructs and tests a model of role conflict in terms of antecedents and consequences, including consideration for job tensions, job satisfaction, and perceived effectiveness.

Morse (FS) finds significant and positive relationships between managers' sense of competence and three measures of managerial performance; *Retondi* (FS) reports a negative relationship between organizational identification and both creativity and effectiveness, suggesting that behaviors related to organizational identification may produce dysfunctional as well as functional outcomes; *Zagoria* (FS) discusses the Nassau County, New York project to improve productivity among 25,000 workers by developing procedures and unifying job descriptions; and *Zenger* (TC) indicates how productivity can be increased by applying behavioral research findings to ten management areas, including executive attitudes, managerial behavior, and communication and feedback.

In the area of motivational theory and performance, *Hamner* (PD) indicates how behavior modification techniques can improve employee performance; *Ivancevich* (FS) notes the effects of goal-setting on performance, reporting that participative and assigned goal-setting were both more effective than no-training goal-setting in improving performance and satisfaction after nine months, but this effect disappeared within twelve months; *Karmel* (LS) analyzes data supplied by practicing managers and reports four dimensions of managerial performance, viz., perceived managerial competence, activity level, role centrality, and purposefulness; and *Lawler* (LS) explores the subject of job choice and post-decision dissonance theory.

Lawler (TC) examines the relationship between reward systems, the quality of work-life, and organizational effectiveness; *Mainstone* (FS) measures the impact of twelve individual organizational variables upon six expectancy theory cognitions, and employee performance; *Mansperger* (FS) reports that motivation was found to be significant in promoting excellent performance of program managers, but feedback from the job itself did not always aid the manager's perception of performance effectiveness; *Silverman* (FS) discusses organizational goals of professionals in a research and development organization, giving attention to the impact of motivation on productivity; and *Steers* (FS) investigates the effects of job scope and need for achievement on management commitment and performance, finding support for the hypothesis that high scope jobs are positively related to increased organizational commitment and increased performance.

In the area of the influence of job characteristics on performance and effectiveness, *Cummings, L.L.* (TC) considers the impact of organizational structure on managerial attitudes and performance, furnishing many conclusions relating satisfaction and performance to position in hierarchy, line and staff positions, number of persons supervised, departmental size, and tall vs. flat organizations; *Forber* (LS) notes that performance and satisfaction are related to the congruence of individual abilities and task design; *O'Reilly* (FS) reports that two indices of work orientation on the part of individual personalities, expressive and instrumental, interact with challenging and nonchallenging job types to affect job performance and attitudes; *Powers* (FS) discusses the generic behaviors involved in technical job task performance; *Umstot* (FS) concludes that job enrichment has a substantial impact on job satisfaction and little effect on productivity, while goal-setting has a major impact on productivity and a lesser impact on satisfaction; and *Umstot* (TC) examines the empirical literature as to job enrichment and goal-setting, indicating how these factors aid productivity and job satisfaction.

In the area of communication influence on performance, *Badawy* (TC) examines management by objectives programs, explaining how employee awareness of "where they stand" relates to effective performance on the job; *Pennings* (TC) describes a new conceptual framework for the concept of organizational effectiveness; *Schuler* (FS) in two empirical studies resulting in separate publications, concentrates on the variables of role perceptions, satisfaction and performance, and moderating influences—1) organizational level and participation in decision-making and 2) employee ability; and *Stone* (LS) studies differences in perceptions and reactions by relating personality variables to task characteristics.

Adaptiveness-Innovation Studies:

Books and Dissertations: In the area of decisions, decision-making processes, and participation, *Cerullo* (FS) notes that the formal organizational structure provided few opportunities for the informal structure to participate in decision-making; *Curtis* (FS) studies decision-making in critical incidents, reporting that the team approach resulted in more satisfactory solutions than those formulated by a single person; *Henry* (TC) examines methods used by President Truman in the decision-making process and finds that initial defects were later rectified by a more aggressive communication style; *Lambright* (TC) analyzes the adoption of urban technology, suggesting that innovation occurs over stages, depending on the capacity of local entrepreneurs to recognize the barriers that inhibit technology; and *March* (FS) discusses a theory of decision-making termed by the authors as "the garbage can" theory, positing that decision-making is largely irrational and ritualistic.

Mitchell (FS) observes that administrators believe students and staff to be involved in participatory management to a greater extent than perceived by the same students and staff; *Neveaux* (FS) concludes that decentralization resulted in an improvement in the flexibility, speed, and quality of decision-making of school principals in two school districts; *Randolph* (FS) finds that overall morale levels do not affect risk behaviors of school administrators, noting the tendency for risk-taking to decrease with longevity; *Schoppert* (TC) develops a model for participatory goal-setting involving manifest goals, hidden goals, public relations goals, and latent goals; and *Sheldon* (FS) notes that principals in "open" organizational climate schools participated in more school-related discussions than principals in "closed" organizational climate schools, and that discussion in "open" schools tended to take place in more informal areas as lounges and halls.

Steiner (TC) adopts a problem-solving method in handling problems of human service organizations relative to communication, conflict, and motivation; and *Weinberg* (FS) presents a case study of four state agencies, explicating a rational model and a crisis model of decision-making.

In the area of innovation, innovative behavior, and receptivity to change, *Burke* (FS) finds that the decision to reorganize an elementary school structure supplied insufficient information for proper implementation, and that participation by change agents was proportionate to the available information; *Page* (FS) reports no significant relationship between a school administrator's management style and the success of change efforts; *Steinhauer* (FS) analyzes a technology transfer innovation in a decentralized government organization, concluding that success was limited due to emphasis on administrative aspects of program and hierarchical conflict within the organization; and *Zerla* (FS) studies educational innovations, finding no significant relationship among openness of climate, change agent style of principals, and the occurrence of innovations.

In the area of morale influence on adaptiveness and innovation, *Struzziery* (FS) indicates that school climate variables can affect racial attitudes toward a voluntary busing program related to the introduction of a school integration program; and *Vegso* (FS) studies the organizational characteristics that influence innovative behavior, finding moderate support for hypothesis that management innovation is significantly correlated with organizational climate.

Articles, Papers, and Reports: In the area of decisions, decision-making processes and participation, *Berman* (TC) presents arguments for the acceptance of insight as the key element in effective decision-making; *Hespe* (TC) emphasizes the importance to workers of participation in decisions concerning practices in their own workplace; *Hilgendorf* (FS) reports that workers' attitudes toward participation are affected by job experience and decision-making opportunities; *Jago* (FS) finds a greater propensity for use of participative managerial methods at higher organizational levels; and *Knoop* (FS) concludes that individuals who are affected by decisions should partake in making those decisions.

The *National Institute of Education* (TC) analyzes decision-making under conditions of goal ambiguity; *Owens* (TC) develops a technique for assessing teachers' views to guide principals in deciding whom to involve in dealing with problems; *Rubinstein* (PD) related participative problem-solving to increasing organizational effectiveness via increased motivation, job satisfaction, and productivity; and *Sakkal* (PD) discusses the fundamental aspects of executive plan preparation, attempting to improve the quality of decision-making and communication within and among state government agencies.

Schuler (FS) finds participation to be satisfying to low authoritarian subordinates regardless of the degree of task repetitiveness but satisfying to high authoriatarian subordinates only when tasks were low in repetitiveness, noting that highly repetitive tasks were less conducive to ego involvement than low repetitive tasks; *Seeborg* (LS) studies the influence of employee participation in job redesign, concluding that satisfaction is improved; and *Singhal* (FS) reports that participation leads to reduced absenteeism, indicating that absenteeism was also affected by interpersonal perception, interpersonal communication, group cohesiveness, and personal correlates as length of service, union-ization, and anxiety.

In the area of innovation and change, *Acker* (TC) discusses professional aspects of contemporary management, relating change in society to demand for adaptive management.

In the area of job design and innovation, *Gyllenhammar* (PD) describes how job satisfaction and productivity can be increased by using work-teams instead of assembly lines, explaining how Volvo adapted work to people; and *Moch* (FS) presents a model of innovation adoption, testing it against empirical data.

In the area of communication influences on innovation, *Stahl* (FS) finds that communication with others in workgroup, and levels of participation in goal-setting, were significantly related to innovation and productivity of scientists and engineers; and *Vogt* (TC) presents a conceptual model to analyze conflict in the planning process of a university.

Leadership Studies:

Books and Dissertations: In the area of leadership roles and role perceptions, *Bennis* (TC) discusses problems inherent to leadership in organizations, including inadequate information, conflict resolution, innovation, and structure; *Finley* (FS) indicates there were no significant differences between principals and subordinates on perceptions of the principal's leadership behavior, but there were differences among the subordinates; *Hedrick* (FS) states that college administrators tend to agree as to role-expectations and need-dispositions, while subordinates tend not to agree on the same variables; *Jackson* (FS) concludes that the perceived and expected leadership role of school principals differed significantly when secretaries, building representatives, and principals were compared to each other; and *Kirchoff* (FS) compares leadership behavior of principals in operating schools with principals in recently closed schools and finds that teachers give higher ratings to principals in operating schools.

Lichtenfeld (FS) concludes that similar administrative skills are necessary to provide effective educational leadership in both public and private schools; *Nontasak* (FS) studies the leadership behavior of school superintendents in Thailand, finding that no significant differences exist among superintendents in terms of desirable leadership traits; *Rings* (FS) analyzes communication variables in a public utility, concluding that supervisors have a key role as facilitators of two-way communication behavior and role definition; *Rundle* (FS) indicates that school size does not affect subordinates' perceived satisfaction with formal leadership; and *Whiting* (FS) finds a positive relationship between accuracy of the perception of leadership and success criteria, as measured by productivity and group status.

In the area of leadership style, *Bandy* (FS) reports that the situational variables of school setting, instructional type, size, and principal's sex were not good predictors of principal's administrative style; *Bartley* (FS) concludes that school superintendents tend to use consensus as means of gaining compliance, although Board of Education members perceived superintendents as using manipulation, and principals viewed superintendents as using coercion; *Blumstein* (FS) indicates that principals who view teachers as self-actualized and rational beings tend to involve teachers more in the decision-making process; *Bonen* (FS) states that a relationship exists between the cognitive style match of principal and faculty, and the staffs' perception of the principal's leadership effectiveness; and *Cox* (FS) finds significant differences among teachers, principals, and school board members as to their perceptions of the real and ideal leadership behavior of school superintendents.

Mead (FS) reports that the preferred leadership behavior of principals included a high degree of initiative and delegation of responsibilities to subordinates; *Milburn* (FS) analyzes teacher perception of female school principals, finding no significant differences between male and female teacher views; *Perkins* (FS) states that the team management approach to the administration of public schools was not considered effective in the schools studied, noting significant differences between the ideal and actual team management approach in use; *Quinn* (FS) examines the self-perceptions of male and female school principals as to administrative behavior, finding significant differences in the areas of leadership style and decision-making; *Schou* (FS) studies flexibility of leadership style and the contingency theory, reporting that subordinate managers perceived superiors as able to alter style to the nature of the problem, but subordinates experienced different degrees of satisfaction at various levels of flexibility; and *Stevens* (FS) surveys the leadership behavior of community college presidents, reporting their difficulty integrating the needs of the individual with the needs of the institution.

Articles, Papers, and Reports: In the area of leadership roles and role perceptions, *Bennis* (PD) suggests that the role of the leader is changing, offering seven guidelines to aid leaders in coping with such change; *Downey* (FS) finds weak support for House's path-goal theory of leadership effectiveness, suggesting need for considering moderator variables; and *Hazelwood* (TC) discusses documented research relative to executive aids for crisis management.

In the area of leadership style, *Adams* (FS) develops a code of ethics for managers in response to public demand for a clearer picture of the ethical responsibilities of today's leaders; *Gleason* (LS) explores the effects of high and low structure of procedural instructions on leadership style, employing the Machiavellianism Scale to indicate high, low, and medium machs; *Kaufman* (FS) compares leadership hierarchies of small communities in terms of complexity, coordination, and openness, analyzed by age, schooling, occupation, and race, and reports a high correlation between coordination and degree of participation; and *Mowday* (FS) finds consistent relationships between methods of leader influence, and principals' needs for achievement and years of supervisory experience.

Paterson (FS) discusses leader behavior in terms of initiating structure and consideration as related to the variables of job satisfaction, organizational climate, organizational size, and hierarchical level; *Schou* (FS) investigates a U.S. Navy installation, discussing leadership flexibility as a function of the situation, nature of problem, evaluations and satisfactions of subordinates, and least-preferred-coworker scores; *Schriesheim* (FS) examines and resolves some differences in the various definitions and conceptualizations of leader initiating structure; and *Sinha* (TC) contrasts three leadership styles, proposing a continuum from authoritarian to participative, with the middle position being labeled authoritative leadership.

Communication Studies:

Books and Dissertations: *Lagios* (FS) presents a formal plan for a principal to get feedback from faculty for the purpose of improving leadership behavior; and *Waters* (TC) studies organizational sanctions, identifying mechanisms within an organization that discourage exposure of illegal and unethical acts.

Articles, Papers, and Reports: *Kennedy* (FS) assesses influence of managerial style on communication in the program management environment, suggesting instrument to measure impact; *Lawler* (LS) finds support for dissonance theory in the area of job choice and post-employment attitudes; and *Rogers, D.L.* (LS) concludes that interorganizational variables account for the largest amount of variance in role conflict, while intraorganizational variables account for the largest amounts of variance in role ambiguity.

Motivation Studies:

Books and Dissertations: *Remmert* (FS) analyzes the relationship of organizational climate and teacher turnover, noting that teachers remaining on job perceived climate to be more interactive and collaborative; *Manning* (FS) studies the satisfiers and dissatisfiers of Virginia Superintendents of Schools, noting that superintendents consider interpersonal relations with teachers and community as a dissatisfier, while relations with school boards was viewed as a satisfier; and *Roberts* (FS) examines leadership characteristics of principals as predictors of teacher job motivation, finding no relationship as teachers ranked challenging work and interpersonal relations as prime motivators.

Articles, Papers, and Reports: *Brief/Munro/Aldag* (FS) present the argument for job enlargement, reporting that correctional employees responded more positively to jobs offering variety and feedback than to jobs perceived as dull and monotonous; *Brief/Aldag/Wallden* (FS) study correlates of supervisory style among policemen, reporting that consideration correlates positively with organizational commitment, and initiating structure correlates negatively with defensive posture and positively with experienced meaningfulness and responsibility of work, general job satisfaction, job involvement, and organizational commitment; *Cummings, T.G.* (FS) supports Lawler and Hall's conclusion that job attitudes of satisfaction, job involvement, and intrinsic motivation are conceptually distinct and empirically independent; *Faunce* (TC) discusses the relationship between occupational achievement and self-esteem employing the self-investment theory; and *Gemmill* (FS) examines factors leading to promotion in large, complex organizations, finding that "politics" and public image are part of the folklore that may not be correct.

Greenberg (LS) explores the use of overreward to motivate performance, giving higher rewards to members of failing groups vs. successful groups, and to lazy workers vs. well-motivated workers; *Hamner* (PD) asserts that behavior modification techniques, involving the use of both positive reinforcement and

verbal feedback by managers, can improve employee performance; *Lawler* (PD) emphasizes that the pay system is an important motivator helping organizational effectiveness if used in
harmony with the total organizational system; *McAlindon* (PD)
outlines how to develop organizations in which self-actualizing
executives flourish; and *Pinder* (LS) investigates the additivity
versus nonadditivity of intrinsic and extrinsic incentives, concluding that they are not additive in determining organizational
attitudes and behaviors.

Scott (TC) studies the effects of extrinsic reward on intrinsic
motivation, maintaining that there is no acceptable evidence
that extrinsic reinforcers disrupt other reinforcing events, noting that the meaning of intrinsic motivation is obscure, and that
a reinforcement analysis is more fruitful; *Singhal* (FS), in the
Indian Journal of Social Work, writes on subject of need gratification and job incentives, reporting that safety was found to
be the most important need, and the important job incentives
included opportunity for promotion, training, and good working conditions; *Srivastava* (TC) evaluates money as a motivating
force, stating that money itself is a secondary motive for working efficiently and that other job characteristics are just as
important; *Stewart* (TC) looks at motivation in the U.S. Navy,
concluding that effective incentives differ in relation to goals of
individuals—e.g., promotion motivates career-minded personnel,
training opportunities motivate occupation-oriented personnel,
and pay is high motivator for those unlikely to reenlist; and
Thompson (FS) indicates that organizational obsolescence, not
individual obsolescence, results in low motivated employees.

Specialized Texts, Anthologies, Bibliographies, and Reviews:

Books: *Caplow* (Text) synthesizes the empirical research on
organizational effectiveness and translates findings into suggestions for the practicing manager including consideration for
communication, productivity, morale, and change; *Rothman*
(Text) presents a planning manual for promoting innovation
and change in organizations and communities; *Sutermeister*
(Text) analyzes the human and mechanical factors which affect
worker productivity; *Steers* (Text) reviews and interprets the
literature on organizational effectiveness, providing guidelines
for improving in the areas of communication, personnel training,
job design, organizational change, and goal setting; *Steele* (Text)
analyzes organization climate in terms of leadership, physical

structures, communication patterns, and group norms, suggesting activities for diagnosing and implementing changes in climate; and *Trotta* (Text) discusses grievances in the workplace, indicating the causes, avoidance procedures, and methods to settle them peacefully when they arise.

Articles, Papers, and Reports: *Goodman* (Review) supplies five original papers on organizational effectiveness presented at Carnegie-Mellon University in 1976; *McKillip* (Review) summarizes research findings concerning the use of biographical data in predicting job performance; *Motowidlo* (Review) describes the major concepts and theories that differentiate and define motivation, satisfaction, and morale, concentrating on those most likely to be usefully applied in the U.S. Army; *Slovic* (Review) presents an overview of decision-making research conducted in the working environment; and *Umstot* (Review) provides a literature review of job enrichment and goal-setting, describing how these two factors aid productivity and job satisfaction.

Skill Improvement and Training in Organizational Communication

Forty-five books and twenty-five articles/papers relate to Skill Improvement and Training in Organizational Communication. Books accounted for ten percent of all books and dissertations, and articles/papers were eight percent of all articles, papers, and reports.

The frequency of specific subclasses is shown below:

Subclasses	Books		Articles/Papers	
	Quantity	Percent	Quantity	Percent
Training Feedback and Evaluation	11	24	3	12
Training Techniques	5	11	7	28
Training Media	7	16	2	8
Training Programs	10	22	7	28
Training Needs	2	5	4	16
Training Resources and Administration	1	2	1	4
Texts, Anthologies, Reviews	9	20	1	4
TOTALS	45	100	25	100

A comparison of the frequency rank order of articles/papers to books/dissertations follows:

	Books	Articles
Training Feedback and Evaluation	1	4
Training Programs	2	1-2
Texts, Anthologies, Reviews	3	6-7
Training Media	4	5
Training Techniques	5	1-2
Training Needs	6	3
Training Resources and Administration	7	6-7

For the classification Skill Improvement and Training in Organizational Communication, the most popular writing areas, when considering books and articles, were Training Programs, Training Feedback and Evaluation, and Training Techniques, followed closely by Texts and Reviews, and Training Media. The least popular subclasses were Training Needs, and Training Resources and Administration.

Table 6 presents the names of authors relevant to each of the subclasses of Skill Improvement and Training in Organizational Communication; and the commentary below furnishes a guide and overview as to the contents and findings of selected works.

Training Feedback and Evaluation:

Books and Dissertations: *Anglin* (FS) reports that college students with communication training experienced more openness and more positive self-concept changes than students receiving no training; *Burke* (FS) finds that a ten-week program in communication skills increased active listening skills and empathy of elementary school teachers; *Easley* (FS) evaluates a modular methodology for developing teacher communication, concluding that special facilitative training did not result in skills being applied to classroom; *Hemphill* (FS) examines the effectiveness of a one-semester graduate course in communications for special education support personnel, concluding that it significantly improved specific skills as paraphrasing and evaluator responses; *Madden* (LS) concludes that human relations training and group discussion results in more accurate decisions than otherwise obtainable; and *Main* (FS) studies the effects of training problem high-school students in communication skills.

Maynard (FS) reports that specialized training did not materially improve the organizational climate of schools studied; *Ollier* (FS) assesses the efforts to improve communication within the

Table 6

Skill Improvement and Training in Organizational Communication—1977
Classification of Authors
by Subclass, Publication Format, and Nature of Research

Subclasses	Books & Dissertations	Articles, Papers, Reports
Training Feedback and Evaluation:	Anglin . . . . FS Burke. . . . . FS Easley . . . . LS Hemphill. . . . . . LS Madden. . . . . . LS Main . . . . FS Maynard . . . . . FS Ollier . . . . FS Rowzee. . . . . . LS Shean. . . . . . . LS Terry . . . . LS	Adams . . . . FS Buckner . . . . . . FS Guyot . . . . PD
Training Techniques:	Davison. . . . . . LS Elliott . . . . . . LS Griffin . . . . . . FS Hubbard . . . . . LS Wilson . . . . . . LS	Cooper . . . . TC Cooper . . . . LS Falcione . . . . . . TC Stilwell . . . . TC Stone . . . . FS Wholey . . . . PD Wittmer . . . . . . TC
Training Media:	Anderson. . . . . . PD Day . . . . PD Greenberg . . . . PD Jones, J. . . . . . . PD Melrose. . . . . . . PD Pfeiffer. . . . . . . PD Roach . . . . . . LS	Braby . . . . PD Carpenter . . . . . FS
Training Programs:	Allman . . . . . . FS Barber . . . . . . FS Bateman . . . . . FS Bryngleson. . . . FS Buchholz. . . . . LS Chiosso. . . . . . FS Coleman . . . . . LS Hopkins . . . . . LS Maurer . . . . . . FS Melton . . . . . . FS	Brown . . . . TC Burstiner. . . . . . FS Crowley . . . . . . FS Horan. . . . . FS Jandt . . . . TC Mendoca . . . . . . LS National Project. . . PD
Training Needs:	Brannen . . . . . FS Robson. . . . . . FS	Fiedler . . . . LS Joint Center . . . . . PD Penrose. . . . . . . FS Research Group Inc. PD
Training Resources/Administration:	Bunning . . . . . FS	Warsylik . . . . FS
Texts and Tradebooks:	Bartel Doyle Egan, G. Egan, K. Hargreaves Hart Nadler Silvern Steinmetz	
Reviews:		Wakefield

government agency responsible for U.S. Dependents Schools European Area, concluding that the instructional programs were effective in terms of communication criteria derived from statements of educational objectives; *Rowzee* (LS) determines that short-term communications training improved the facilitative communications skills and self-concepts of Upward Bound students (low socio-economic level, and under-achieving); *Shean* (LS) finds that a fifteen hour training program in creative problem-solving improved creative thinking ability, fluency, flexibility, and originality; and *Terry* (LS) notes that training in listening skills did not affect learning retention or student attitudes toward a business communications course.

Articles, Papers, and Reports: *Adams* (FS) studies 56 first-line supervisors to determine if training programs increase satisfaction; *Buckner* (FS) compares personnel training with Transaction Analysis to conventional training; and *Guyot* (PD) suggests that training produces a placebo effect in that trainee's improve simply because they are expected to, not because the training was actually effective.

Training Techniques:

Books and Dissertations: *Davison* (LS) compares simulation versus case study approaches, noting 1) a simulation strategy was feasible for developing teacher verbal communication, and 2) a more positive relationship between teachers and students in the case study approach; *Elliott* (LS) observes no difference in student attitudes whether taught by lecture, simulation or videotape, reporting that all three methods improved on control-group performance; *Griffin* (FS) finds that a T-group marathon produced behavioral changes in participants behavior, with individual differences attributed to participant's experience, sex, and level of teaching reponsibilities; *Hubbard* (LS) compares the incident case and the in-depth case method of instruction, finding no significant differences on an objective test but noting students' preference for the incident case method when measured on a subjective test; and *Wilson* (LS) studies real and nominal brainstorming groups, finding no difference in the number of unique ideas generated, although nominal groups (combined efforts of individuals brainstorming independently) were superior in the production of nonoverlapping ideas.

Articles, Papers, and Reports: *Cooper* (TC) examines the impact of sensitivity training on participants' self-actualization in the United Kingdom, Turkey, and Japan, suggesting that individuals respond to experimental learning groups in direct relationship to economic and social conditions; *Cooper* (LS) finds that managers in structured exercise-based groups have more negative personality changes than managers in unstructured experiential learning groups after training; and *Falcione* (TC) outlines an instructional paradigm applicable to any learning environment, presenting four instructional strategies for organizational communication—viz., case studies, role playing, internships, and field research; *Stilwell* (TC) provides a learning development consultant model as a prototype for counselor training in the future; *Stone* (FS) investigates effects of instructions, modeling, and rehearsal in training college students in empathic communication, finding that instruction was a critical factor in facilitating written work and modeling was effective for interviewing; *Wholey* (PD) describes the training plan developed by HRA (Human Resources Agency), working with the Urban Institute, including training modules, data collection and analysis methods, and evaluation techniques for managers; and *Wittmer* (TC) suggests a model intended to assist correctional counselors in facilitating communication between prison guards and inmates of different races.

Training Media:
Books and Dissertations: *Anderson* (PD) studies problems in the selection of media for instruction, covering print, video, and computer media; *Day* (PD) discusses methods for learning communication skills including interviewing, simulations, and group exercises; *Greenberg* (PD) considers effective methods of communication with the elderly patient; *Jones* (PD) supplies a series of group exercises and questionnaires for practitioners and trainers in human relations training; *Melrose* (PD) provides materials for simulating the communication activities of a large corporation including exercises relative to information overload, lack of information, inaccurate data, performance evaluation, and authority delegation; *Pfeiffer* (PD) presents a collection of 23 group exercises designed for utilization in human relations training leadership development, self-awareness, and problem-solving; and *Roach* (LS) reports that use of two communications skills training models (Ivey's Microcounseling Paradigm and Carkhuff's Systematic Human Relations Model) produced significant differences.

Articles, Papers, and Reports: *Braby* (PD) discusses the design of U.S. Navy technical manuals to better support training programs; and *Carpenter* (FS) finds that videotaped role playing (VTR) is an effective training technique for improvement of nurses' therapeutic communication skills.

Training Programs:

Books and Dissertations: *Allman* (FS) indicates that the orientation process of new school board members is inadequate despite utilization of multi-media presentations; *Barber* (FS) reports significant differences between the perceptions of school superintendents and teachers towards principals who completed in-service training sessions involving planning, monitoring, and feedback processes; *Bateman* (FS) notes a considerable improvement in organizational climate after in-service training was administered to elementary school teachers; *Bryngleson* (FS) explains a staff development program involving constructs from transactional analysis, teacher effectiveness training, and values clarification, concluding that a one semester course resulted in higher levels of empathy and interaction skills; and *Buchholz* (LS) indicates that participation in a two-day course improved behavior in interpersonal communication encounters.

Chiosso (FS) states that a high school curriculum emphasizing learning of role-taking skills resulted in the gaining of valuable interpersonal skills by students; *Coleman* (LS) discusses a special training program designed to raise the level of empathic understanding, noting that results were significantly superior to the use of written instructions; *Hopkins* (LS) concludes that an effectiveness communications program lasting 12 weeks had no significant effect on the level of teachers' self-concept; *Maurer* (FS) finds that a self-instruction program in facilitation and communication skills furnishes an effective method of training teachers in interpersonal skills; and *Melton* (FS) explores school board communication problems, determining that an informal training program, consisting of reading and self-help, was the most valuable method for reducing barriers to communication into, through, and out of school systems.

Articles, Papers, and Reports: *Brown* (TC) presents a conceptual framework for studying the development stages of training programs relative to race relations, equal opportunity, and education; *Burstiner* (FS) reports good results from a workshop in "creative management" theory including training in creative thinking and problem solving, leadership, group dynamics, and motivation; *Crowley* (FS) notes that teaching communication skills to clients has become an important function of the counseling psychologist and examines language patterns of trainees in an instruction program; and *Horan* (FS) describes intercultural communication training programs, including a needs-attitudes survey of trainees moving from one cultural area to another.

Jandt (TC) studies communication and conflict resolution, suggesting ways to enhance conflict resolution skills; *Mendoca* (LS) finds that a combination of anxiety management training and problem-solving training results in greater gains than either method alone, with respect to vocational exploratory behavior of college students; and the *National Project on Education for Management of Social Welfare* (PD) develops a syllabus for a course on management of conflict and change, providing a model that indicates people will respond to an influencer only when it results in need satisfaction.

Training Needs:

Books and Dissertations: *Brannen* (FS) analyzes training needs of management personnel, concluding that greatest need is in areas of people management skills and top management skills; and *Robson* (FS) prepares an inventory of perceived management skills of school superintendents, finding that superintendents consider themselves most proficient in planning skills, but most deficient in areas of evaluation skills and decision-making skills.

Articles, Papers, and Reports: *Fiedler* (LS) examines the applicability of an expectancy-decision model to assertiveness in a nonclinical population, noting that participants consider the consequences of being assertive when making a decision about how to behave, and recommending that training programs focus on changing participants' perceptions of the risks involved in being assertive; The *Joint Center for Human Services Development, San Jose State University, California* (PD) proposes five training objectives to improve the processes for managing, planning, and integrating programs; *Penrose* (FS) describes a survey of business attitudes as to the importance of communication skills, indicating the educational and business background of survey respondents; and the *Research Group, Inc. of Atlanta, Georgia* (PD) presents training guidelines and materials used in a two-day needs assessment program, discussing techniques for needs assessment, including structured and unstructured surveys and interviews.

Training Resources and Administration:

Books and Dissertations: *Bunning* (FS) reports that "skill of communicating" was considered a significant skill in adult educators.

Articles, Papers, and Reports: *Warsylik* (FS) reports on a study designed to quantify the nature and extent of in-house communications training.

Specialized Texts, Anthologies, Bibliographies, Reviews:

Books: *Bartel* (Text) covers preparation, selection, application, and development of educational materials for training instructors; *Doyle* (Text) presents a new interaction method of making meetings work; *Egan, G.* (Text) assumes that many group experiences require people to use new skills, and provides training in self-disclosure, listening, confrontation, and other interpersonal behavioral elements; and *Egan, K.* (Text) explains structural communication is a new methodogy to improve communication in discussion groups on basis of Skinner's and Brunner's ideas.

Hart (Text) discusses the basic elements of writing, covering letters, memorandums, proposals, progress reports, and investigative reports; *Hargreaves* (Text) gives checkpoints for success in management communication; *Nadler* (Text) indicates how to improve workshops and conferences; *Silvern* (Text) writes on topics related to occupational instruction, including planning, curriculum development, and program analysis; and *Steinmetz* (Text) aims to help individuals learn the art of delegating and to assist those who teach delegation in company training programs.

Articles, Papers, and Reports: *Wakefield* (Review) provides a summary of research relative to perception and communication, including practical suggestions to improve student-teacher communication ability.

Communication Media in Organizations

Fifty books and twenty-four articles/papers were selected as relating to Communication Media in Organizations. Books within this classification accounted for 11 percent of all books and dissertations, and articles/papers were eight percent of all articles, papers, and reports.

The frequency of specific subclasses of Communication Media is shown below:

Subclasses	Books Quantity	Books Percent	Articles/Papers Quantity	Articles/Papers Percent
Oral Media[1]				
Written Media	5	10	3	13
Nonverbal Media[1]				
Telephonic Media	-		1	4
Audiovisual Media	-		4	17
Electronic Media	3	6	2	8
Comparative Media Studies	1	2	1	4
Information Systems	20	40	6	25
Communication Programs	10	20	7	29
Media Organization & Administration	2	4	-	
Texts, Anthologies, Reviews	4	18		
TOTALS	**50**	**100**	**24**	**100**

[1] Oral media and nonverbal media are listed but show no publications for the reason that writings relative to these media are classified under the major classes of Interpersonal, Intragroup, and Intergroup Communication. To a lesser extent, this is also true of written media.

A comparison of the frequency rank order or articles/papers to books/dissertaions follows:

	Books	Articles
Information Systems	1	2
Communication Programs	2	1
Texts, Anthologies, Reviews	3	8-9
Written Media	4	4
Electronic Media	5	5
Media Organization	6	8-9
Comparative Media Studies	7	6-7
Audiovisual	8-9	3
Telephonic	8-9	6-7

For the classification Communication Media in Organizations, the most popular writing areas were Information Systems, and Communication Programs. These two subclasses ranked first or second in both books and articles. The least popular subclasses were Comparative Media Studies, Media Organization and Administration, and Telephonic Media.

Table 7 presents the names of authors relevant to each of the subclasses of Communication Media in Organizations; and the commentary below furnishes a guide and overview as to the contents and findings of selected works:

Table 7

Communication Media in Organizations—1977
Classification of Authors
by Subclass, Publication Format, and Nature of Research

Subclasses	Books & Dissertations	Articles, Papers, Reports
Written Media:	Gibbins. . . . . LS Leach. . . . . TC Phillips . . . . PD Simpson . . . . . . FS Worthington. . . . . TC	Alderson . . . . LS Lunine . . . . PD Timm. . . . . TC
Telephonic Media:		McGough. . . . . . FS
Audiovisual Media:		A. F. Occ. Cntr.. . . FS Burns. . . . . TC Fisher. . . . . FS Rizzo . . . . FS
Electronic Media:	Kidane . . . . FS Roberts. . . . . . . FS Terry . . . . FS	Flory . . . . FS Sylvia. . . . . PD
Comparative Media Studies:	Cureton . . . . . . FS	Grace . . . . FS
Information Systems:	Boland . . . . FS Cerveny . . . . FS Craft . . . . FS Diran . . . . FS Geary. . . . . FS Gehrmann . . . . . . FS Jump . . . . FS Kroeber . . . . FS London. . . . . PD McClurg . . . . FS Murdick . . . . PD Reck . . . . FS Shutt . . . . FS Smith, H.. . . . . . . LS Spiegler. . . . . TC Spurgat. . . . . FS Sugarman . . . . . . FS Waller. . . . . FS Walstrom. . . . . . . FS Wolfe . . . . FS	Alter . . . . PD Applied Mgmt. Sci. . FS Colorado Social Ser. FS Cross . . . . TC Human Ser. Info . . FS Puma . . . . FS
Communication Programs:	Berman. . . . . FS Bhandari . . . . FS Carter. . . . . FS Johnson . . . . FS Lewis. . . . . FS	Argyris. . . . . PD Hall. . . . . TC Likert. . . . . PD Nadler . . . . PD NC Dept. of Human Resources. . . . . . PD

Table 7, Continued

Subclasses	Books & Dissertations	Articles, Papers, Reports
Communication Programs (con.):	Ryan . . . . TC	Odiorne . . . . PD
	Scaggs . . . . FS	Scott . . . . PD
	Springer . . . . FS	
	Troisi . . . . FS	
	Van Zandt . . . . . . FS	
Media Organization & Administration:	Brooks . . . . FS	
	Lyons. . . . . FS	
Texts and Tradebooks:	Burton	
	Fear	
	McIntosh	
	Nadler	
	Roman	
	Schramm	
	Ulanoff	
	Wells	
	Winfrey	

Written Media:

Books and Dissertations: *Gibbins* (LS) indicates that accounting information is not entirely factual and credibility of accountants was affected by readers' perception of factualness; *Leach* (TC) reports need for State Boards of Education to develop policy manuals, stressing the necessity for preliminary meetings and continuous policy drafting; *Phillips* (PD) emphasizes written communication including writing skills (grammar, effectiveness, mechanics, revisions), letter writing, and report writing; *Simpson* (FS) finds no differences between perceptions of business educators and business communicators with regard to error acceptability in written business communication; and *Worthington* (TC) concludes that financial statement footnotes are generally difficult to comprehend by the average investor, recommending that footnotes consist of short sentences with understandable vocabulary geared to the audience.

Articles, Papers, and Reports: *Alderson* (LS) reports on experiments designed to determine if a relationship exists between the order of information in a persuasive request letter and the effectiveness of the message; *Lunine* (PD) considers the procedure writer as a catalyst for implementing change insofar as the writer interacts with employees throughout the organization; and *Timm* (TC) explores internal organizational communication, emphasizing economical and effective means of utilizing the bulletin board as a medium for information dissemination.

Telephonic Media:
Articles, Papers, and Reports: *McGough* (FS) presents a summary of a two-year experience with the TIE-LINE, a statewide, telephone-accessed information and referral system.

Audiovisual Media:
Articles, Papers, and Reports: *The Air Force Occupational Measurement Center* (FS) describes the development of an Audiovisual Media Career Ladder; *Burns* (TC) discusses basic research questions relative to instructional television, interaction, and learning objectives; *Fisher* (FS) studies the effects of a Model-Reinforced Videotape relative to increasing information-seeking behavior in a self-instruction information resource center; and *Rizzo* (FS) compares sound-microfiche audiovisual programs to sound-slide programs, recommending sound-microfiche for further development.

Electronic Media:
Books and Dissertations: *Kidane* finds that EXIR (Executive Information Retrieval) is an inadequate method of storing and retrieving records due to requirement for numerous individual data banks and lack of clarity in some responses; *Roberts, A.* (FS) assesses the use of an electronic feedback system in the decision-making process of school districts and reports that the system was a valuable aid, especially in the final phases of decision-making; and *Terry* (FS) surveys school district usage of electronic data processing, finding a positive correlation with size of district and noting that administrative applications greatly outnumber instructional applications.

Articles, Papers, and Reports: *Flory* (FS) surveys computerization aspects of personnel functions in fifty state governments, considering factors that promote, hinder, or have little effect on computer applications; and *Sylvia* (PD) explains TOSS, a computerized system that presents information about a company's manpower.

Comparative Media Studies:
Books and Dissertations: *Cureton* (FS) studies the methodology in political public-opinion polling and reports that telephone interviewing and face-to-face interviewing produced similar data, but the face-to-face method derived added information and a more positive response by the interviewees.

Articles, Papers, and Reports: *Grace* (FS) evaluates the effectiveness of four multi-media presentations designed to support the Navy Career Counseling Program.

Information Systems:

Books and Dissertations: *Boland* (FS) examines two systems of analyst and user interaction in designing information systems, concluding that a high degree of analyst-user interaction is superior to the traditional approach wherein the analyst is more detached from the user; *Cerveny* (FS) notes that computerized information systems lowered claim costs for insurance companies; *Craft* (FS) indicates that most college libraries in negro universities favored membership in an automated communication network system despite required staff and organizational changes; *Diran* (FS) analyzes failures of a management information system in a large college, finding breakdown attributable to unattainable expectations plus assumptions that system would not alter human power structure, and that "obvious benefits" would generate support; and *Geary* (FS) discerns that perceived organizational support for management information systems is most important correlative with perceived success in the system.

Gehrmann (FS) finds that the organization's external environment plays an important role in management information system design and the effective application of such design; *Jump* (FS) stresses the need for prior training of personnel involved in the development and implementation of management information systems; *Kroeber* (FS) evaluates the current state of information systems evolution and constructs a matrix indicating the sophistication level and the performance level of computer systems; and *London* (PD) provides a useful guide for designing and implementing information systems with concern for the part of humans in the process.

McClurg (FS) concludes that computer-assisted management information systems in public higher education are not being utilized to maximum potential, noting that systems are incomplete due to financial constraints, costs of hardware acquisition, and personnel policy conflicts; *Murdick* (PD) provides an introduction to management information systems with the focus on management; *Reck* (FS) reports that a computer-based management information system is an effective tool in community colleges; *Shutt* (FS) finds that top-management in a university failed to assume responsibility for planning, guidance, and development of the management information system; *Smith, H.* (LS) examines various forms of computerized data base inquiry (basic, extended alpha-numeric reformatory, extended graphical reformatory) and concludes that the extended forms do not result in better decision-making performance; and *Spiegler* (TC) proposes a computer-aided methodology for linking three conventional methods of building information processing systems, so as to diminish difficulties as to cost, documentation, updating, and coordination.

Spurgat (FS) presents a study of the implementation and use of Management Information Systems (MIS) in a Federal Research agency, noting that the use of MIS showed the interdependence of three groups: 1) administrative-functional group, 2) manager-client user group, and 3) the technical designer; *Sugarman* (FS) reviews the Localized Job Search Information System designed to increase job entry applicants to the California State Employment Department; *Waller* (FS) evaluates budgetary control of management information systems, emphasizing need for close linkage between corporate and system development; *Walstrom* (FS) reports that management information systems in universities were used for many purposes including instructor evaluation and program evaluation; and *Wolfe* (FS) reports that computer use in the personnel function is directly related to company size.

Articles, Papers, and Reports: *Alter* (PD) explains how managers can use computers to help them make decisions, and communicate decisions, giving examples of seven types of computer support systems; *Applied Management Sciences, Inc.* (FS) analyzes the components of social service information and referral systems from the level of the State Agency on Aging to the level of the local social service center; *Colorado Department of Social Services* (FS) provides an overview of an information system, outlining management activities which contribute to a successful implementation at the local level, including feedback to caseworkers; *Cross* (TC) reviews potential benefits of implementing a central management information system for the U.S. Army Satellite Communications Agency; *The Human Services Information System Project of Lancester County, Pennsylvania* (FS) studies the five steps involved in developing a Human Services Information System for the purpose of obtaining more efficient and effective service agency operations; and *Puma* describes the operational components and special features of the Wyoming Social Service Information System.

Communication Programs:

Books and Dissertations: *Berman* (FS) observes no significant differences in managerial effectiveness of community colleges using management by objectives (MBO); *Bhandari* (FS) indicates need for communications to combat negative feelings towards proposed social programs; *Carter* (FS) reports favorable attitudes towards MBO on part of community college administrators, but finds some negative reactions generated by time pressures, paperwork, and difficulty in setting objectives; *Johnson* (FS) finds that an MBO program in a school district did not meet original objectives due to lack of organizational objectives, coordination, in-service preparation, and communication; and *Lewis* (FS) examines administrative perceptions of certain MBO programs, noting that superintendents and principals disagreed on some practices and plans while agreeing with the program's principles.

Ryan (TC) surveys federal involvement in MBO programs and notes lack of success; *Scaggs* (FS) finds the use of MBO has a significant effect on the self-concept of government agency directors; *Springer* (FS) reports that implementation of an MBO program in Pennsylvania school districts did not insure the solution of administrative problems; *Troisi* (FS) maintains that school use of MBO programs is complicated by school organizational structure, the authoritarian mode of school administration, and the excessive retraining needed; and *Van Zandt* (FS) assesses the effects of an MBO model on student and teacher evaluation of school guidance programs.

Articles, Papers, and Reports: *Argyris* (PD) describes "double-loop learning in organizations," a method that permits underlying assumptions and objectives to be openly questioned, and one that decreases game-playing and ineffective communication; *Hall* (TC) reports favorably on the effectiveness of the assessment center process as an evaluation instrument for selecting participants in an Upward Mobility Program; *Likert* (PD) asserts that management by *group* objectives (MBGO) has advantages over MBO that include higher motivation to reach objectives, more loyalty to co-workers and superiors, and better teamwork; *Nadler* (PD) indicates that an on-going feedback system is a useful management tool, and describes the implementation of one such system; *The North Carolina Department of Human Resources* presents a manual for the use of management by objectives in human service programs; *Odiorne* (PD) notes reasons causing organizations to fail with MBO and sees the need for quality training in MBO; and *Scott* (PD) couples MBO and TA (transactional analysis), observing that they are compatible and complementary tools leading to higher productivity and profits.

Media Organization and Administration:

Books and Dissertations: *Brooks* (FS) compares practices and perceptions of leaders in school-media relations, noting that finance-related news items were viewed as the most important school news by superintendents, newspaper editors, and television news directors; and *Lyons* (FS) discusses the role of media professionals in business and industry, noting their need for a comprehensive background in communications.

Specialized Texts, Anthologies, Bibliographies, and Reviews:

Books: *Burton* (Text) furnishes an extensive coverage of advertising fundamentals including media planning, media research, marketing research, and creativity; *Fear* (Text) presents a work in technical communication relative to writing and speaking including oral presentation, group discussion, telephone conversations, grammar, word usage, and research papers; *McIntosh* (Text) reviews techniques of business communication including letter writing, report writing, and oral communication; and *Nadler* (Text) discusses procedures for facilitating the exchange of information in conferences and workshops.

Roman (Text) provides a series of guidelines for effective advertising, including media selection, media production, media planning, and advertising testing; *Schramm* (Text) presents media tools and techniques for instruction including economics of instruction and multi-media comparisons; *Ulanoff* (Text) emphasizes advertising media use and evaluation, including discussions of copywriting, layout, organizational structure, and campaigns. *Wells* (Text) studies written business communication primarily, including chapters on letters, memos, job applications, and report writing; and *Winfrey* (Text) concentrates on technical and business report preparation including laboratory reports, interviews, and verbal reports.

Communication System Analysis in Organizations

Forty-one books and thirty-six articles/papers relate to Communication Analysis in Organizations. Books accounted for nine percent of all books and dissertations, and articles/papers were twelve percent of all articles, papers, and reports.

The frequency of specific subclasses is shown below:

Subclasses	Books Quantity	Percent	Articles/Papers Quantity	Percent
Empirical Case Studies Testing Specific Hypotheses	7	17	5	14
Communication Evaluation and Feedback Studies	6	15	6	17
Communication Network and Direction Studies	5	12	6	17
Models	5	12	3	8
The Systems Approach	2	5	3	8
The Organizational Development Approach	5	12	11	30
Information Processing and Requirement Studies	6	15	2	6
Texts, Anthologies, Bibliographies, and Reviews	5	12	-	
TOTALS	**41**	**100**	**36**	**100**

A comparison of the frequency rank order of articles/papers to books/dissertations follows:

	Books	Articles
Empirical Case Studies Testing Specific Hypotheses	1	4
Communication Evaluation and Feedback Studies	2-3	2-3
Information Processing and Requirement Studies	2-3	7
Communication Network and Direction Studies	4-5-6-7	2-3
Models	4-5-6-7	5-6
The Organizational Development Approach	4-5-6-7	1
Texts, Anthologies, Reviews	4-5-6-7	8
The Systems Approach	8	5-6

For the classification Communication System Analysis in Organizations, the most popular subclasses for books were Empirical Case Studies, Evaluation and Feedback Studies, and Information Processing Studies, with all other subclasses following very closely except for The Systems Approach that ranked last.

The most popular subclass for articles/papers was The Organizational Development Approach, with almost twice the writings of any other subclass. Other popular subclasses in the articles/papers format included Communication Evaluation and Feedback Studies and Communication Network and Direction Studies. Least popular were subclasses on Information Processing, Models, and the Systems Approach.

Table 8 presents the names of authors relevant to each of the subclasses of Communication System Analysis in Organizations; and the commentary below furnishes a guide and overview as to the contents and findings of selected works:

Table 8

Communication System Analysis in Organizations—1977
Classification of Authors
by Subclass, Publication Format, and Nature of Research

Subclasses	Books & Dissertations	Articles, Papers, Reports
Empirical Case Studies Testing Specific Hypotheses:	Brandt . . . . FS Brannen . . . . . . FS Dunning . . . . . . FS Lundy . . . . FS Nichols . . . . FS Pugh . . . . FS Spencer . . . . FS	Allied Health . . . . FS American Indian . . FS George . . . . FS Martino . . . . FS Schuelke . . . . FS
Communication Evaluation and Feedback Studies:	Barker . . . . FS Kaye . . . . FS Koenig . . . . FS Mazzaroppi . . . . FS Papageorgio . . . . FS Tate . . . . FS	Bass . . . . FS Goldhaber . . . . . . TC Rosenberg . . . . . . FS Wergin . . . . TC Wiio . . . . FS
Communication Network and Direction Studies:	Burns . . . . TC Coburn . . . . FS Kusterer . . . . . . FS Sanders . . . . FS Yeager . . . . FS	Housel . . . . FS Krivonos . . . . FS Schwartz . . . . FS Shapero . . . . FS Taylor . . . . FS Wigand . . . . FS
Models:	Bowey . . . . TC Lachenmeyer . . . TC Midgley . . . . TC Nelson . . . . LS Wigand . . . . . . FS	Comm. Serv. Agcy. . TC Hanson . . . . FS Spector . . . . FS
The Systems Approach:	Kilmann . . . . . . TC Pasmore . . . . . . FS	Goyer . . . . TC Pennings . . . . TC Roberts, K. . . . . . TC
The Organization Development Approach:	Duncan . . . . FS Eich . . . . FS Klein . . . . FS Lipshitz . . . . . . FS	Baker . . . . FS Bowers . . . . PD Burke . . . . PD Carlson . . . . PD

Table 8, Continued

Subclasses	Books & Dissertations	Articles, Papers, Reports
The Organization Development Approach (con.):	Roeber . . . . FS	Cook . . . . PD Frame . . . . PD Friedlander . . . . . TC Lourenco. . . . . . . FS Patten . . . . PD Tichy . . . . FS Wergin . . . . TC
Information Processing and Requirement Studies:	Aragona . . . . . . FS Bonett . . . . FS Smith, T.. . . . . . PD Torres . . . . FS Gorodezky. . . . . FS Hackathorn . . . . FS	Jacobson. . . . . . . TC Wilde . . . . TC
Texts and Tradebooks:	Alan Coyle Dyer	
Anthologies:	Hawley Mirvis	

Empirical Case Studies Testing Specific Hypothesis:

Books and Dissertations: *Brandt* (FS) compares product and service organizations as to critical variables (leadership, communication, decision-making) finding similar management systems but less managerial satisfaction in service industries; *Brannen* (FS) provides a case study of the worker-director plan in the British Steel Corporation, arguing that worker participation in corporate management is not likely to result in significant social changes; *Dunning* (FS) reports that communication in three police organizations was negatively affected by lack of propinquity and lack of perceived ability to participate in decision and control processes, noting that job satisfaction correlated positively with horizontal and vertical communication satisfaction; *Lundy* (FS) suggests that the types of communication used to attract members accounts for differences in types of members in Common Cause, a voluntary organization; *Nichols* (FS) reports a three year study of worker politics in a large English chemical company; *Pugh* (FS) surveys 82 firms as to the relationships of organizational size, structure, and technology, concluding that structure is a function of size as opposed to technology; and *Spencer* (FS) studies Presidential communication in terms of information and decision-making, finding that

the President's use of the information system available to him
shapes his role and his relationships with the members of the
system.

Articles, Papers, and Reports: The *Allied Health Manpower
Council of Santa Clara, California* (FS) examines the adequacy
of management information in Santa Clara County Nursing education, and the effectiveness of the county programs in terms of
coordination in utilization of health-care facilities, articulation
between various nursing programs, and personnel staffing; the
American Indian Journal (FS) provides insight on the content,
flow, timeliness, and usefulness of management information
generated and communicated throughout the Bureau of Indian
Affairs; *George* (FS) supplies a case history of the task-team
building program of the Litton Microwave Cooking Division;
Martino (FS) describes a manager's experience running a
medium-size engineering organization, including problem-solving
events; and *Schuelke* (FS) indicates the effects of a technology-
monitoring program on communication activites, and attitudes
of employees.

Communication Evaluation and Feedback Studies:

Books and Dissertations: *Barker* (FS) develops and imple-
ments a communication audit, finding that communication barriers between subsystems interfere with production; *Kaye* (FS)
assesses communication patterns and attitudes of management
personnel in a technical assistance network, finding that the
development of an organizational communication system is a
viable and worthwhile innovation; *Koenig* (FS) examines the
relationship between participation, feedback, and performance
efficiency in organizational planning, noting that extreme care
and effort are needed to achieve positive results from participation and feedback; *Mazzaroppi* (FS) investigates the area of
communication audit standards; *Papageorgio* (FS) evaluates
faculty written communication regarding an Affirmative Action
Program, selected as a study of imposed compliance; and *Tate*
(FS) reports inadequate communication between faculty and
administrative personnel in a university foreign exchange student program.

Articles, Papers, and Reports: *Bass* (FS) examines the problem of providing systems feedback for management and organizational development, describing a survey instrument that yields
feedback as to factors operating in the workgroup situation;

Goldhaber (TC) discusses the development of the ICA measurement system for analysis of communication in organizations; *Rosenberg* (FS) evaluates the components of the human services information system of the Utah Department of Social Services; *Wergin* (TC) suggests a framework for evaluating organizational policy-making; and *Wiio* (FS) summarizes the communication audit studies (1970-1977) conducted by the Helsinki Research Institute in Finland, concluding that 1) organizational communication is situational, 2) dissatisfaction increases with organizational distance between source and receiver, and 3) direction of communication flow has an effect on communication satisfaction, with receivers being less satisfied than senders.

Communication Network and Direction Studies:

Books and Dissertations: *Burns* (TC) presents ideas and case studies on social network theory, examining corporate interconnections through interlocking directorates and stability of structures; *Coburn* (FS) finds that incongruence between the formal and informal communication nets accounts for a significant portion of the variance in organizational climate; *Kusterer* (FS) concludes that workers establish communal networks throughout the work organization to reduce own alienation; *Sanders* (FS) reports that higher level administrators tend to know more information, know more accurate information, and relay more information than lower level administrators; and *Yeager* (FS) studies upward communication in a large organization, reporting that a subordinate's trust in immediate superior has impact on perceived accuracy of communication, directionality of communications, and overall satisfaction with communications.

Articles, Papers, and Reports: *Housel* (FS) presents a field study of the effects of three different channel communication methods (face to face, telephone, and written) on four levels of management, finding significant differences in subjects' satisfaction and perception of openness; *Krivonos* (FS) analyzes message-biasing of upward communication in organizational hierarchies utilizing simulated situations to determine effects of favorable and unfavorable situations on message content; *Schwartz* (FS) examines the liaison communication role in organizational communication network analysis, supporting the validity of employing a sociometric procedure for identifying liaison persons; *Shapero* (FS) maps the information-communication behavior of an engineering division in a research organization; *Taylor* (FS) employes a sociometric questionnaire and a communication matrix, finding that neither communication network efficiency nor network stability was significantly related to school size; and *Wigand* (FS) explores communication and information flow in relation to organizational concepts, generating four communication networks from interview responses and constructing communication maps as to client referrals, planning/innovation, interpersonal relations, and other areas.

Models:

Books and Dissertations: *Bowey* (TC) employs a cultural anthropological approach to the study of organizations, including discussions of roles, systems theory, and human relationships; *Lachenmeyer* (TC) presents a system model for the analysis, evaluation, and design of organizations and jobs, including consideration for performance evaluation and job structure; *Midgley* (TC) collects information about consumer behavior from different disciplines, then formulates a general theory of innovative behavior applicable to diverse market situations; and *Nelson* (LS) uses simulation and linear programming to study beef marketing, finding that ineffective communications as to prices and production hindered moves to a more efficient marketing system; and *Wigand* (FS) finds that a preliminary path-analytic model of interorganizational relationships did not achieve satisfactory results, but an expanded model incorporating variables as communication and goal attainment was statistically significant.

Articles, Papers, and Reports: The *Community Service Agency of Washoe County, Nevada* (TC) provides a decision-maker's model with four steps including 1) needs assessment, 2) policy conference, 3) priority setting, and 4) resource allocation; *Hanson* (FS) presents the Interacting Spheres Model to clarify the decision-making ramifications of professional employees working in bureaucratic organizations; and *Spector* (FS) develops a contingency model of organization structure that projects organization structures in terms of different task force environments.

The Systems Approach:

Books and Dissertations: *Kilmann* (TC) presents MAPS (multivariate analysis, participation, and structure) as an organizational control system based on humanistic psychology, statistics, and modeling; and *Pasmore* (FS) studies organizational change effects of socio-technical systems, job redesign, and survey feedback interventions on task accomplishment and human fulfillment.

Articles, Papers, and Reports: *Goyer* (TC) suggests that "communication" and "process" be viewed together as the goal-oriented combination of variables designed to produce a single communicative event, a process that lends itself to the use of a systems approach; *Pennings* (TC) presents a conceptual framework for considering organizational effectiveness, viewing organizational effectiveness, viewing organizations as open systems with distinct but interdependent subsystems; and *Roberts* (TC) indicates a systemic approach to understanding organizations in terms of interpersonal, workgroup, and organizational communication.

The Organizational Development Approach:

Books and Dissertations: *Duncan* (FS) determines that the success of organizational change depends on the presence of a skilled change agent who is either an outsider or has previous experience outside the system; *Eich* (FS) describes the practices of organizational communication consultants, concluding there is a need for training, practical organizational experience, and classroom discussion; *Klein* (FS) details experiences in the implementation of social science research programs in a large oil corporation, providing insight into the role of "in-house" social scientists; *Lipshitz* (LS) examines effectiveness of third party process interventions as a function of consultant's prestige and style, finding that teams improved by using process analysis with or without consultation; and *Roeber* (FS) describes a large scale innovation in a major British chemical corporation.

Articles, Papers, and Reports: *Baker* (FS) stresses the importance of correct diagnosis, as opposed to guesswork, through data gathering, feedback, and joint diagnosis; *Bowers* (PD) views O.D. as a fad marked by superficiality, commercialism, and incorrect assumptions about the role of the consultant; *Burke* (PD) describes changes within the organizational development area during the past 12 years, and provides recommendations for the future; *Carlson* (PD) explains the approach of General Motors to organizational research and organizational change; and *Cook* (PD) presents the techniques and strategies used in organizational development, motivating participants to work toward organizational objectives as a way of achieving their own goals.

Frame (PD) argues the case for handling organizational development (OD) as a personnel department's function; *Friedlander* (TC) discusses three values underlying O.D., viz., rationalism, pragmatism, and existentialism; *Lourenco* (FS) analyzes the strategies by which change was introduced into an organization over a three year period,—participant observation, historical analyses, and informal interviews; *Patten* (PD) identifies various ways in which the factor of time influences OD's success or failure, considering the adequacy of time on the part of the organization, the consultant, and the environment; *Tichy* (FS) classifies change agents into four types, viz., outside-pressure type, analysis-for-the-top type, organizational development type, and people-change-technology type; and *Wergin* (TC) presents a model of university faculty development, beginning with low mutual knowledge and trust and evolving into greater mutual knowledge, trust, and collaboration.

Information Processing and Requirement Studies:

Books and Dissertations: *Aragona* (FS) notes that school district statistics for expenditure per pupil were not significantly related to information received by chief school officers as to curriculum programs, costs, student achievement, and media use; *Bonett* (FS) examines the information processes in a State Legislative system, reporting that major sources of substantive information were outside the legislature, and verbal communication between peers was the principal method of the internal communication system; *Smith, T.* (PD) emphasizes information needs, decision-making, and information feedback in formulating dynamic business strategy; *Torres* (FS) develops a three-step information collecting procedure for government agencies; *Gorodezky* (FS) reports no significant relationship between accurate input into management information systems and the level of bureaucratization in the work setting; and *Hackathorn* (FS) presents a methodology called "Activity Analysis" as an effective method of describing work flow activity.

Articles, Papers, and Reports: *Jacobson* (TC) concentrates on the economics of information, examining strategies for organizational adjustment; and *Wilde* (TC) outlines a management information framework to reduce costs, emphasizing need to closely adhere to information needs of individual decision-makers.

Specialized Texts, Anthologies, Bibliographies, Reviews:
Books: *Alan* (Text) combines text, case histories, and readings in an exposition of behavioral and technical aspects of management control and decision systems; *Coyle* (Text) presents techniques of management system dynamics, examining the mechanisms in a company able to produce appropriate behavior under conditions of change; and *Dyer* (Text) provides insight to strategies for interpersonal and organizational change, supplying related communication concepts and techniques; *Hawley* (Anthology) brings together several articles on organizational change and innovation in public administration and urban management; and *Mirvis* (Anthology) includes cases and essays covering a variety of organization development activities by private and public sector organizations.

Research Methodology in Organizational Communication

There were 71 publications selected in the area of Research Methodology in Organizational Communication. The 33 books and dissertations represented 7 percent of all books, and the 38 articles, papers, and reports represented 12 percent of all articles/papers.

The frequency of specific subclasses of Research Methodology is shown below:

Subclass	Books Quantity	Percent	Articles/Papers Quantity	Percent
Data Collection Instruments	16	49	15	40
Analytical and Processing Methods	1	3	2	5
Models and Theories	4	12	8	21
Experimental Designs	3	9	5	13
Research Strategies and Special Techniques	7	21	7	18
Texts, Anthologies, Reviews	2	6	1	3
TOTALS	**33**	**100**	**38**	**100**

A comparison of the frequency rank order of articles/papers to books/dissertations follows:

Subclass	Books	Articles/Papers
Data Collection Instruments	1	1
Research Strategies and Special Techniques	2	3
Models and Theories	3	2
Experimental Designs	4	4
Texts, Anthologies, Reviews	5	6
Analytical and Processing Methods	6	5

For the classification, Research Methodology in Organizational Communication, the six subclasses show approximately the same relative popularity in both the books format and the articles/papers format. The most popular subclass, by far, was Data Collection Instruments, followed by Models/Theories, and Research Strategies/Special Techniques. The least popular subclasses were Analytical/Processing Methods and Experimental Designs.

Table 4 presents the names of authors relevant to each of the subclasses of Research Methodology in Organizational Communication; and the commentary below furnishes a guide and overview as to the contents and findings of selected works:

Table 9

Research Methodology in Organizational Communication—1977
Classification of Authors
by Subclass, Publication Format, and Nature of Research

Subclasses	Books & Dissertations	Articles, Papers, Reports
Data Collection Instruments: Observation	Flanders . . . . FS Hatfield . . . . FS McGill . . . . FS	Sykes . . . . TC
Questionnaire	Aghamirmohamodali . FS Armstrong . . . . . . FS Fields . . . . FS Kelliher . . . . FS Shockley . . . . LS Smith, C . . . . FS Veal . . . . FS	Analytic Systems . . FS Duffy . . . . FS Ellison . . . . FS Felsinger . . . . FS Hopp . . . . FS Hurt . . . . FS Kirton . . . . FS Langdale . . . . FS Steers . . . . FS
Interview	Neal . . . . FS	
Comparative Analyses	Cole . . . . FS Elbert . . . . TC Ellsworth . . . . LS Munzenrider . . . . . TC Rooney . . . . FS	Alexander . . . . . . FS Bolyard . . . . FS Sussman . . . . TC Sykes . . . . FS

Table 9, Continued

Subclasses	Books & Dissertations	Articles, Papers, Reports
Analytical and Processing Methods:	Wilson . . . . FS	Chase . . . . TC Hammons . . . . . . FS
Models and Theories:	Janz. . . . . LS Sellick . . . . FS Tomlinson . . . . TC Vadhanapanich . . . . TC	Grunig . . . . TC Lederman . . . . . . TC Nebeker . . . . FS Pressemier . . . . . . TC Roloff . . . . TC Roloff . . . . LS Scoville. . . . . FS Young . . . . FS
Experimental Designs:	Green. . . . . TC Lynch . . . . FS Mullins . . . . TC	Alley . . . . FS Ettlie . . . . LS Wilborne . . . . FS Yelland. . . . . TC Zytowski. . . . . . . FS
Research Strategies and Special Techniques:	Isaacson . . . . LS Morrison . . . . FS Niehoff. . . . . FS Rahim . . . . LS Robinson. . . . . FS Rollins . . . . LS Seltzer . . . . LS	Buck . . . . FS Crecine. . . . . TC Goetzman . . . . . . FS Jones . . . . FS Meyer. . . . . TC Sackman . . . . FS Selvidge . . . . TC
Texts, Anthologies, Reviews:	Wesolowsky Linstone	Vroom

Data Collection Instruments:

Books and Dissertations: *Flanders* (FS) finds that the use of daily logs constitutes an effective technique for measuring organizational behavior and decision-making in a unversity; *Hatfield* (FS) constructs two interaction category sets (Superior-Subordinate Interaction Analysis System—Form A and B) designed to record and analyze the oral message content of superior-subordinate communications; and *McGill* (FS) concludes that Bales' Interaction Process Analysis does contribute to the study of communication behavior in health-care organizations; *Aghamirmohamodali* (FS) notes that the Likert Profile of Organizational Characteristics was developed for business organizations and questions the ability of that instrument to distinguish management styles in educational organizations; *Armstrong* (FS) reports that the Survey of Organizations Questionnaire, originally designed for industrial organizations, is applicable in an educational setting; *Fields* (FS) develops a questionnaire instrument to identify humanistic administrative style; *Kelliher* (FS) creates a new instrument, the Principal Leadership Behavior Monitoring Questionnaire, as an effective device for determining the potential for curriculum innovation; *Shockley* (LS) presents an instrument for measurement of public's attitude towards schools; *Smith, C.* (FS) develops a questionnaire to test the application of Lawrence-Lorsch differentiation-integration theory concepts in a university; and *Veal* (FS) analyzes the Organizational Climate Description Questionnaire (Halpin and Croft), as part of a study of teacher behavior and organizational climate, concluding that the abbreviated score for openness in the OCDQ differs significantly from total scores.

Neal (FS) describes the development and validation of a structured interview to identify potentially effective teachers; *Cole* (FS) compares four instruments as to ability to predict teacher openness and finds the Kerlinger Education Scale VII more accurate than the Rokeach Dogmatism Scale, the Walberg-Thomas Educational Beliefs Questionnaire, and the FIRO-F (Fundamental Interpersonal Relations Questionnaire—Feelings); *Elbert* (TC) studies three measures of organizational climate and satisfaction (Organizational Practices Questionnaire of House and Rizzo; Organizational Climate Questionnaire of Campbell and Pritchard; and Job Description Index of Smith, Kendall, and Hulin), concluding that they are sufficiently different in structure and content to refute the argument that climate and satisfaction are redundant; *Ellsworth* (LS) tests the relationships among the Carkhuff Communication Index Scale, the Dogmatism Scale, and a behavioral assessment of a counseling situation, finding that the three measures do not correlate with each other; *Munzenrider* (TC) investigates three organizational climate instruments, Likert's Profile of Organizational Characteristics, Litwin-Stringer-Meyer's Organizational Climate Survey, and Halpin-Croft's Organization Climate Description Questionnaire, finding considerable commonalities among them; and *Rooney* (FS) reports significant correlations between teacher perception of organizational climate as measured by the Organizational Climate Description Questionnaire (Halpin-Croft) and the condition variables of the Pennsylvania Educational Quality Assessment Inventory.

Articles, Papers, and Reports: *Sykes* (TC) describes a technique for studying the frequency of interaction by observers of large, spontaneous groups; *Analytic Systems Inc.* (FS) provides an instrument for measuring the productivity of state employment service agencies; *Duffy* (FS) develops the Job Proficiency Appraisal Form incorporating eight performance dimensions relative to 30 specialty fields of the Officer Personnel Management System; *Ellison* (FS) evaluates the Management Audit Survey (100 item questionnaire) as a predictor of employment service office productivity, finding the most significant validities in the scores relating to operational efficiency, performance feedback, work satisfaction, morale, and satisfaction with pay; and *Felsinger* (FS) considers the problem of measuring productivity on U.S. Navy ships, concluding that the level of productivity was related to adequacy of supplies, planning, tools, and extent of teamwork.

Hopp (FS) constructs and tests two sets of behaviorally-oriented rating scales to measure worker attitudes; *Hurt* (FS) reports on the development of a 25 item self-report measure of perceived organizational innovativeness (PORGI), indicating that it was found to be a significant predictor of four measures of employee job satisfaction; *Kirton* (FS) describes the development and validation of a measure distinguishing adaptors from innovators; *Langdale* (FS) creates a measure of bureaucratic organizational design and human relations organizational design, noting that neither design strategy is universally appropriate across all organizational settings; and *Steers* (FS) develops and validates an instrument measuring the four needs of achievement, affiliation, autonomy, and dominance.

Alexander (FS) examines the relationships among measures of work orientation, job attribute preferences, personality measures, and abilities, indicating that different measures are neither operationally nor conceptually equivalent; *Bolyard* (FS) studies measures of job satisfaction, comparing Hoppock's measure of satisfaction to the Job Description Index of Smith, Hulin, and Kendall; *Sussman* (TC) suggests procedures to improve measurement of upward distortion, reviewing four data collection methods—disparity scores, questionnaire-interview data, actual encoding of messages, and selection-transmission of messages; and *Sykes* (FS) compares various scales for measuring effects of structural and attitudinal similarity on interaction and attraction.

Analytical and Processing Methods:

Books and Dissertations: *Wilson* (FS) finds that CONTENT (a computerized form of communications content analysis) is a reliable form of interaction analysis.

Articles, Papers, and Reports: *Chase* (TC) compares the statistical power in the field of applied psychology to the fields of social psychology, education, and communication; and *Hammons* (FS) presents the Functional Responsibility Chart as a key to effective decision-making.

Models and Theories:

Books and Dissertations: *Janz* (LS) tests various models intending to provide optimal personnel selection utilizing multivariate prediction and Monte Carlo comparisons of configural and combinational techniques; *Sellick* (FS) develops an assessment model designed to identify the strengths and weaknesses of ongoing management by objectives programs; *Tomlinson* (TC) constructs a planning model designed to use educational decision information; and *Vadhanapanich* (TC) presents a cost model and an effectiveness model to assist in the analysis of instructional technology.

Articles, Papers, and Reports: *Grunig* (TC) presents a multisystem theory of communication behavior relative to individuals and organization-related systems, giving consideration to communities, families, and social systems; *Lederman* (TC) relates some of the important features of general systems theory and modern organizational theory to organizational communication theory; *Nebeker* (FS) discusses and tests a new conceptualization of Vroom's (1964) expectancy model, predicting that an individual chooses from among levels of performance rather than from among levels of effort to exert; and *Pressemier* (TC) provides a model designed to allow communication analysts to predict the most promising approach for improving acceptance of a competitive service or idea.

Roloff (TC) supplies a conceptual model to explain why a person selectively exposes oneself to information; *Roloff* (LS) utilizes a model in a laboratory experiment to clarify the relationship between persuasive messages and attitudes; *Scoville* (FS) conducts a test of Herzberg's two-factor theory of job satisfaction, reporting that significant relationships were found between several variables that contradicted the basic premises; and *Young* (FS) designs a field research study to test the validity of Maslow's theory and finds no support for the theory.

Experimental Designs:

Books and Dissertations: *Green* (TC) surveys research employing the Organizational Climate Description Questionnaire in studies of elementary schools, concluding that little attention has been given to the reliability and validity of the instrument; *Lynch* (FS) concludes that PEEL (Performance Evaluation of the Educational Leader) as a measurement instrument is a valid and reliable indicator of administrative competence; and *Mullins* (TC) summarizes research using the Organizational Climate Description Questionnaire (excluding elementary schools), finding that the instrument is both reliable and valid.

Articles, Papers, and Reports: *Alley* (FS) describes the process for validation of an Air Force Vocational Interest Inventory, indicating that the Vocational Interest-Career Examination proved reliable and significantly predicted job satisfaction; *Ettlie* (LS) indicates that critical incident techniques have low convergent validity even when attempts are made to remove selective retention bias; *Wilborne* (FS) discusses potential usefulness of nonverbal measures in future testing of enlisted military personnel, noting that findings substantiate their validity and utility; *Yelland* (TC) notes the feasibility of using multiple choice questions as a reliable procedure in testing trainees; and *Zytowski* (FS) analyzes the predictive validity of the Kuder Occupational Interest Survey through a study of 1000 persons located 12 years after taking the survey.

Research Strategies and Special Techniques:

Books and Dissertations: *Isaacson* (LS) concludes that the Interpersonal Skills Interaction Analysis Technique is a valid and reliable method of measuring interpersonal communication skills in small group settings; *Morrison* (FS) reports that the Delphi Technique provides opportunity for subordinate input into decision-making, supplying recommendations for more effective use; *Niehoff* (FS) employs the Delphi Technique in a study of comparative strategies for university goal attainment; *Rahim* (LS) finds that organizational designs using MAPS (Multivariate Analysis, Participation, and Structure) generated less intragoup and intergroup conflict than other designs; *Seltzer* (LS) examines possible modification of MAPS, viewed as a system of clustering congruent people in groups, so as to differentiate operational routine work from strategic planning work; *Robinson* (FS) demonstrates the use of the Systems Semantics Profile, a semantic differential instrument, in a study of the lines of communication within a university; and *Rollins* (LS) agrees that the Mehrabian Formula, assigning various weights to communications content, vocal expression, and facial expression, is functional for educational administrators.

Articles, Papers, and Reports: *Buck* (FS) reports on the development of a test to decode affect in others through the use of videotaped sequences of facial expressions and gestures; *Crecine* (TC) discusses ways to conduct research on educational institutions and their development and adaptation to the environment; *Goetzman* (FS) studies subject of survey-response-bias by examining introductory approaches and feedback promises, finding no support for hypothesis that a humanistic approach and promise of results information would reduce bias; and *Jones* (FS) reviews the basic theories related to the use of aggregated psychological climate scores to describe organizational climate, concluding that this procedure is useful for homogeneous subunits.

Meyer (TC) examines research techniques for empirical studies comparing innovation processes in private and public sector organizations; *Sackman* (FS) investigates Participating Polling as a technique for more effective use of expert opinion in relation to long-range planning, comparing it to other techniques, such as Delphi; and *Selvidge* (TC) discusses the effectiveness of decision analysis techniques, encouraging users to retrospectively evaluate each experience and maintain statistics as to results.

Specialized Texts, Anthologies, Bibliographies, Reviews:
Books: *Linstone* (Anthology) presents 26 papers primarily concerned with the Delphi Technique, a system for group problem-solving which minimizes problems with communication; and *Wesolowsky* (Text) discusses errors in the interpretation of various coefficients and tests, presenting guidelines for selecting or excluding variables for regression.

Articles, Papers, and Reports: *Vroom* (TC) provides a general perspective of research areas in leadership including methods for studying leadership and leadership development and training.

Texts, Anthologies, Reviews, and General Bibliographies

This category of the literature includes 54 books and 12 articles/papers, representing 12 percent of all books and dissertations and 4 percent of all articles, papers, and reports.

The frequency of specific subclasses is shown below:

Subclasses	Books Quantity	Books Percent	Articles/Papers Quantity	Articles/Papers Percent
Textbooks:				
Management-Oriented	18	33		
Communication-Oriented	5	9		
Organizational Communication	11	20		
Tradebooks	8	15		
Anthologies	9	17		
Reviews	1	2	5	42
General Bibliographies	2	4	7	58
TOTALS	54	100	12	100

As indicated in the introduction to this OVERVIEW CHAPTER, specifically in the presentation of Table 1, the classification TEXTS, ANTHOLOGIES, REVIEWS, AND GENERAL BIBLIOGRAPHIES excludes specialized works devoted to only one of the other classifications (e.g., Interpersonal Communication) as such specialized works are listed under the particular area concerned. Therefore, in addition to the 66 writings covered by this immediate discussion, there are additional specialized texts, anthologies, bibliographies, and reviews in each of the other eight classifications.

Table 10 presents the names of authors relevant to each of the subclasses, and the commentary below furnishes a guide and overview as to the contents of selected works:

Table 10

Texts, Anthologies, Reviews, General Bibliographies, and References—1977
Classification of Authors
By Major Subclass and Publication Format

Subclasses	Books & Dissertation		Articles, Papers, Reports
Textbooks:			
Management-Oriented	Behling	Hall, R.	
	Bowen	Huse	
	Cohen	Jacques	
	Davis	Landy	
	Duncan	Lusato	
	Evan	Melcher	
	Finch	Richardson	
	Galbraith	Scott	
	Hall, D.	Simon	

Table 10, Continued

Subclasses	Books & Dissertations		Articles, Papers, Reports	
Communication-Oriented	Faules Lillico Reitz	Rosenblatt Vogel		
Organizational Communication	Allen Baird Bowman DiSalvo Farace Harlem	Hatch Johnson Oaks Rockey Wofford		
Tradebooks: Organization Design	Bernstein			
Leadership	Bowers Levinson	Maccoby		
Communication	Brennan Hargreaves	Hopper		
Motivation	Ingalls			
Anthologies:	Arnold Eakins Craig Gilmer Huseman	Pugh Gruneberg Hackman Ruben		
Reviews:	Rosenfeld		James Kirschenbaum Lau	Rabinowitz Richetto
General Bibliographies:	Balachandran Falcione/Greenbaum		Bolch Earles Grooms	Shonyo (3) Young

Textbooks:

Include 18 management-oriented works, and 5 communication-oriented works. In addition, 11 books were directed specifically to the field of organizational communication, authored by *Allen; Baird; Bowman; DiSalvo; Farace; Harlem; Hatch; Johnson; Oaks; Rockey;* and *Wofford.*

Tradebooks:

Defined as books not judged to be university texts, include eight publications in the subject areas of organization design, leadership, communication, and motivation. The three works in the communication area are authored by *Brennan; Hargreaves;* and *Hopper.*

Anthologies:

Arnold presents readings on the elements of communication and communication settings including organizational communication; *Eakins* brings together papers on various communication subjects including interpersonal communication between the sexes and sex differences in language, speech, and nonverbal communication; *Craig* supplies a training development handbook including articles in communication training, group methods, programmed instruction, instructional systems, and organizational development; *Gilmer* provides a 4th edition on industrial and organizational psychology including traditional and new studies covering nonverbal communication, leadership, and motivation; and *Huseman* selects outstanding articles in interpersonal and organizational communication including the areas of organization structure, motivation, conflict, persuasion, evaluation, interviews, small groups, and listening.

Pugh presents and discusses several experiments relevant to organizational structure and performance; *Gruneberg* includes readings on 1) the Herzberg theory of satisfaction, 2) the effects on job satisfaction of participative decision making, and 3) the relationship between satisfaction, turnover, absenteeism, and work performance; *Hackman* furnishes a collection of works relating to organizational change including career development, work design, reward systems, and managerial style; and *Ruben* compiles the first annual publication of outstanding papers presented at the International Communication Association convention in April 1977.

Reviews:

Rosenfeld examines recent theory and research on nonverbal experience and behavior; *James* synthesizes research on organizational structure as it relates to individual attitudes and behavior; *Kirschenbaum* summarizes early research on values clarification theory, reviewing nineteen recent studies; *Lau* discusses the literature on organizational climate, indicating the place of communication; *Rabinowitz* reviews the literature on job involvement via definitions, theoretical perspectives, correlates, and profiles; and *Richetto* traces the history of organizational communication from the 1920's through the mid 1970's, providing detailed comments as to the research in the middle 1970's in the areas of special groups within the organization, effects of communication training, feedback, interorganizational communication, communication and organizational development, and shortcomings of organizational communication research.

General Bibliographies:

Balachandran provides an annotated bibliography of writings since 1965 on subject of employee communication, including the categories of management communication, communication in personnel management, reports to employees, and employee publications; and *Falcione/Greenbaum* further develop a reference manual for the field of organizational communication by furnishing 900 abstracts of relevant writings in 1976, analyzed with nine major literature groups and 56 subclasses, indexed by author, data collection instruments, and organizational type subject to field studies, and overviewed by a prefatory chapter.

Bolch presents a collection of abstracts in the field of information and referral services prepared by the staff of the Institute for Interdisciplinary Studies; *Earles* includes research studies relative to assessment centers and reports that assessment center evaluations are more predictive of future management success than traditional evaluations; *Grooms* reviews decision-making research on federal, state, and local governments; *Shonyo* supplies three works, 1) selected abstracts of studies on civilian and military job satisfaction, 2) a summary of research on measurement of human work, and 3) a review of government reports on the theoretical and applied aspects of physical work environment, attitudes, and public relations; and *Young* cites reports dealing with mathematical models of manpower and personnel management.

chapter 3

Classified abstracts of organizational communication literature 1977

INTERPERSONAL COMMUNICATION IN ORGANIZATIONS

BOOKS AND DISSERTATIONS

Alessandra, Anthony J. *Buyer-Seller Similarity as a Determinant of Success in Industrial Sales.* Ph.D. Dissertation, Georgia State University—School of Business Administration, 1976. DAI, Vol. 37, No. 5, p. 3140-A.

Concludes that buyer-seller demographic similarity (height, weight, sex, hair length, and beard similarities) has a positive effect on sales success. In addition, observable demographic similarity variables are more important than nonobserved demographic similarity variables. FS.

Arams, John D. *Dilemmas of Administrative Behavior.* Englewood Cliffs, NJ: Prentice-Hall, 1976.

Disregards the theory and research of the administrative sciences, and focuses solely on five paradoxes or dilemmas faced by managers; for example, satisfying individual needs while promoting efficiency. P/D.

Beebe, Steven A. *Effects of Eye Contact, Posture, and Vocal Inflection upon Comprehension and Credibility.* Ph.D. Dissertation, University of Missouri—Columbia, 1976. DAI, Vol. 37, No. 9, p. 5436-A.

Maintains that eye contact was a determinant of enhanced credibility and increased comprehension; and that speaker posture and vocal inflection had little effect on either credibility or comprehension. LS.

Brittingham, Linda L. *An Analysis of the Effects of Subordinate Feedback on Superordinate Task Assistance and Personal Support Behaviors.* Ph.D. Dissertation, University of Maryland, 1976. DAI, Vol. 38, No. 2, p. 559-A.

Indicates that negative personal support was the only variable that influenced change in superordinate behavior. Positive personal support, negative task assistance, and positive task assistance did not affect superordinate behavior. LS.

Caine, Bruce T. *Leadership Orientation and Self Presentation: A Leader's Impression of Management Under Stress.* Ph.D. Dissertation, University of Florida, 1976. DAI, Vol. 38, No. 1, p. 412-B.

Low LPC leaders described themselves more positively than high LPC leaders especially when dimensions of leadership are emphasized. FS.

Charlier, Peter J. *A Study of the Relationship Between Selected Personal and Interpersonal Dimensions of Elementary Principals and Their Leadership Behavior.* Ed.D. Dissertation, Temple University, 1977. DAI, Vol. 37, No. 12, p. 7425-A.

States that it is difficult to determine relationships between personality dimensions and leadership behavior in complex settings. FS.

Cibotti, Thomas M. *Conceptual Levels as a Determinant of the Relationship Between the Cooperating Teacher and the Student Teacher.* Ph.D. Dissertation, Boston College, 1977. DAI, Vol. 38, No. 2, p. 561-A.

Determines that Conceptual Level is a determinant of perceived productivity on the part of student teachers, but is not a determinant of the quality of student teacher—cooperating teacher interpersonal relations. FS.

Cohn, Richard M. *The Consequences of Unemployment on Evaluations of Self.* Ph.D. Dissertation, University of Michigan, 1977. DAI, Vol. 38, No. 3, p. 1465-B.

Individuals who become unemployed evidence greater dissatisfaction with self, lower self-confidence and greater discounting of the importance of others' evaluations of self, relevant to the stably employed. FS.

Ezell, Annette S. *Power, via Machiavellianism, in Educational Decision-Making: A Study of Selected Educators, State Officials, and Lobbyists in the 1975 Nevada Legislative Session.* Ed.D. Dissertation, Brigham Young University, 1977. DAI, Vol. 38, No. 2, p. 566-A.

Indicates no significant difference in the level of interpersonal manipulative orientations of registered lobbyists, boards of education and educational administrators. FS.

Fahs, Michael L. *The Effects of Self-Disclosing Communication and Attitude Similarity on the Reduction of Interpersonal Conflict.* Ph.D. Dissertation, University of Southern California, 1976. DAI, Vol. 38, No. 3, p. 1119-A.

Indicates that self-disclosure as a method of controlling conflict in communication transactions was effective as a conflict-reducing strategy. Conflict reduction was also observed in communications involving subjects expressing attitude similarity. LS.

Farrow, Dana L. *A Path Analytic Approach to the Study of Contingent Leader Behavior.* Ph.D. Dissertation, University of Rochester, 1977. DAI, Vol. 38, No. 2, p. 942-B.

Tight subordinate-boss structure, clear task objectives and an assertive attitude of the manager promotes a directive leader style. A short-term objective perspective on the part of managers and organizations with unplanned and unordered activities influence a more negotiative leader style. FS.

Feingold, Paul C. *Toward a Paradigm of Effective Communication: An Empirical Study of Perceived Communicative Effectiveness.* Ph.D. Dissertation, Purdue University, 1976. DAI, Vol. 37, No. 8, p. 4697-A.

Indicates that the effective communicator is perceived as "other-oriented," able to adapt communication to the respondent, committed to the message, and recognized as an empathetic listener. LS.

Ferraro, Mario F., Jr. *Principals' Orientation Toward Interpersonal Interaction, Manipulative Technique Preferences, Curriculum Change, and Shared Decision Making.* Ph.D. Dissertation, Fordham University, 1976. DAI, Vol. 37, No. 5, p. 2531-A.

Reports no significant difference between altruistic and manipulative principals with respect to participative decision making with teachers and students. Principals perceived both punishment and rewards as preferable techniques for eliciting desired behavior, but did not perceive withholding or substitution of information and postponed decision making as preferred techniques for eliciting such behavior. FS.

Fujii, Donald S. *A Dyadic, Interactive Approach to the Study of Leader Behavior,* Ph.D. Dissertation, Purdue University, 1976. DAI, Vol. 37, No. 10, p. 5415.

Follower performance is positively related to increases in compatibility between leader and members in terms of subjective measures of performance. Extrinsic satisfaction was a linear function of leader-member compatibility. The degree of leader-member compatibility was positively related to the interpersonally-oriented leader behaviors. LS.

Gaymon, Donald L. *Exploring Personal Values in an Organizational Context.* Ph.D. Dissertation, University of Washington, 1976. DAI, Vol. 37, No. 7, p. 4467-A.

Recommends that organizations should encourage managers to be aware of the values and ethical factors involved in organizational decisions. FS.

Gellerman, Saul W. *Managers and Subordinates.* Hinsdale, IL: The Dryden Press, 1976.

Critically discusses the importance of motivation and suggests that because human relationships are so complex, the manager must learn specific communication skills, rather than adhering to "cookbook" approaches to motivation. P/D.

Hall, Kirby D. *Leadership Style, Perceived Leader Behavior and Job Function Emphasis of Secondary School Principals.* Ph.D. Dissertation, The Ohio State University, 1976. DAI, Vol. 37, No. 8, p. 4742-A.

Finds that task-oriented principals are perceived by teachers to vary leadership behavior more from situation to situation than relationship-oriented principals. FS.

Kasperson, Conrad J. *An Exploratory Analysis of Information Use by Innovative, Productive, and Non-Productive Scientists and Engineers.* Ph.D. Dissertation, Rensselaer Polytechnic Institute, 1976. DAI, Vol. 38, No. 1, p. 9-A.

Concludes that scientists are information processors, and that creativity, can be explained by the information-seeking behavior of the innovative scientist. Non-innovative scientists were found to rely more upon superiors as information sources, while innovative scientists rely upon a wide range of information exposure. FS.

King, Donald M. *A Study of Formal Performance Appraisal by Supervisors in an Industrial Environment.* Ph.D. Dissertation, The University of Michigan, 1976. DAI, Vol. 37, No. 6, p. 3360-A.

Indicates that the best rating of employee performance is secured from a combination of direct and indirect supervision. The rater organizationally closest to the ratee is not best able to appraise the individual; and indirect supervisors tend to be inconsistent in their assessments. FS.

Larson, Richard J. *Interpersonal Relationships of Elementary and Senior High Principals and Compatability with Their Superintendents.* Ph.D. Dissertation, Iowa State University, 1976. DAI, Vol. 37, No. 8, p. 4752-A.

Concludes that the most effective high school principals exhibited a greater desire to initiate interaction than did the least effective principals. FS.

Lefton, Robert E., *et al. Effective Motivation Through Performance Appraisal.* Psychological Associates, Inc., 1977.

Provides a step-by-step guide to performance appraisal, using two models which explain why and how people behave as they do in appraisals. Shows how to strengthen relationship between supervisor and employees. Presents a new system for preparing appraisals, and includes actual dialogue to highlight key points. T/C.

McGovern, Thomas V. *The Making of a Job Interviewee: The Effect of Nonverbal Behavior on an Interviewer's Evaluations During a Selection Interview,* Ph.D. Dissertation, Southern Illinois University, 1976. DAI, Vol. 37, No. 9, p. 4740-B.

Interviewees high in nonverbal behavior during an interview are evaluated more positively and are more likely to receive a second interview than applicants low in nonverbal behavior activity. LS.

Metzler, Ken. *Creative Interviewing.* Englewood Cliffs, NJ: Prentice-Hall, 1977.

Designed primarily for the college journalism student, this text provides a practical guide to question formulation, use of recording media, and preparation, etc. P/D.

Minder, Charles. *Teacher Openness as a Function of Race.* PhD. Dissertation, The University of Alabama, 1976. DAI, Vol. 37, No. 12, p. 7644-A.

Finds that openness of elementary school teachers differs significantly according to race, with black teachers more closed to experience than white teachers, regardless of the predominant race in the school building. No difference between races was determined at the secondary level. FS.

Morrison, James H., and John J. O'Hearne. *Practical Transactional Analysis in Management*, Addison Wesley, 1977.

A simple, A-B-C approach to transactional analysis—a way to understand and improve human interactions. The authors, a management consultant and a physician, believe by using TA, managers can increase their skills in dealing with people. P/D.

Nirenberg, Jesse S. *Breaking Through to Each Other*. New York: Harper & Row Publishers, 1976.

A book about how to use persuasion as a method to change thinking to conform to reality. The author demonstrates what to do and what not to do through the use of typical conversations as examples, in situations calling for persuasive communication in organizational settings. P/D.

Rogers, Jean L., and Walter L. Fortson. *Fair Employment Interviewing*. Reading, MA: Addison Wesley Publishing Company, 1976.

Discusses interviewing techniques, the impact of recent legal decisions, reference checks, the analysis of application information, personnel correspondence, and recruitment sources. P/D.

Royal, Robert F., and Steven P. Schutt. *The Gentle Art of Interviewing and Interrogation: A Professional Manual and Guide*. Englewood Cliffs, NJ: Prentice-Hall, 1976.

Discusses such topics as the mechanics of questioning, preparatory work, developing rapport, physical influence factors, psychological factors, and so on. T/C.

Ryan, Samuel G. *Some Relationships Between Supervising Conflict Management Behaviors, Situational Factors and Subordinate Perceptions of Conflict in Organizational Settings*, Ph.D. Dissertation CUNY, 1977. DAI, Vol. 38, No. 4, p. 1958-B.

A positive relation exists between conflict and supervisory nonroutinization, supervisory personal influence and subordinate dogmatism. A negative relationship exists between supervisory adherence to chain of command and subordinate personal influence. FS.

Stano, Michael E. *Dimensions of Productive and Unproductive Performance Appraisal Interviews*. Ph.D. Dissertation, University of Minnesota, 1977. DAI, Vol. 38, No. 3, p. 1124-A.

Provides a set of explicit guidelines for interview behavior geared to the interviewee. Finds no new variables to indicate "productive" or "unproductive" performance appraisal interviews. FS.

Sterrett, John H. *A Study of the Relationship Between Nonverbal Communication and Perceptions of Qualities Associated with Effectiveness in the Insurance Industry*. Ph.D. Dissertation, Georgia State University —School of Education, 1976. DAI, Vol. 37, No. 10, p. 6380-A.

Maintains that men and women tend to perceive themselves negatively if they pause for long periods of time in midlevel management job interviews. Male interviewers react positively to aggressive body language by males, while female interviewers react positively to more passive body language behavior. LS.

Stetler, Cheryl B. *Empathy, Communication and Related Variables Among Registered Nurses.* Ph.D. Dissertation, University of Kansas, 1976. DAI, Vol. 37, No. 8, p. 4707-A.

Reports that neither verbal nor vocal communicative behavior plays a major role in the perception of empathetic understanding among registered nurses. LS.

Tucker, Jeffrey H. *Leadership in Autonomous Group Environments, Task/Person Orientation and Interpersonal Competence.* Ph.D. Dissertation, Georgia State University, 1976. DAI, Vol. 37, No. 8, p. 4202-B.

Competence relates to the ability of a person to exhibit both task and person oriented behaviors. Task and person oriented behaviors are not opposite poles of a single leadership dimension. LS.

Van Hoeven, Shirley A. *A Study of Competitiveness Between Sexes and the Effect of Communication Messages upon the Building of Trust.* Ed.D. Dissertation, Western Michigan University, 1976. DAI, Vol. 37, No. 10, p. 6209-A.

Determines that sex of person sending message has no effect upon the level of trust between sender and receiver. Content or type of message communicated does increase or decrease trust. LS.

Weigand, Gerald L. *Social Psychological Exchanges of Interpersonal Power and Obligation Between U.S. Army Infantry Superordinates and Subordinates,* Army Command and General Staff College, Ft. Leavenworth, KS, Masters Thesis, June 1976, 141 p.

Indicates that decentralized authority and responsibility to subordinates improves the upward flow of communications within an organization, thereby contributing to organizational effectiveness. Investigations show that leadership style preferences improve with level among officer personnel, but do not improve with level among noncommissioned officers. Reports other findings relating to preferred leadership. T/C.

Wortman, Randy J. *Leadership Behavior of Secondary School Assistant Principals.* Ed.D. Dissertation, Indiana University, 1976. DAI, Vol. 37, No. 8, p. 4774-A.

Indicates a difference in the perception of real and ideal leader behaviors of assistant principals, suggesting this is due to inadequate leadership training. FS.

ARTICLES, PAPERS, AND U.S. GOVERNMENT PUBLICATIONS

Allen, T. Harrel. "How Good a Listener are You?" *Management Review,* Vol. 66, No. 2, February 1977.

Discusses the eight ways that Dr. Ralph Nichols has found will improve listening effectiveness: resist distractions, listen to complex material, work at it, use thought-speed, focus on meaning, listen for main ideas, seek interest, and beware of emotional filters. P/D.

Bartol, K. M., and A. D. Butterfield. "Sex Effects in Evaluating Leaders," *Journal of Applied Psychology,* Vol. 61, No. 4, August 1976, pp. 446-454.

Female managers were seen as more positive on consideration style than male managers. Initiating structure behavior was valued more highly when engaged in by male managers. LS.

Becker, Walter A., Gerald M. Dupree, and James E. George. "Decision Making Processes of Natural Dyadic Groups," Air Force Institute of Technology, Wright-Patterson AFB, OH, School of Systems and Logistics, June 1976, 130 p. Report No. SLSR-41-76A.

Discusses an experiment conducted to observe the decision-making process of natural dyadic groups. Results confirmed the hypothesis that natural dyadic groups would utilize a decision process for a nonprogrammed decision-making task that would: 1) search beyond the 1st acceptable alternative, 2) reduce alternatives to two before final decision, 3) not compare alternatives until after search terminates, 4) choose an earlier acceptable alternative rather than the last one. Results also showed that the importance of the decision to the decision makers did not influence the decision process. LS.

Bernardin, J. H., and K. Alvares. "The Managerial Grid as a Predictor of Conflict Resolution Method and Managerial Effectiveness," *Administrative Science Quarterly,* Vol. 21, No. 1, March 1976, pp. 84-92.

Studied the relation between ratings of leadership effectiveness and conflict resolution methods. Results indicate that grid placement was a poor predictor of either managerial effectiveness or conflict resolution method employed. FS.

Bodden, Jack L., and Leonard E. James. "Influence of Occupational Information on Cognitive Complexity," *Journal of Counseling Psychology,* Vol. 23, No. 3, May 1976, pp. 280-282.

Describes an experiment designed to evaluate the effects of occupational information giving on subjects' cognitive complexity level. Results of the experiment indicate that information giving reduces subject's cognitive differentiation of occupational/vocational constructs compared to control subjects. Theoretical research and professional practice implications of these findings are discussed. LS.

Bonoma, Thomas V., and Leonard C. Felder. "Nonverbal Communication in Marketing: Toward a Communicational Analysis," *Journal of Marketing Research*, Vol. 14, No. 2, May 1977, pp. 169-180.

Reviews pertinent articles dealing with research concerning 136 specific nonverbal behaviors in a marketing frame of reference. Includes cataloging method and relationship to interactions. FS.

Burlem, William S. "The Recognition and Characteristics of Effective Executives," Naval Postgraduate School, Monterey, CA, September 1976, 118 p.

Discusses the effectiveness of selected individuals whose professional endeavors are known to their peers outside the organization. This selected group was compared to those individuals who were not recognized as effective executives. Results indicated differences in perception of management function, leadership style, and motivational needs. FS.

Cahn, D. D. "The Employment Interview: A Self Validation Model," *Journal of Employment Counseling*, Vol. 13, No. 4, December 1976, pp. 150-155.

Applies a development theory of interpersonal communication to the initial job interview. T/C.

Civikly, Jean M., Wayne Pace, and Richard M. Krause, "Interviewer and Client Behaviors in Supportive and Defensive Interviews," in *Communication Yearbook I*, Brent D. Ruben ed., Austin, TX: International Communication Association, pp. 347-361.

Gibb's (1961) supportive-defensive paradigm was used as the conceptual basis for an investigation of the pattern of verbal and nonverbal behaviors manifest in such interviews. Communicative behaviors were examined to identify situations rated as defensive, supportive, or intermediate. The results suggest the paradigm's validity and further indicate that individual behaviors may be less important than are behavioral repertories. LS.

Constantin, S. W. "An Investigation of Information Favorability in the Employment Interview," *Journal of Applied Psychology*, Vol. 61, No. 6, December 1976, pp. 743-749.

Judges rate information that deviates from social norms more extremely than information that is normative. Judges respond to relevant unfavorable information more negatively than they do to irrelevant unfavorable information. Judges respond to favorable information by rating the applicant high regardless of the relevancy of the information. LS.

Dansereau, F., G. Green, and W. J. Haga. "A Vertical Dyad Linkage Approach to Leadership Within Formal Organizations: A Longitudinal Investigation of the Role Making Process," *Organizational Behavior and Human Performance*, Vol. 13, No. 1, February 1975, pp. 46-78.

Leadership is conceptualized as an exchange relationship which develops within the .vertical dyad overtime during role-making activities. The degree of latitude a superior grants a member to negotiate his/her role is predictive of subsequent behavior on the part of both superior and member. FS.

DeGise, Robert F. "Recognizing and Overcoming Defensive Communication," *Supervisory Management,* Vol. 22, No. 3, March 1977, pp. 31-38.

Dispels the notion that defensive and supportive climates exist independently and illustrates with examples how to interact or coexist in organizations. The perceptions of the receiver, not the intentions of the source determine the climate for each receiver. Constant awareness is necessary. P/D.

Demers, Robert W. "Ask and Ye Shall Receive," *Supervision,* Vol. 38, No. 9, September 1976, pp. 18-19.

Lists six ways administrators can put questions to subordinates and warns that the content has less importance than the tone of voice used. Includes examples. P/D.

Dipboye, R. L. "A Critical Review of Korman's Self Consistency Theory of Work Motivation and Occupational Choice," *Organizational Behavior and Human Performance,* Vol. 18, No. 1, February 1977, pp. 108-126.

Reviews research on Korman's theory. Chronic self esteem and situational self esteem appear to be important determinants of performance, choice and satisfaction. Offers a number of critiques. T/C.

————, Richard D. Arvey, and David E. Terpstra. "Equal Employment and the Interview," *Personnel Journal,* Vol. 55, No. 10, October 1976, pp. 520-524.

Argues that a personnel interview is no substitute for well designed and valid objective tests as predictors of job success. In order for the interview to be valid it should be structured and used in conjunction with other objective tests. P/D.

Dolgoff, Thomas. "The Psychological Meaning of Work," *Management Review,* Vol. 66, No. 1, January 1977, pp. 39-42.

Discusses how work determines one's self-concept, self-esteem, and identity. Motivation, promotions, work loss, and fear of failure are also discussed in terms of a person's attitudes, beliefs, and sense of self. P/D.

Drucker, Peter F. "How to Manage Your Boss," *Management Review,* Vol. 66, No. 5, May 1977, pp. 8-12.

Advises how to analyze and adapt to the boss to communicate more effectively. Suggests some general rules to follow and discusses various strategies. P/D.

Entine, A. D. "The Mid-Career Counseling Process," *Industrial Gerontology,* Vol. 3, No. 2, Spring 1976, pp. 105-111.

Discusses the additional demands and potential counseling solutions available to deal with the growing number of persons considering mid-life career changes. P/D.

Farrant, Alan W. "Boss, Are You Listening?" *Supervision*, Vol. 38, No. 9, September 1976, p. 9.

Warns managers than when employees shun contact with them, it indicates a lack of genuine personal interest in subordinates. Describes a defensive and an open climate on the job.

Herold, D. M., and M. M. Greller. "Feedback: The Definition of a Construct," *Academy of Management Journal*, Vol. 20, No. 1, March 1977, pp. 142-147.

Five factors of feedback emerged from a three stage study. They were: Negative feedback, Positive feedback from sources above the respondent in the hierarchy, positive feedback from nonhierarchial others, internal criteria and work flow feedback. FS.

Hester, Larry R. *et al.* "Supervisor Attraction as a Function of Level of Supervisor Skillfulness and Supervisees' Perceived Similarity," *Journal of Counseling Psychology*, Vol. 23, No. 3, May 1976, pp. 254-258.

Investigates the effects of perceived supervisor attraction on attitudes toward supervisor skillfulness and perceived similarity between supervisor and supervisee. LS.

Housel, Thomas J., and Patrick J. McDermott. "The Perceived Credibility and Persuasiveness of a Message Source as Affected by Initial Credibility, Styles of Language, and Sex of Source," paper presented at the Annual Meeting of the International Communication Association, Portland, OR, April 1976, 31 p. ERIC ED 122 317.

Studies four problem areas of communication research: 1) source credibility, 2) language intensity, 3) the gender of source as it affects the source's persuasiveness and credibility and 4) the scarcity of multifactor studies using gender of source as one of the independent variables. Results indicate that a source's initial credibility is not affected by the source's gender of language usage and that low credible sources were more persuasive than the high credible sources. LS.

Jones, Dean C. "Spatial Proximity, Interpersonal Conflict, and Friendship Formation in the Intermediate Care Facility," Indiana University-Purdue University at Indianapolis, IN, 1975, 5 p.

Discusses spatial proximity in relation to friendship formation and interpersonal conflict in nursing homes. Results indicated that interpersonal conflict occurred more often between patients living within a distance of two rooms, that close spatial proximity did not produce positive interaction, and that patients living at a greater distance sustained positive interaction. FS.

Kavanagh, M. J. "Expected Supervisory Behavior, Interpersonal Trust and Environmental Preferences: Some Relationships Based on a Dyadic Model of Leadership," *Organizational Behavior and Human Performance*, Vol. 13, No. 1, February 1975, pp. 17-30.

The popular hypothesis arguing for higher preferences for freedom and self actuatization opportunites in the work role was not completely supported by leadership preference results. Being employed affects one's preference for "ideal" leadership. Preferences for organizational climate is related to the patterns of leadership behavior preferred. FS.

Kennedy, Thomas Francis. "The Influence of Management Style on Effective Communication in the Program Management Environment," Defense Systems Management School, Fort Belvoir, VA, November 1974, 32 p.

Assesses the influence that managerial-style has on communication in the program management environment. Couples Blake and Mouton's Managerial Grid with the Johari Awareness Model of Luft and Ingham to provide a conceptual framework for assessing the various managerial styles. Analyzes the effects of managerial styles on communication. Suggests use of the Styles of Management Inventory Test of Teleometrics International to assess communication impact. FS.

Knight, Philip H., and Carolyn K. Bair. "Degree of Client Comfort as a Function of Dyadic Interaction Distance," *Journal of Counseling Psychology*, Vol. 23, No. 1, January 1976, pp. 13-16.

Male undergraduate volunteers (N=27) were interviewed by nine male counseling students using an intake interview. Each student counselor saw three subjects, one in each of three counselor-client distance conditions: 18 inches, 30 inches, and 48 inches. Subject's degree of comfort scores ranged from highest for 30 inches to lowest for 18 inches with intermediate scores at 48 inches. LS.

Kotter, John P. "Power, Dependence, and Effective Management," *Harvard Business Review*, Vol. 55, No. 4, July-August 1977, pp. 125-136.

Presents a case that managers need to use power for effectiveness. Discusses four types of power over others: sense of obligation, belief in expertise, identification, and perceived dependence. P/D.

Kreck, L. A. "Semantic Distance and Job Satisfaction in Formal Organizations," *Etc.*, Vol. 31, No. 3, September 1974, pp. 249-256.

Managers and nonmanagers appear to have similar frames of reference. Semantic distances between superiors and subordinates were unrelated to job satisfaction. FS.

Landy, F. J. "The Validity of the Interview in Police Officer Selection," *Journal of Applied Psychology*, Vol. 61, No. 2, April 1976, pp. 193-198.

On-the-street performance of policemen could be successfully predicted from average interview factor scores derived from trait ratings made by interviewers. FS.

London, M., and J. R. Poplawski. "Effects of Information on Stereotype Development in Performance Appraisal and Interview Contexts," *Journal of Applied Psychology*, Vol. 61, No. 2, April 1976, pp. 199-205.

Ratings of individual members of groups were different from overall group perceptions. Sex differences, contrast effects, and factors affecting voter's overall impressions were also found. FS.

Matteson, M. T. "Attitudes Toward Women as Managers: Sex or Role Differences?" *Psychological Reports*, Vol. 39, No. 1, August 1976, p. 166.

Females have a more favorable attitude towards women as managers than males. A negative relationship was observed between number of years of work experience and total attitude scores for the total sample (with age partialled out). FS.

Nisberg, Jay N., and Daniel Spurr. "Getting the Facts: How to Set Up a Communications Framework for Interviewing," *Management Review*, Vol. 66, No. 3, April 1977, pp. 13-17.

The authors state that an interviewer must obtain relevant, valid, and reliable information. Potential problems, and inhibitors of good communication that hinder this goal are discussed. Seven factors that promote exchange of information are detailed. P/D.

Norton, Linda, and Russell Dobson. "Perceptions of Teachers' Nonverbal Behaviors by Children of Different Race, Age, and Sex," *Humanist Educator*, Vol. 14, No. 3, March 1976, pp. 94-101.

Discusses the quality of teacher-pupil interaction. Investigates whether differences exist in elementary school children's perceptions of nonverbal behaviors of teachers in this organizational hierarchy. The study specifically investigates effects of race, sex, and age. FS.

Oldham, D. R., J. Hackman, and J. Pearce. "Conditions Under Which Employees Respond Positively to Enriched Work," *Journal of Applied Psychology*, Vol. 61, No. 4, August 1976, pp. 395-403.

Employees who had strong growth needs and also were satisfied with the work context (i.e., with their pay, job security, co-workers, and supervisors) responded more positively to enriched jobs than employees who had weak needs for growth and/or who were dissatisfied with the work context. FS.

Reichman, Walter, and Marguerite Levy. "Personal Power Enhancement: A Way to Executive Success," *Management Review*, Vol. 66, No. 3, March 1977, pp. 28-34.

A "how-to" article on ways to increase one's personal power so that one can exert stronger pressure on others to counteract pressures being exerted on them. Discusses ten ways to increase power and three communication strategies to use in conjunction with them.

Roloff, Michael E. "A Model of the Selective Exposure Phenomenon," paper presented at the Annual Meeting of the Speech Communication Association, Houston, TX, December 1975, 35 pp. ERIC ED 117 761.

Presents a conceptual model to explain why a person selectively exposes himself to information. This model enhances the development of a theory for predicting accurately the existence of selective exposure and increases the ability to control the selective exposure phenomenon. T/C.

Rosen, B., and T. H. Jerdee. "The Influence of Age, Stereotypes on Managerial Decisions," *Journal of Applied Psychology*, Vol. 61, No. 4, August 1976, pp. 428-432.

Stereotypes regarding older employees' physical, cognitive, and emotional characteristics lead to discrimination against them. LS.

————. "The Nature of Job Related Age Stereotypes," *Journal of Applied Psychology*, Vol. 61, No. 2, April 1976, pp. 180-183.

Business students rated a hypothetical 60 year old lower on performance capacity and on potential development while rating a 30 year old lower on stability. LS.

Rosenfeld, Lawrence B., and Jean M. Civikly. "With Words Unspoken: The Nonverbal Experience," New York: Holt, Rinehart, & Winston, 1976.

Examines recent theory and research on nonverbal experience and behavior. In addition, provides examples of the nonverbal experience in contemporary social experience. Can be applicable to training activities. P/D.

Schmitt, N., and B. W. Coyle. "Applicant Decisions in the Employment Interview," *Journal of Applied Psychology*, Vol. 61, No. 2, April 1976, pp. 184-192.

Perceived interviewer personality, manner of delivery, and adequacy of job information affected interviewee evaluations of the interviewer and his company and the interviewee's likelihood of job acceptance. FS.

Schneider, Joseph. "The Greener Grass" Phenomenon: Differential Effects of a Work Context Alternative on Organizational Participation and Withdrawal Intentions." *Organizational Behavior and Human Performance*, Vol. 1, No. 2, August 1976, pp. 308-333.

The attraction or instrumentality of the current work context was correlated significantly with organizational participation/withdrawal intentions. Participation and withdrawal intentions are also affected by evaluations of outcome in an alternative context. FS.

Shaffer, D., P. V. Mays, and K. Etheridge. "Who Shall be Hired: A Biasing Effect of the Buckley Admendment on Employment Practices?" *Journal of Applied Psychology*, Vol. 61, No. 5, October 1976, pp. 571-575.

Individuals with confidential placement files were judged more attractive as prospective employees, preferable as job supervisors, and somewhat more socially attractive than individuals with open files. LS.

Shapira, Z. "A Facet Analysis of Leadership Styles," *Journal of Applied Psychology*, Vol. 61, No. 2, April 1976, pp. 136-139.

Five leadership styles (direction, negotiation, consultation, participation, and delegation) were defined by a facet analysis of three facets— the leader's behavior, the lack of power, and the lack of information within a management-subordinate system. FS.

Siegman, Aaron Wolfe. "Do Noncontingent Interviewer Mm-hmms Facilitate Interviewee Productivity?" *Journal of Consulting and Clinical Psychology*, Vol. 44, No. 2, April 1976, pp. 171-181.

Discusses two studies that investigate the hypothesis that noncontingent interviewer "mm-hmms" facilitate interviewee verbal productivity. FS.

Sykes, Richard E. "A Theory of Proximity and Attraction," Minnesota Systems Research Inc., Minneapolis, February 15, 1977, 21 p. Report No. TR-1 Contract N00014-75-C-0075.

Suggests a new explanation of the relationship between proximity and attraction based on the variables of territoriality and likelihood of common occupancy. Includes review of the literature since 1950. T/C.

————. "Friendship and Social Structure: A Preliminary Outline of a Social Psychological Theory," Minnesota Systems Research Inc., Minneapolis, February 1977, 45 p. Report No. TR-2 Contract N00014-75-C-0075.

Attempts to distinguish between attraction and friendship. Friendship is defined as the co-occurrence of attraction and relationships, examining those factors which lead to each. Attraction is defined in terms of social desirability and etiquette norms. T/C.

————, "Informal Social Network Formation in Navy Training Units," Minnesota Systems Research Inc., Minneapolis, April 1977, 23 p. Report No. TR-1 Contract N00014-75-C-0075.

Discusses the theory of informal group formation relating similarity, proximity, and social structure variables to interpersonal attraction. Empirical results of the analysis are given. FS.

Weiss, Howard M. "Subordinate Imitation of Supervisor Behavior: The Role of Modeling in Organizational Socialization," *Organizational Behavior and Human Performance*, Vol. 19, No. 1, 1977, pp. 89-105.

Data collected from 141 pairs of subordinates and supervisors demonstrated that the degree of behavior similarity displayed by subordinates and their direct supervisors was positively correlated with subordinates' perceptions of their supervisors' success and competence. FS.

Zaleznik, Abraham. "Managers and Leaders: Are They Different?" *Harvard Business Review*, Vol. 55, No. 3, May-June 1977, pp. 67-78.

Argues that managers and leaders are different types of people and require different conditions for growth. Traces a leader's psychological development, attitudes, goals, and relationships with others. In order to develop fully, leaders need to form a one-to-one relationship with a mentor. P/D.

SEE ALSO

Intragroup Variables: Eckloff & Petelle, Greene, Parker
Intergroup Variables: Hall
Communication Factors and Organizational Goals: Dipboye & Arvey & Terpstra, Faunce, Gleason & Seaman & Hollander, Kostick & Pearse, McAlindon, Merryman & Shani, Powers, Roach, Silverman
Skill Improvement and Training: Cooper & Bowles, Crowley & Elvey, D'Augelli & Danish, Egar, Fiedler & Beach, Imberman, Mendoca & Siess, Scott, Steinmetz, Wakefield, Wittmer *et al.*, Yorks
Research Methodology: Buck, Hopp, Roloff, Steers & Braunstein, Sykes, Wilbourne & Guinn & Leisey
Texts, Anthologies, Reviews, and General Bibliographies: Dyer, Eakins, Ingalls, Kirschenbaum, Rogers & Fortson, Royal & Schutt

 **you have a professional interest in the communications of business...**

you are invited to join the American Business Communication Association. Teacher, administrator, or practitioner, you will find ABCA the association for all who are seriously interested in business communication — written, oral, and graphic.

ABCA was founded in 1935 and now has a membership of more than 1500, including professors of world-wide reputation, well-known authors, training directors, business executives, and consultants. Association with such people will allow you the opportunity to keep up with professional research and developments, as well as share your own ideas and work experience.

For example, four times a year you'll receive **The Journal of Business Communication** with its papers on important aspects of business communication and its reviews of major books. You are encouraged to submit articles for consideration.

You'll also receive a second quarterly publication, **The ABCA Bulletin,** which carries course descriptions for senior college, junior college, and high school; company training programs; bibliographies; class problems and solutions; and other useful material.

ABCA's publication program makes a number of other books and pamphlets available: a casebook, comprehensive bibliographies, a career booklet, and an anthology of articles on the teaching of business communication.

Finally, regional meetings and the national convention will enable you to meet and talk with leaders in the profession.

To enjoy these opportunities, just ask ABCA for a membership application. When you return it, along with your check for $25, you will be enrolled immediately and receive the current issues of the **Journal** and **Bulletin**. Write to Francis W. Weeks, Executive Director, The American Business Communication Association, 911 South Sixth, University of Illinois, Champaign, Illinois 61820.

You'll be glad you did. And we'll be glad to meet you.

INTRAGROUP COMMUNICATION IN ORGANIZATIONS

BOOKS AND DISSERTATIONS

Absher, Harold, Jr. *A Study of the Relationship Between Involvement in Decision-Making and Morale Among Virginia Public Elementary School Teachers.* Ed.D. Dissertation, Virginia Polytechnic Institute and State University, 1976. DAI, Vol. 38, No. 3, p. 1136-A.

Concludes that teachers underinvolved and overinvolved in decision-making areas had lower morale than teachers moderately involved. FS.

Baird, John E., and Sanford B. Weinberg. *Communication: The Essence of Group Synergy.* Dubuque, IA: Wm. C. Brown, 1977.

Covers such traditional topics in group processes as norms, roles, leadership, decision making, motivation, group formation and development, and verbal and nonverbal communication. T/C.

Barbanell, Lester H. *The Relationship of the Task and Interpersonal Dimensions of Conflict to the Effectiveness of Child Study Team Decision Groups.* Ed.D. Dissertation, Columbia University Teachers College, 1976. DAI, Vol. 37, No. 4, p. 1891-A.

Concludes that teams that do not recognize or resolve conflict are less effective than teams that do discuss and resolve conflict. Ineffective teams tend not to make recommendations quickly enough, while effective teams tend to focus less on formal tasks. FS.

Brill, Naomi. *Team Work: Working Together in Human Services.* New York: J. B. Lippincott Company, 1976.

Suggests that teamwork, or working in groups, is becoming more important as technology continues to advance, and that teams (or groups) are characterized by a developmental pattern that can be understood and controlled. Views teams as systems involved in a complex set of interrelationships with their environment. T/C.

Broom, Glen M. *Community Consensus-Building: A Communication Experiment in Two Rural Wisconsin Communities.* Ph.D. Dissertation, The University of Wisconsin—Madison, 1977. DAI, Vol. 38, No. 2, p. 531-A.

Reports that use of feedback increased awareness of community problems among community leaders, elected officials, and citizens. After the experiment, however, agreement as to severity of problems decreased between citizens and elected officials. FS.

Cooper, C. L., ed. *Developing Social Skills in Managers. Advances in Group Training.* New York: Wiley and Sons, 1976.

Examines and evaluates the range of methods based on participation and group experience designed to develop social skills, which are available to teachers and trainers of managers from Britain and the U.S. Identifies the characteristics of successful methods to aid in designing successful management and organizational development programs. T/C.

Courtright, John A. *Groupthink and Communication Processes: An Initial Investigation.* Ph.D. Dissertation, The University of Iowa, 1976. DAI, Vol. 37, No. 8, p. 4695-A.

Finds no significant difference in the number and quality of solutions for groups of different cohesiveness. Cohesive groups tended to have a higher degree of error in judgments. LS.

Drake, Bruce H. *An Experimental Study of the Effects of Vertical and Horizontal Power on Behavioral Commitment, Satisfaction, and Involvement in Decision Making.* Ph.D. Dissertation, University of Washington, 1976. DAI, Vol. 37, No. 7, p. 4464-A.

Finds that increases in the horizontal power within groups resulted in higher commitment by the members of the groups. Less commitment by members was observed in groups after increases in vertical power. LS.

Eldridge, Larry D. *The Effects of Nominal and Brainstorming Decision-Making Procedures on Group Productivity.* Ph.D. Dissertation, University of Rochester, 1977. DAI, Vol. 38, No. 2, p. 941-B.

Groups provided with decision structures generated more ideas than control groups. The number of alternatives generated were related to the number of good alternatives which were related to the quality of the final decision. Participation was suggested as a means for member influence. LS.

Forys, Karen A. O. *Helper Response Behaviors of Administrators in Small Groups.* Ph.D. Dissertation, The University of Arizona, 1977. DAI, Vol. 38, No. 3, p. 1146-A.

Shows that group leaders maintaining minimum or better levels of facilitative conditions led more productive groups, used a more democratic interaction style, and were better accepted by group members. Leaders not maintaining minimum levels were ineffective group leaders. LS.

Griffin, Richard A. *The Effect of Interpersonal Behaviors Within A Superintendency Team on the Principals' Perception of the System's Organizational Climate.* Ed.D. Dissertation, University of Houston, 1976. DAI, Vol. 38, No. 1, p. 43-A.

Finds that the team management approach to the school superintendency is an effective means of administering a school district. The "team within a team" concept was found to be in use in many districts. FS.

Gulley, Halbert E., and Dale G. Leathers. *Communication and Group Process: Techniques for Improving the Quality of Small Group Communication.* New York: Holt, Rinehart, and Winston, 1977.

Adopts a systems theory perspective in its treatment of small group communication. Communication topics discussed include interaction phrases, nonverbal communication, and communication quality. Includes other topics such as: leadership, task, outcomes, interpersonal outcomes, and preparation for group interaction. T/C.

Hare, Paul A. *Handbook of Small Group Research* (2nd Edition). New York: Free Press, 1976.

Summarizes the major trends and findings in group theory and research from 1898 to 1974. Over 6,000 references are included. T/C.

Harnack, R. Victor, Thorrel B. Fest, and Barbara S. Jones. *Group Discussion: Theory and Technique* (2nd Edition). Englewood Cliffs, NJ: Prentice-Hall, Inc., 1977.

Covers such traditional topics as evidence, reasoning, problem solving, and functions of discussion in society. Also includes chapters on group dynamics, communication principles, leadership, and group effectiveness. Emphasizes practical skills necessary to work in problem solving groups. T/C.

Harvey, Ruth B. *A Study of Communication Change in Group Process Seminars Using the Sequential Analysis of Verbal Interaction.* Ph.D. Dissertation, Bryn Mawr College, 1976. DAI, Vol. 37, No. 9, p. 5605-A.

Finds that T-group seminar sessions produced no change in communication processes within small groups. Areas investigated were communication changes across the life of the group, changes in group communication within the training session, and the effects of trainer modeling on the groups. LS.

Hills, G. S. *Managing Corporate Meetings: A Legal and Procedural Guide.* New York: Wiley and Sons, 1976.

Covers the law and practice of meetings as recorded in the case law and parliamentary manuals, and emphasis is on meetings of business and membership cooperations. Considers basic legal requirements of meetings. Includes the application of common parliamentary law; rights and duties of the chairperson; standards of fairness; and more. T/C.

Hoffman, David B. *Work Unit Structure and Decision Making Influence.* DBA Dissertation, Kent State University, 1976. DAI, Vol. 37, No. 7, p. 4469-A.

Finds that highly structured work units have less influence over work decisions than less structured units. FS.

Kozan, Memmet K. *Work Group Flexibility: Development and Construct Validation of a Measure.* Ph.D. Dissertation, University of California—Los Angeles, 1976. DAI, Vol. 37, No. 9, p. 5927-A.

Indicates that work groups with high flexibility had higher autonomy and higher supervisory leadership, but low peer leadership and a lack of a collaborative or compromise approach to internal conflict management. FS.

Leth, Pamela C., and Jo Ann Vandemark. *Small Group Communication.*
Menlo Park, CA: Cummings, 1977.

Covers the following topics: problem solving, interaction, listening, conflict, leadership, and group evaluation. Each topic is accompanied by
exercises designed to facilitate the acquisition of group skills. Includes
a programmed review. T/C.

MacKenzie, Kenneth D. *Theory of Group Structure* (2 Volumes). New
York: Gordon & Breach Science Publishers, 1976.

Describes, in volume one, basic theory: defining group structure, task
processes, roles, structure levels and efficiency, span of control, and
change and rate of change. Presents in volume two, empirical tests of
the theory: group preferences for type of structure and a model for interpersonal hostility. T/C.

Marshak, Robert J. *Committee Decision Making Using the Special Majority
of Unanimous Consent: An Empirically Based Theoretical Inquiry.* Ph.D.
Dissertation, The American University, 1977. DAI, Vol. 38, No. 2, p.
1015-A.

Determines that committee outcomes were a function of the decision
rule of majority consent and the size of the committee. Support was
not found for the theory that informal conflict resolution processes,
such as seniority, prestige, position, and special knowledges, are influential in committee decisions. FS.

Merton, Karol K. *Peer Review Among Professionals: The Application of
Group Communication Criteria.* Ph.D. Dissertation, University of Denver, 1976. DAI, Vol. 37, No. 7, p. 3983-A.

Obtains low reliability results when peer review by professionals is cate-
gorized into six problem-solving behaviors: problem formulation, number of relevant issues, range of relevant issues, issue frequency, conflict,
conflict resolution and deferred evaluation. More training sessions for
participants is recommended. FS.

Mills, Esther R. *A Descriptive Model of Verbal Decision-Making Behavior
in Task-Oriented Dyads.* Ph.D. Dissertation, University of Washington,
1976. DAI, Vol. 38, No. 3, p. 1122-A.

Finds that regulation of dyadic conflict was achieved by means of unilateral peaceable behavior, prior intention by participants to agree,
commitment to a common community, and civility. LS.

Miner, Frederick C., Jr. *The Effectiveness of Problem Centered Leadership, Nominal Leadership, and the Delphi Process in a High Quality-
High Acceptance Problem.* Ph.D. Dissertation, University of Minnesota,
1976. DAI, Vol. 37, No. 10, p. 6608-A.

Concludes that the quality of decision making in small groups was highest where the leader followed a structured decision-making approach
placing emphasis on the expression of feelings prior to attempting to

solve the problem. Anonymous written decisions and group-generated decisions were of lower quality. LS.

Nykodym, Gilbert F., II. *An Evaluation of Transactional Analysis as a Strategy of Organization Development.* Ph.D. Dissertation, The University of Nebraska—Lincoln, 1976. DAI, Vol. 38, No. 1, p. 371-A.

Determines that Transactional Analysis in work groups improved some measures of supervisory behavior, including information flow and organizational climate. Suggests that Transactional Analysis be used as a Team Skills Training device in a total Organizational Development program. FS.

Pendell, Sue D. *The Influence of Room Design on Small Group Communication.* Ph.D. Dissertation, University of Utah, 1976. DAI, Vol. 37, No. 10, p. 6144-A.

Concludes that room design had no effect on communication behavior, indicating that neither the shape of the room nor the level of interior decoration exerted any influence on the activity within the room. LS.

Penley, Larry E. *An Investigation of the Relationship Between Communication and the Explanatory Structure of Organizational Work Groups.* Ph.D. Dissertation, University of Georgia, 1976. DAI, Vol. 37, No. 5, p. 3022-A.

Concludes that there is a strong relationship between communication and the explanatory structure of work groups. Work groups can be classified on the basis of their explanatory structure and comparable communication. FS.

Reinheimer, Robert E. *Interpersonal Attractiveness and Distribution of Task Relevant Information as Contributors to an Influence Base in Task Oriented Groups.* Ph.D. Dissertation, University of Kansas, 1976. DAI, Vol. 37, No. 8, p. 4705-A.

Determines that attitudinal attractiveness in a task-oriented discussion group was directly related to a person's ability to influence the group. LS.

Richman, Harold S. *Facilitating Problem-Solving in Student-Teacher Planning Groups.* Ph.D. Dissertation, The University of North Carolina—Chapel Hill, 1976. DAI, Vol. 37, No. 8, p. 5333-A.

Finds that the atmosphere in groups of high school students with a facilitator present was more confrontative and less easy-going. Group members played a more active role in group discussion and teacher domination was less prevalent in facilitated groups. FS.

Schindler-Rainman, Eva, Ronald Lippitt, and Jack Cole. *Taking Your Meetings Out of the Doldrums.* La Jolla, CA: University Associates, 1977.

Includes practical suggestions and principles for conducting meetings. Emphasizes preplanning and discusses many pitfalls and common problems that occur during meetings. Includes specific recommendations for a series of situations such as goal setting and stimulating creativity. P/D.

Stead, Walter E. *Comparison of the Nominal Grouping and Sequenced Brainstorming Techniques of Creative Idea Generation.* Ph.D. Dissertation, The Louisiana State University and Agricultural and Mechanical College, 1976. DAI, Vol. 37, No. 6, p. 3760-A.

Concludes that, in terms of overall effectiveness, quantity, and satisfaction, sequenced brainstorming groups were more effective than nominal brainstorming groups, although both approaches provided management with high quality ideas. FS.

Wilkinson, David. *Cohesion and Conflict: Lessons From the Study of Three-Party Interaction.* New York: St. Martin's Press, 1976.

Synthesizes previous research on triads and the stability of structure. Reports the results of a study as well as measures of power and conflict which are used to construct models to predict coalition formation and to predict the outcome of three-party interaction. T/C.

ARTICLES, PAPERS, AND U.S. GOVERNMENT PUBLICATIONS

Allen, W. R., and J. A. Ruhe, "Verbal Behavior by Black and White Leaders of Biracial Groups in Two Different Environments," *Journal of Applied Psychology*, Vol. 61, No. 4, August 1976, pp. 441-445.

No significant differences were found in verbal patterns by leaders of groups varying in racial composition. LS.

Brownlee, Don. "The Supreme Court as a Small Group," paper presented at the Annual Meeting of the Speech Communication Association, Houston, TX, December 1975, 13 p. ERIC ED 123 694.

Investigates the Supreme Court as a decision-making small group from October 1969 to October 1974. Areas investigated are group interaction, decision-making techniques, type and degree of dissent, coalition formation, the effect of personnel change, and value systems as measured by the Guttman scale. FS.

Dowling, W. F. "Consensus Management at Graphics Control," *Organizational Dynamics*, Vol. 5, No. 3, Winter 1977, pp. 22-47.

Describes the development, implementation, and effectiveness of consensus management policies in a manufacturing firm. FS.

Eckloff, Maurine C., and John Petelle. "Cognitive Abstractness, Interpersonal Perception, Factual and Social Problem Solving," paper presented at the Annual Meeting of the International Communication Association, Portland, OR, April 1976, 40 p. ERIC ED 123 691.

Investigates the effects of cognitive abstractness levels, interpersonal perception abilities, and task type (factual or social problem solving) on group performance as measured by time used and quality of solutions. The results of the investigation has implications for real world task groups. LS.

Graves, Gordon R. "How Can a Chief Negotiator Influence His School Board to Set Realistic Guidelines for Negotiations?" 1976, 8 p. ERIC ED 125 056.

Advocates awareness of group dynamics on the part of the group leader. Discusses in detail the four phases of group decision-making: orientation stage, conflict stage, emergence stage, and reinforcement stage. P/D.

Greene, Les R. "Body Image Boundaries and Small Group Seating Arrangements," *Journal of Consulting and Clinic Psychology*, Vol. 44, No. 2, April 1976, pp. 244-249.

Examines the effects of body image boundaries on preferred and avoided seating choices in small groups and the personal meanings associated with these measures of spatial behavior. The findings indicate a tendency toward greater defensive distancing by the boundary-indefinite subjects. LS.

Hackman, J. Richard. "The Design of Self-Managing Work Groups," Yale University, New Haven, CT, School of Organization and Management, December 1976, 52 p. Report No. TR-11 Contract N00014-75-C-0269.

Proposes a model for the design and maintenance of self-managing work groups in organizations. Three design factors in constructing such groups are emphasized in the model. Implications of this model focus on the management of work groups and the advantages of designing work by interacting groups rather than by individuals. T/C.

Hill, Raymond E. "Managing Interpersonal Conflict in Project Teams," *Sloan Management Review*, Vol. 18, No. 2, Winter 1977, pp. 45-61.

Identifies personality conflict as the most constant type of conflict common to project teams in various phases of project life cycles. In a large oil company, the writer separates the coping responses of high as well as low producing managers. Isolates managerial style characteristics figuring into such conflict. FS.

Hill, Timothy A. "The Relationship of Male and Female Deviance to Member Perceptions of Group Outcome," paper presented at the Annual Meeting of the Southern Speech Communication Association, San Antonio, TX, April 1976, 13 p. ERIC ED 120 829.

Investigates the effects of male versus female deviants on the small discussion group. Subjects were presented with a decision-making task under the auspices of an exercise in consensus. Confederates were planted in the groups with instructions to perform deviant behaviors and prevent the group from reaching consensus. The results were: female deviant behavior affected the goals less negatively than male deviant behavior. LS.

Kruger, Gerald P. "Conferencing and Teleconferencing in Three Communication Modes as a Functioning of the Number in Conferences," Johns Hopkins University, Baltimore, MD, February 1977, 115 p. Report No. TR-6 Contract N00014-75-C-0131.

Discusses a study which investigated the relationship between group size (2, 3, 4) to performance and communication activity under three communication modes in problem solving. Results showed that an increase in group size resulted in an increase in communication as measured by the number of messages, words, speed, and message variability. LS.

Lauenstein, Milton C. "Preserving the Importance of the Board," *Harvard Business Review*, Vol. 55, No. 4, July-August 1977, pp. 36-48.

A tongue-in-cheek article that demonstrates how common mistakes of the chief executive officer of board meetings make members impotent and himself more exalted and powerful rather than encouraging contributions. P/D.

London, Manuel and Greg R. Oldham. "A Comparison of Group and Individual Incentive Plans," *Academy of Management Journal*, Vol. 20, No. 1, 1977, pp. 34-41.

In a lab experiment, the effects of three variations of group incentive plans were compared. The nature of the incentive system significantly affected goal setting and performance of coacting pairs. LS.

Morley, Eileen and Andrew Silver. "A Film Director's Approach to Managing Creativity," *Harvard Business Review*, Vol. 55, No. 2, March-April 1977, pp. 59-70.

The production of Arthur Penn's film "Night Moves" is analyzed as a temporary creative work group. Working relationships, motivation, leadership, stress and conflict, and how creativity is stimulated are examined. P/D.

Parker, W. S. "Black-White Differences in Leader Behavior Related to Subordinates' Reactions," *Journal of Applied Psychology*, Vol. 61, No. 2, April 1976, pp. 140-147.

The behavior of supervisors toward their subordinates is a complex function of a) the supervisor's own race and role in combination with, b) the race of the subordinate, and c) the majority or minority position of racial groups within the group supervised. FS.

Purinton, Michael. "The Development, Implementation, and Evaluation of a Values Clarification Program," *School Guidance Worker*, Vol. 30, No. 6, August 1975, pp. 23-25.

Describes the values clarification approach as a novel and exciting method of working with students in groups. This article describes a pilot project in values clarification initiated by the Student Personnel Services Branch of the Manitoba Department of Education. P/D.

Richards, T. "Brainstorming: An Examination of Idea Production Rates and Level of Speculation in Real Managerial Situations," *R & D Management*, Vol. 6, No. 1, October 1975, pp. 11-14.

In a considerable proportion of brainstorming exercises by industrial managers the material produced was low level speculations within the groups. In real situations the intrusion of longer-term belief systems may be influencing the group in the brainstorming process. FS.

Schlenker, Barry R. "Egocentric Perceptions in Cooperative Groups: A Conceptualization and Research Review," Florida University, Gainesville, FL, November 10, 1976, 41 p. Report No. TR-76-6 Contract N00014-75-C-0901.

Examines the various aspects of egocentrism on group behavior. Results indicated that egocentric perceptions produce self-enhancement and self-protection. Egocentrism also affects other communication factors such as leadership patterns, interpersonal agreement, and group performance. LS.

——— and Rowland S. Miller. "Style of Group Interaction, Anonymity, and Group Performance as Determinants of Egocentric Perceptions," Florida University, Gainesville, FL, Dept. of Psychology, September 1976, 52 p. Report No. TR-76-4, Contract No. N00014-75-C-0901.

Discusses the various aspects of egocentrism with cooperative groups. An additional hypothesis tests the concept of face-to-face interaction among group members during the problem/solving phase. It was estimated that during this type of interaction, egocentrism would decrease and group identification would increase. LS.

———. "The Effects of Group Performance and Evaluative Feedback from Other Group Members on Egocentric Perceptions," Florida University, Gainesville, FL, Dept. of Psychology, September 1976, 42 p. Report No. TR-76-5 Contract No. N00014-75-C-0901.

Examines the effects of group performance and the effects of personal evaluative feedback from fellow group members on retrospective perceptions of group activities. Findings show that failing groups' peer evaluations had no effects on the amount of relative responsibility subjects took for their group's performance. In successful groups, however, the favorability of the peer evaluations was directly related to the amount of responsibility subjects perceived. Self-ratings of leadership were directly related to peer feedback following group failure, but unrelated following group success. LS.

Seaver, David A. "Assessment of Group Preferences and Group Uncertainty for Decision Making," Decisions and Designs Inc., McLean, VA, June 1976, 65 p. Contract N00014-76-C-0074.

Reviews the literature concerning the relative merits of individual versus group judgments. Concludes that no entirely satisfactory method for determining either group utilities or probabilities exists. T/C.

Taylor, James A. and Richard V. Farace. "The Referential Function of Internal Communication Groups in Complex Organizations: An Empirical Analysis," paper presented at the Annual Meeting of the International Communication Association, Portland, OR, April 1976, 41 p. ERIC ED 122 314.

Asserts that people who repeatedly interact create a conjoint information space determined by common values, attitudes, and beliefs. Results of the study indicate that members of informal groups feel less inclined to trust their work team members, less willing to advocate staying with the work team, less willing to rate highly the performance of their group, and less likely to see themselves as important to the team's productivity. FS.

Vallacher, Robin, George E. Seymour, and E. K. Eric Gunderson. "The Relationship Between Cohesiveness and Effectiveness in Small Isolated Groups: A Field Study," Naval Health Research Center, San Diego, CA, July 1974, 27 p. Report No. 74-50.

Discusses the relation between group effectiveness and cohesiveness among groups of men at U.S. Antarctic research stations. Cohesiveness was found to be unrelated to supervisors' and group members' perceptions of performance. Conflict, however, was related to perceptions of supervisor performance. FS.

Whitmore, Paul G. "Analysis of Human Relations Problem Situations: The Group Process Approach," Human Resources Research Organization, Alexandria, VA, January 1976, 49 p. Report No. HumRRO-FR-WD-TX-75-27 Contract DAHC19-74-C-0056.

Discusses various aspects of analyzing realistic problem situations through group problem solving methods. T/C.

SEE ALSO

Interpersonal Variables: Hill, Sykes
Intergroup Variables: Elkins, Mace
Communication Factors & Organizational Goals: Greenburg & Leventhal, Gyllenhammer, Likert & Fisher, Rubinstein, Streker, Viall
Skill Improvement/Training: Egan, Kirkpatrick, Nadler
System Analysis: George
Media: Software & Hardware: London, Polit
Research Methodology: Sykes
Texts, Anthologies, Reviews, & General Bibliographies: Behling & Schrieheim, Hare, MacKenzie, Wilkinson

INTERGROUP COMMUNICATION IN ORGANIZATIONS

BOOKS AND DISSERTATIONS

Acton, Milton E. *The Organizational Behavior of Elementary Principals as Perceived by Teachers.* Ph.D. Dissertation, The Florida State University, 1976, DAI, Vol. 37, No. 7, p. 3997-A.

Finds that the elementary school principals who rate high on the consideration scale of the Organization Climate Description Questionnaire communicate better with their faculty, show more concern for their staff, work longer hours, and have greater insight as to teachers' needs. FS.

Archer, Robert K. *An Examination of Three Citizen Participation Styles in Federal Grant Administration as Seen in the Model Cities Programs, 1966-1974.* Ph.D. Dissertation, Wayne State University, 1976. DAI, Vol. 37, No. 5, p. 3167-A.

Reports that peak efficiency and citizen satisfaction occurred in those governmental programs in which elected and appointed officials controlled the decision process; and, indicates the value of meaningful citizen participation in public policy formation. T/C.

Barnett, Andrew H. *Communication in Auditing: An Examination of Investors' Understanding of the Auditor's Report.* DBA Dissertation, Texas Tech University, 1976. DAI, Vol. 38, No. 2, p. 864-A.

Finds that neither professional investors nor nonprofessional investors sufficiently understand the standard auditor's report. A revised format for auditing reports is presented for possible adoption. FS.

Bouch, Richard F. *Perceptions of Supervisory Techniques by Black and White Teachers and Principals in Selected Florida Schools.* Ed.D. Dissertation, The University of Florida, 1976. DAI, Vol. 37, No. 7 p. 4004-A.

Finds significant differences in perception of supervisory techniques by black and white supervisors and black and white teachers. FS.

Boyle, John M. *Service Integration and Urban Field Administration: Interdependence and Coordination in New York City's Field Services.* Ph.D. Dissertation, Columbia University, 1976. DAI, Vol. 37, No. 7, p. 4611-A.

Finds that substantial problems of service integration exist among urban field services, including overlapping responsibilities and inter-service conflicts. Field services are under environmental pressure to change more rapidly than organizational structure permits. Informal coordination is not seen as a viable alternative. T/C.

Brant, Roy, Jr. *Collective Bargaining in Pennsylvania's Public Schools.* Ph.D. Dissertation, West Virginia University, 1976. DAI, Vol. 36, No. 4, p. 2411-A.

Concludes that the Pennsylvania Public Employee Relations Act has failed to provide a means of effective communication and that collective bargaining is the only viable alternative to unilateral policy-making by Boards of Education. T/C.

Burke, John P. *Organizations and Clients: A Method for the Investigation of Verbal Exchanges Between Agents and Clients.* Ph.D. Dissertation, Saint Louis University, 1976. DAI, Vol. 37, No. 12, p. 7977-A.

Analyzes verbal interaction between college advisors and students, finding variations in verbal patterns but no relationship between these variations and student outcomes. LS.

Buroker, Charles D. *College Presidents' Perceptions of Student Participation in Administrative Decision Making in the Two-Year College.* Ph.D. Dissertation, Bowling Green State University, 1976. DAI, Vol. 37, No. 5, p. 2527-A.

Reports that junior college administrators felt student participation was most extensive in areas such as recognition of student groups, outside speakers, student newspapers, and discipline procedures. Areas traditionally under administrative control, such as promotion and tenure of faculty and admission standards, remained so. T/C.

Capie, Robert M. *A Study of the Attitudes and Opinions of Administrators and Board Members with Respect to the Involvement of Teachers, Parents, and Students in Decision-Making.* Ph.D. Dissertation, St. John's University, 1977. DAI, Vol. 38, No. 2, p. 560-A.

Reports that school board members believed in significantly less involvement of teachers, parents, and students than did school administrators. FS.

Childress, Roger R. *A Study of the Organizational Climate and Satisfaction with First Year Negotiations as Perceived by Principals in Selected Impasse and Non-Impasse School Corporations in Central Indiana.* Ed.D. Dissertation, Indiana University, 1976. DAI, Vol. 37, No. 8, p. 4733-A.

Notes that there is a direct relationship between the degree of impasse in collective bargaining negotiations and principal dissatisfaction with teachers. FS.

Clark, Noreen M. *Citizen Participation in Health Organization Decision Making: Implications for Education.* Ph.D. Dissertation, Columbia University, 1976. DAI, Vol. 37, No. 7, p. 4154-A.

Notes that the local community board under a central governmental agency is required to balance local needs and organizational mandates; and that there is a need for agency/board collaboration, including delineation of jurisdiction and open and consistent communication. FS.

Cook, Philip J. *Towards a Practice Theory of Citizen Participation in Public Programs.* Ph.D. Dissertation, State University of New York—at Buffalo, 1976. DAI, Vol. 37, No. 5, p. 3168-A.

Discusses the role of practice theory (activity cannot occur unless the participants have some theory implicitly guiding their actions) in the organizational structure. Fifteen specific agency goals, including transmission of information, are examined. T/C.

Crosby, Willis H., Jr. *A Survey of Principal Attitudes Toward Community Involvement in a Southern Public School System.* Ed.D. Dissertation, University of Massachusetts, 1977. DAI, Vol. 38, No. 1, p. 39-A.

Indicates that principals held positive attitudes towards community involvement, but expressed negative attitudes for parent membership on school committees and parent evaluation and selection of teachers. FS.

Davenport, Irvin W. *Analysis of the Perceived Leader Behavior of Male and Female Elementary School Principals.* Ed.D. Dissertation, University of Missouri—Columbia, 1976. DAI, Vol. 37, No. 9, p. 5476-A.

Finds no significant differences between the overall leader behavior of male and female school principals; noting that male superordinates favored male principals over female principals. FS.

Ehrman, Hope J. *Public Information About Schools: A Dissemination Strategy Using Systems Concepts and Principles from the "Change" Literature.* Ph.D. Dissertation, Northwestern University, 1976. DAI, Vol. 37, No. 7, p. 4011-A.

Indicates that school administrators exhibited a moderately favorable response to the introduction of nine techniques of information dissemination. Barriers to the introduction of new techniques were considered to be a lack of time and qualified staff. FS.

Ford, Charles W. *A Description and Analysis of the Community Involvement Committee as it Functions in the Elementary Schools of the Lansing School District and as Perceived by its Members.* Ph.D. Dissertation, Michigan State University, 1977. DAI, Vol. 38, No. 3, p. 1211-A.

Recommends that all community elements be involved early in the initial planning. Views committee chairperson selection as an area of primary importance. FS.

Forrer, Stephen E. *A Comparison of Two Information Dissemination Systems in University Parent Orientation.* Ph.D. Dissertation, University of Maryland, 1972. DAI, Vol. 37, No. 11, p. 6949-A.

Compares the effects of two methods of university parent orientation (oral and written on-campus vs. written off-campus) finding that on-campus communication was more effective. FS.

Gauldfeldt, Frank I. *Interorganizational Relations of United States Voluntary Health Organizations in Their Host Countries.* DPA Dissertation,

The George Washington University, 1976. DAI, Vol. 37, No. 9, p. 6045-A.

Reports little communication between U.S. government agencies overseas and host countries. Frequency of interaction and number of different contacts were few. FS.

Gibbins, Michael. *Persuasive Communication and Accounting.* Ph.D. Dissertation, Cornell University, 1976. DAI, Vol. 38, No. 3, p. 1485-A.

Indicates that accounting information is not entirely factual and credibility of accountants was affected by the perception of factualness by readers. LS.

Hale, George E. *A Field Interview Study of the Effects of Executive Leadership Style on the State Budgetary Process in Delaware Under the Peterson and Tribbit Administrations.* Ph.D. Dissertation, Syracuse University, 1975. DAI, Vol. 36, No. 4, p. 2414-A.

Reports that, in two state administrations, the budgetary processes of state agencies were highly responsive to different executive priorities. However, bureaucratic constraints did hinder the full implementation of budgetary decisions. FS.

Hall, Edward T. *Beyond Culture.* New York: Anchor Books, 1977.

Not oriented toward business communication specifically, but much of what is written is readily adaptable. It should be particularly useful for businessmen who work in cross-cultural contexts. T/C.

Heim, Joseph P. *Decision-Making in the Wisconsin Legislature: A Case Study of the Merger of the University of Wisconsin and The Wisconsin State University Systems.* Ph.D. Dissertation, The University of Wisconsin—Milwaukee, 1976. DAI, Vol. 37, No. 7, p. 4613-A.

Concludes that the governor was the single most salient influence on state legislators in reference to the merger of the university systems. Interest groups, however, were found to play a significant role in influencing some legislators. FS.

Heiting, William A. *A Comparison of Secondary Science Teachers' and Students' Perceptions of the Interpersonal Relationship Existing Between Them in the Classroom.* Ph.D. Dissertation, The University of Iowa, 1976. DAI, Vol. 37, No. 8, p. 5015-A.

Reports significant differences between secondary teachers' perceptions of their interpersonal classroom behavior and students' perceptions of that behavior. FS.

Howe, Elizabeth A. *Intergovernmental Dependence as a Constraint on Urban Reform: New York City's Relationship with the New York State Legislature During the Second Lindsay Administration.* Ph.D. Dissertation, University of California—Berkeley, 1976. DAI, Vol. 37, No. 9, p. 6046-A.

Examines relationships between New York City and New York State in areas of urban reform legislation. Communications between the city and interest groups in the city were shown to influence legislative priorities. T/C.

Jorgenson, Spike C. *A Comparison of Three Degrees of Teacher Participation in Policy Development and the Effects of Each on the Attitudes of Power Structure Teachers; and an Outline for a Policy on Teacher Participation in the Selection of Teachers.* Ed.D. Dissertation, University of Wyoming, 1976. DAI, Vol. 37, No. 8, p. 4747-A.

Notes that perceived levels of satisfaction by teachers were affected by the degree of involvement in school district policy development. Lack of administrative implementation of teacher participative decisions caused dissatisfaction. FS.

Keener, Barbara J. *An Analysis of the Perceptions of the Leadership Behavior of Male and Female University of Florida Administrators.* Ed.D. Dissertation, The University of Florida, 1976. DAI, Vol. 37, No. 7, p. 4023-A.

Reports little difference in the leadership behavior of male and female college administrators, but some differences in career orientation, career development, and career aspirations. FS.

Lambert, Henry L. *Level of Community Participation of Selected School Principals and Parents' View of the School.* Ed.D. Dissertation, The University of Florida, 1976. DAI, Vol. 37, No. 10, p. 6181-A.

Finds that parental view of a school is related to both the principal's membership in community organizations and the time spent in community activities. FS.

Lamoreaux, James W. *Receptivity of Specific Subaudiences to Family Planning Communications in Iran: A Typological Approach.* Ph.D. Dissertation, Syracuse University, 1976. DAI, Vol. 37, No. 11, p. 6821-A.

Concludes that messages from government agencies to small subaudiences may be more effective than messages to influentials when subaudiences are selected on basis of age, sex, urbanization, media exposure, and community involvement. FS.

Leenhouts, Thelma K. *Communication Similarities and Differences of the Female and Male Legislators in the 1975 Michigan House of Representatives.* Ph.D. Dissertation, The University of Michigan, 1976. DAI, Vol. 37, No. 6, p. 3266-A.

Finds that women state legislators tend to function in a male-dominated environment by adapting to the existing communication patterns. Length of service is a determinant of increasing legislator-constituent relationships and increasing participation in floor debates. FS.

Leonard, Rebecca. *Communication in the Total Institution: An Investigation of Prisoner-Guard Interaction in a State Penitentiary.* Ph.D. Dissertation, Purdue University, 1976. DAI, Vol. 37, No. 8, p. 4703-A.

Notes that both prisoners and guards indicate a negative intergroup attitude in a state prison. Finds that group interaction is infrequent, institutional, brief, and generally hostile. FS.

Locander, Robert G. *Presidential Communications.* Ph.D. Dissertation, The University of New Mexico, 1976. DAI, Vol. 38, No. 2, p. 1000-A.

Examines the methods used by seven presidents to communicate with the public and concludes that the president is the head of a communications team, interacting with the press and the public. T/C.

McCamey, Wade B. *The Relationship Between Selected Factors of Leadership Behavior and Selected Factors of Teacher and Principal Self-Concepts.* Ed.D. Dissertation, East Tennessee State University, 1976. DAI, Vol. 37, No. 7, p. 4031-A.

Finds a positive relationship between principal's perception of leader behavior and teacher self-concept, and a negative relationship between teachers' perception of leader behavior and teacher self-concept. FS.

McFillen, James M. *The Effects of Reward and Penalty Power and Subordinate Performance upon the Attributions and Behaviors of a Supervisor.* DBA Dissertation, Indiana University, Graduate School of Business, 1976. DAI, Vol. 37, No. 7, p. 4425-A.

Finds that successful subordinates are perceived to be more trustworthy, more favorable towards their supervisors, and more internally motivated. They tend to be supervised less and rewarded more than unsuccessful subordinates. LS.

Midgley, D. F. *Innovation and New Product Marketing.* New York: Wiley & Sons, 1977.

Collects information about consumer behavior from different disciplines, then formulates and presents a general theory of innovative behavior applicable to diverse market situations. Demonstrates how the theory can be applied, indicating which management techniques are relevant to new product management. T/C.

Mikrut, John J., Jr. *Teachers' Attitudes Toward Collective Negotiations: The Relationship of Personality, Organizational Morale and Selected Demographic Characteristics.* Ed.D. Dissertation, University of Missouri —Columbia, 1976. DAI, Vol. 37, No. 9, p. 5500-A.

Indicates that organizational morale was a significant factor in attitudes towards collective bargaining but personality was not significantly related to negotiation attitudes. FS.

Moller, Iver H. *The Effectivenss of Shop Stewards and Supervisors.* Teknisk Forlag, Kobenhavn Socialforskningsinstituttet Studie 33, 1976.

Presents an empirical study of eighteen Danish industries. Results indicate that steward effectiveness is related to union strength, worker perceptions of union, and steward-management relations. Effectiveness of superior is associated with their relationships with others, e.g., management. The study has significant implications for bargaining and theories of organizational effectiveness. FS.

Muller, Steven. *A Management Communications Model for Collective Bargaining in Public Schools.* Ph.D. Dissertation, The University of Iowa, 1976. DAI, Vol. 37, No. 8, p. 4757-A.

Emphasizes the development of a management team model to coordinate all aspects of the management side of collective bargaining in public schools. FS.

Newsom, Doug and Alan Scott. *This is PR: The Realities of Public Relations.* Belmont, CA: Wadsworth Publishing Company, 1976.

Gives guidelines for successful public relations. Discusses topics such as communication theory, public relations theory, and interpersonal relations with media people. Includes discussions of report writing. P/D.

Noel, Winifred St. Mary. *Experiencing as Systematic Training: Its Effects on Communication Between Black and White High School Students.* Ed.D. Dissertation, University of Massachusetts, 1976. DAI, Vol. 36, No. 4, p. 1995-A.

Reports that systematic training in experiencing is effective for improving communication between the participants. Neither sex nor race were significant. FS.

O'Connell, James J. *A School and Its Communities: An Effort Toward Effective Communication.* Ed.D. Dissertation, Harvard University, 1976. DAI, Vol. 38, No. 2, p. 579-A.

Analyzes efforts of a school superintendent to reconcile the goals of teachers, community, and board of education by the adoption of a more open and collaborative system of communication. FS.

Orr, Fred L., II. *A Description Study of Selected Organizational Variables in Undergraduate Student Recruitment.* Ph.D. Dissertation, Ohio University, 1976. DAI, Vol. 37, No. 8, p. 4669-A.

Investigates undergraduate recruitment and finds 20 communications variables significantly related to effective student recruitment and retention. FS.

Owen, Brian E. *Business Managers' Influence on Government: Case Study of Participation in Three Processes of Government Policy Formulation in Manitoba.* Ph.D. Dissertation, The University of Western Ontario, Canada, 1976. DAI, Vol. 37, No. 10, p. 6609-A.

States that participation by business managers in the process of government policy formulation was not effective in bringing about outcomes desired by the managers. Suggests that this lack of effectiveness stems from lack of knowledge of government processes, lack of persuasive arguments, and lack of adequate action-planning. FS.

Pavy, Raymond E., Jr. *Guidelines for the Development of Reports for Fact Finders.* Ed.D. Dissertation, Ball State University, 1976. DAI, Vol. 37, No. 10, p. 6193-A.

Identifies a set of guidelines to be used by fact finders in impasse negotiations in the collective bargaining process. The guidelines are divided into seven general categories of information needed for fact finders. FS.

Peitchinis, Jacquelyn A. *Staff-Patient Communication.* New York: Springer Publishing Company, 1976.

Discusses improved communication in the health services field between workers and clients, and among workers themselves. Deals with the meaning and importance of communication in the health and social services field, the factors that influence the communication process, and approaches that may be taken to improve communication between health service workers and their clients. Emphasizes empirical data in a multidisciplinary approach. P/D.

Perry, John K. *A Study of Elementary Principals' Leader Behavior as Perceived by High and Low Status Elementary Teachers.* Ed.D. Dissertation, Mississippi State University, 1976. DAI, Vol. 37, No. 7, p. 4039-A.

Reports no significant difference between high and low status teachers' perceptions of principals' leader behavior. FS.

Piazza, Charles J. *A Study of the Participation of High School Principals in Collective Negotiation for Teachers in Selected School Districts from Forty-Two States.* Ed.D. Dissertation, Duke University, 1976. DAI, Vol. 38, No. 3, p. 1163-A.

Examines role of principals in collective bargaining process, concluding that principals' participation should be on the management negotiating team. Principals were found to function most effectively in an advisory role. FS.

Pollack, Patricia K. B. *Citizen Participation in Urban Renewal Decision Making: A Case Study of Syracuse Hill.* Ph.D. Dissertation, Syracuse University, 1976. DAI, Vol. 37, No. 11, p. 7294-A.

Indicates that citizen planning committees will not influence political decision-making unless citizen input is accepted as a valid and valued contribution. FS.

Rosenthal, Jean S. *Leadership Role Perceptions of Vocational Education Administrators as Related to Job Satisfaction of Teacher-Coordinators in Michigan.* Ed.D. Dissertation, Arizona State University, 1976. DAI, Vol. 37, No. 6, p. 3323-A.

Finds that teacher coordinators of vocational skills tend to view vocational administrators in a negative manner, while the supervisors of vocational administrators tend to be neutral. Interpersonal relationship skills were viewed more favorably by teacher-coordinators than task-oriented skills. FS.

Ross, R. D. *The Management of Public Relations. Analysis and Planning External Relations,* New York: Wiley and Sons, 1977.

Concerns the management of public relations, with emphasis on analysis and planning. Stresses important factors in the environment, such as the negative attitude toward business and profit. Describes the use of Management by Objectives and specific planning, attitudes and the causes, communicative tools (advertising and publicity), public affairs, and the importance of managing change. P/D.

Sherman, Hazel B. *The Relationship Between Teacher Perceptions of Managerial Styles and the Quality of Interpersonal Relationships Between Teachers and Supervisory Personnel.* Ed.D. Dissertation, The College of William and Mary, 1976. DAI, Vol. 37, No. 6, p. 3325-A.

Finds that the quality of interpersonal relationships between teachers and supervisors is negatively affected by teacher perception of limited opportunity to exercise self-direction and self-control, and to participate in goal-setting and goal-evaluation. Teacher perception of ability to participate in the supervisory process positively affects interpersonal relationships. FS.

Shockley, Robert E. *The Development of an Instrument which May Be Used to Measure a Public's Attitude Toward a School System.* Ph.D. Dissertation, The Pennsylvania State University, 1976. DAI, Vol. 37, No. 11, p. 7079-A.

Finds that a special instrument developed to assess community attitudes towards schools did not reveal differences between communities exhibiting positive and negative attitudes. Recommends further research on development of the instrument. LS.

Steinberg, Marcia K. *Consumer Participation in a Health Care Organization: The Case of the Health Insurance Plan of Greater New York.* Ph.D. Dissertation, City University of New York, 1977. DAI, Vol. 38, No. 1, p. 493-A.

Finds that consumer participation in a health care organization was achieved only after internal tensions affected the organization, and not as a result of consumer efforts concentrated in the form of consumer councils. FS.

Stewart, Kenneth L. *A Dramaturgical Model for Analysis of Social Control Through Conflict Management: The Case of a University Ombudsman.* Ph.D. Dissertation, Western Michigan University, 1976. DAI, Vol. 38, No. 1, p. 494-A.

Studies the role of a university ombudsman, and finds it is a useful model for evaluating the conflict management process. FS.

Tannenbaum, Michael A. *An Analysis of Communication Patterns Between Student Teachers and University Supervisors with Training in Transactional Analysis.* Ed.D. Dissertation, University of Oregon, 1976. DAI, Vol. 37, No. 9, p. 5583-A.

Reports that supervisors were uncertain as to the usefulness of transactional analysis skills in supervising student teachers. FS.

Tepper, Leon. *The Relationship Between District Negotiations on the Perceived Leader Behavior of the Principal and Teacher Representative in Selected New York State High Schools.* Ed.D dissertation, Hofstra University, 1976. DAI, Vol. 37, No. 5, p. 2572-A.

Finds that leadership behavior by principals is greater than that of teacher-leaders during the negotiations process. However, teacher leadership behavior increased as collective bargaining reached the picketing and strike stages. The need for developing teacher leadership and teacher-principal communications to obtain mutually acceptable goals was stressed. FS.

Tharpe, Edith M. *A Study of Morale of Elementary, Junior-High, and High School Teachers in Louisiana Public Schools.* Ed.D. Dissertation, Northwestern State University of Louisiana, 1976. DAI, Vol. 37, No. 6, p. 3280-A.

Finds that female teachers exhibited higher morale levels than male teachers, while elementary school teachers have higher morale levels than junior- or senior- high school teachers. Morale rises as length of service increases. FS.

Thompson, Charles A. *An Interorganizational Analysis of Four Social Service Agencies.* Ph.D. Dissertation, University of Missouri—Columbia, 1976. DAI, Vol. 37, No. 9, p. 6078-A.

Concludes that organizational cooperation among four government agencies was directly related to a high degree of informational congruence. FS.

Wegner, Margot E. *A Comparative Study of the Interorganizational Relationship Between Mental Health and Retardation Boards and Boards of Prime Service Delivery Agencies in Ohio: A Study of Conflict.* Ph.D. Dissertation, Case Western Reserve University, 1976. DAI, Vol. 37, No. 6, p. 3916-A.

Finds that, although both groups as a whole, deny the existence of intergroup conflict, the individual members of each group reflect perceptions of conflict. FS.

Wood, Donnie A. *A Case Study of a Principal's Attempts to Capitalize on Informal Faculty Groupings in an Elementary-Junior High School.*

Ed.D. Dissertation, University of Illinois—Urbana-Champaign, 1976. DAI, Vol. 37, No. 5, p. 2574-A.

Notes that the use of informal faculty groups was of limited value in helping teachers improve interpersonal relationships with students. FS.

ARTICLES, PAPERS, AND U.S. GOVERNMENT REPORTS

Akinbode, I. A. and R. C. Clark. "A Framework for Analyzing Interorganizational Relationships," *Human Relations*, Vol. 29, No. 2, February 1976, pp. 101-114.

Four types of interagency relationships were identified (cooperation, conflict, competition, and merger). Cooperation is facilitated by dynamic and democratic leadership while competition and conflicts are attributed to change in leadership style and centralized administrative practices. FS.

Alderfer, Clayton P. "Improving the Quality of Work Life: Group and Intergroup Design," Bethany, CT, June 1975, 108 p. Contract L-74-80.

Provides a definition of human groups with emphasis on intergroup relations behavior. Classical studies of group behavior are examined and propositions explaining intergroup conflict are outlined. T/C.

Bobrow, Edwin E. "Communicating for Maximum Results," *Sales and Marketing Management*, Vol. 116, No. 3, February 23, 1976, pp. 32-40.

Carefully explains how national sales managers can insure that useful upward information comes in from the remote sales force. Greatest need identified is for regional sales managers to listen carefully at sales meetings and to care genuinely about the people doing the selling. P/D.

Breaugh, James A. and Richard J. Klimoski. "The Choice of a Group Spokesman in Bargaining: Member or Outsider," *Organizational Behavior and Human Performance*, Vol. 19, No. 2, 1977, pp. 325-336.

In a simulation experiment, constituency member representation experienced greater difficulty in negotiations. LS.

Douglas, John. "Why Worker Directors are Not Working Out," *The Engineer (Brit.)*, Vol. 243, No. 6285, September 9, 1976, p. 44.

Bases conclusion that workers cannot help manage businesses on a report prepared by Lord Bullock's committee. Identifies chief problems as workers' lack of control and their unwillingness to communicate with their co-workers. P/D.

Draznin, Julius N. "Letting the Sunshine into Collective Bargaining," *Personnel Journal*, Vol. 55, No. 10, October 1976, pp. 511-525.

Discusses advantages and disadvantages of the "Sunshine Laws" on collective bargaining. Stresses that these laws will help labor negotiations more than they will hurt. P/D.

Folz, Edna. "An Informal Public: Its Rights to Information and Management Decision Making in Collective Bargaining," 1976, 4 p. ERIC ED 125 060.

The school board members have an obligation to inform the public on its activities and how effectively they are representing the public's interest in collective bargaining. Advocates that school boards make more information available to the public with the hope that the public will in turn support the school boards' position. P/D.

Goerges, Peter. "The Influence of Cooperating School Districts in Defeating the Union Whipsaw," 1976, 4 p. ERIC ED 125 058.

Advocates that school districts cooperate with each other to fend off union assaults. Provides administrators with training and education in all aspects of labor relations. P/D.

Goble, Nick and Albert E. Holiday. "Your Year-Round Communication Planning Calendar," *Journal of Educational Communication*, Vol. 1, No. 1, July-August 1975, pp. 9-13.

Presents a month-by-month list of communication activities intended to assist the school communicator in strengthening school-community relations. The communicator must reach all school constituents (parents, staff, citizens) with his program. P/D.

Grunig, James E. "Organizations and Public Relations: Testing a Communication Theory," Association for Education in Journalism, November 1976, 63 p. ERIC ED 132 580.

Reviews and later field tests a theory of individual communication behavior and the observed activities of public relations practitioners, and discusses the implications of the theory and the research findings of the theory and the research findings for the teaching and practice of public relations. FS.

Heisel, W. D. "What Can Mediators Rationally Expect of Management Negotiators?" 1976, 4 p. ERIC ED 125 064.

Discusses the importance of a mediator's objective assessment and recommendations when communication breaks down between union and management. Also stresses the necessity for good will, openness, honesty, and acceptance in order for collective bargaining and decision-making to be successful. P/D.

Herman, Jeanne B. "Cognitive Processing of Persuasive Communication," *Organizational Behavior and Human Performance*, Vol. 19, No. 1, 1977, pp. 126-147.

Theories of cognitive processing are used to analyze the failure of employer and union campaigning to change employee predispositions to vote for or against union representation. FS.

Hundley, John R. "Listening Posts," *Personnel*, Vol. 53, No. 4, July 1976, pp. 39-43.

Describes the General American Insurance Company's communication setup which includes a monthly meeting between the president and 12 employees chosen at random. Also tells of department-level "RAPP" sessions, attitude surveys, and supervisor-rating programs. P/D.

Hurst, James C. *et al.* "Agency Directionality and Staff Individuality," *Personnel and Guidance Journal,* Vol. 54, No. 6, pp. 314-317.

Discusses the conflict encountered when counseling institution prompts one thing and one's employing institution dictates another. Provides a procedure for bringing this dissonance into harmony. P/D.

Jackson, Barbara. "An Informed Public: Its Rights to Information and Its Claim for Involvement in Influencing Management Decision Making in Collective Bargaining," 1976, 5 p. ERIC ED 125 061.

Advocates that educational institutions must become more a part of the community. Also it is necessary for the community to establish more realistic goals for the educational institutions to bridge the gap between community expectations and reality. Advocates opening up channels of communication and community involvement in decision making of actual school operations. P/D.

Jay, Antony. "Rate Yourself as a Client," *Harvard Business Review,* Vol. 55, No. 4, July-August, pp. 66-74.

Stresses the importance of choosing a good consultant and the client's attitude and behavior which leads to success. Offers 25 principles and pitfalls along with the "7 deadly sins" of advisers and clients. P/D.

King, Albert S. "Differences in Arbitrators Reactions to Incongruent Communication," *The Journal of Business Communication,* Vol. 14, No. 3, Spring 1977, pp. 47-61.

Different patterns of reaction distinguish lawyer and nonlawyer arbitrators' responses to incongruous statements. Nonlawyers pay attention to the details whereas lawyers reject the incongruity. These results are based on 196 responses to 8 statements. FS.

Lancaster Roy, "Dealing with the Press in a Crisis Situation," *Management Review,* Vol. 66, No. 4, April 1977, pp. 38-39.

Offers hints on how to deal with reporters during a crisis. The author emphasizes planning ahead before speaking to the press, and telling the truth in positive terms. P/D.

Lorey, Will. "Mutual Trust Is the Key to Open Communications," *Administrative Management,* Vol. 37, No. 9, September 1976, pp. 70-72, 74, 92.

Provides examples of everyday annoyances (distance between desks, requiring a V.P. to sign an OK for a $15.00 item, separate lunch areas, etc.) which create vast distances between individuals on the job. Suggests many specific behaviors to correct the situation. P/D.

Louis, Arthur M. "In the Grip of 'Hands-On' Management," *Fortune*, Vol. 95, No. 3, March 1977, pp. 170-178.

Shows how one corporation president keeps direct personal contact with each of his 13 division heads as many as eight times a year. This president does not depend on serial communication. He describes three of his plant visits—with dialog. P/D.

Mace, Myles L. "Designing a Plan for the Ideal Board," *Harvard Business Review*, Vol. 54, No. 6, November-December 1976, pp. 20-22+.

Proposes that the current passive role of board members be reassessed and changed to a more active one. Suggests duties and responsibilities for board members along with time requirements and the kind of people needed to fulfill the role of a board member. P/D.

Maloney, Paul W., Charles A. Ekstrom, and H. Parker Lansdale. "Vocational Education and Training Employment Monitoring System," Higher Education Center for Urban Studies, Bridgeport, CT, 1976, 57 p. Contract HUD-H-2196.

Develops a system for monitoring employment demands for graduates of Bridgeport's vocational and training programs. One objective of the study was to facilitate communication and cooperation between the training institutions and the business-industrial sectors of the community. The report presents twelve recommendations relative to the monitoring system, counseling and placement services, and training and cooperative work experience. P/D.

Margulies, Walter P. "Make the Most of Your Corporate Identity," *Harvard Business Review*, Vol. 55, No. 4, July-August 1977, pp. 66-74.

Discusses how a corporate name and logo is an asset. Uses examples to show effective and ineffective ways to change a name. Advises when and how a name should be changed and the benefits which can result; i.e., attracting new customers, recruiting executives, obtaining finances, and stimulating sales. P/D.

Mauser, Ferdinand F. "Losing Something in the Translation," *Harvard Business Review*, Vol. 55, No. 4, July-August 1977, p. 14+.

Points out some of the many problems with translation of both oral and written communication. Offers 17 pointers for Americans conversing in English to foreign businessmen. P/D.

McAdams, Tony. "Speaking Out in the Corporate Community," *Academy of Management Review*, Vol. 2, No. 2, 1977, pp. 196-205.

The author reviews recent legal developments and proposes that the long-term interest of the corporation calls for voluntary adoption of a free speech ethic. T/C.

McConnell, James E. "Promoting U.S. Exports Through More Effective Communication Between Government and Business," *The Journal of Business Communication*, Vol. 14, No. 1, Fall 1977, pp. 3-18.

Negative attitudes toward exporting are discussed, and some attempts by the USDOC to stimulate exporting are examined. Finally, the author proposes a theoretical model which can be used to overcome the negative attributes and stimulate greater exporting. T/C.

Nolan, Richard L. "Controlling the Costs of Data Services," *Harvard Business Review*, Vol. 55, No. 4, July-August 1977, pp. 114-124.

Emphasizes that the individuals who use data processing must learn to control it so that they can be held accountable for services they receive. Author gives seven steps to implement a "charge out" system that achieves this goal and stops misunderstandings between managers and data processors. P/D.

Pacacha, Carl T. "Organizing a Speaker's Bureau for Effective Public Relations," *Clearing House*, Vol. 49, No. 6, February 1976, pp. 281-282.

Article suggests the establishment of a Speaker's Bureau, as an educational program designed to foster communication between the school and its community by providing local citizens first-hand information about the schools on a variety of interesting educational issues. P/D.

Roessler, Richard and Greta Mack. "Strategies for Inter-Agency Linkages: A Literature Review," Arkansas Rehabilitation Research and Training Center, Fayetteville, November 1975, 29 p.

Reviews literature on strategies for interagency linkages in the delivery of human services. The effect of attitudinal factors on the initiation of interagency linkages are discussed as well as approaches to improving these linkages at the program coordination level. T/C.

Schermerhorn, J. R. "Information Sharing as an Interorganizational Activity," *Academy of Management Journal*, Vol. 20, No. 1, March 1977, pp. 148-153.

A positive relationship between information sharing activity and perceived level of task accomplishment was found. Information sharing was also positively related to hospital size and type and negatively related to administrator tenure. FS.

Smith, Howard R. "Waiting for the Other Shoe to Fall," *Management Review*, Vol. 66, No. 4, April 1977, pp. 28-33.

Warns managers that the influence and authority of first-line supervisors has eroded, and that it continues to diminish. Although top managers need dialog with workers, they should not omit the first-line supervisor from such communication. P/D.

Waters, James A. "Organizational Sanctions: A Process of Inquiry into Deviations," Ph.D. Dissertation, Case Western Reserve University, 1976. DAI, Vol. 38, No. 1, p. 420-B.

Identifies mechanisms within an organization which act to discourage people from exposing illegal and unethical acts. Ten specific mechanisms are described. P/D.

Wells, Larry T. "Negotiations with Third World Governments," *Harvard Business Review*, Vol. 55, No. 1, 1977, pp. 72-80.

Negotiations often break down not only because of the differing objectives but also because of poor communication. This article prescribes some of the things that an international manager ought to do in order to overcome problems. P/D.

Williamson, Merritt A. "The Communication Crisis or Mucking Around in the Muddy Middle," *Chemical Engineering Progress*, Vol. 73, No. 2, February 1977, pp. 25-29.

Reports on specific problems faced by engineers and managers as they interact. Lists what members of each group identified as areas of greatest misunderstanding. P/D.

Zack, Arnold M. "Effective Evidence and Presentation for Influencing a Factfinder or Arbitrator," 1976, 6 p. ERIC ED 125 065.

Expresses the importance of factfinding to settle a negotiation impasse and arbitration to settle a grievance to resolve union-management conflict. Presents tactics and practices that impede the efficient collection of evidence in factfinding and makes recommendations for improvement. P/D.

(No author, alphabetized by title)

"Assessing and Improving Communications About School Programs and Services. A Handbook for the Professional Staff," Columbus Public Schools, OH, 1975, 36 p.

Booklet serves as guide to school staffs on improving the flow of information about school programs and services to parents and pupils. In addition, it aids school personnel in assessing school programs and services. Also provides suggestions on how to use the media and the services of the school system's communication specialists. P/D.

"Employee Relations: Who Holds the Trump Card?" *Industry Week*, Vol. 191, No. 2, October 18, 1976, pp. 58-62.

Stresses that employee relations are determined by employees themselves who frequently do not understand the operation of the business. Suggests that managers owe it to themselves and the employees to keep communication lines open with employees and avoid ignoring them. P/D.

SEE ALSO

Interpersonal Variables: Bartol & Butterfield, Matteson

Intragroup Variables: Allen & Ruhe, Brill, Graves, Hills

Communication Factors & Organizational Goals: Emery & Thorsrud, Nord, Roach, Robinson, Rogers & Molnar, Stone, Trotta, Weihrich

Skill Improvement/Training: Agnew, Brown, Coulson, Horan, Malickson & Nason, Wilkinson, Yousef

Media: Software & Hardware: Bagin, Burton & Miller, Deutsch, Nolan, "TV that Competes with Office Grapevine"

System Analysis: Bagin, Burns & Buckley, Nichols & Armstrong, Wigand

Texts, Anthologies, Reviews, and General Bibliographies: Peitchinis, Young

HUMAN COMMUNICATION RESEARCH

Editor: JAMES C. McCROSKEY
(West Virginia University, Morgantown)

Publication of the International Communication Association

Human Communication Research is devoted to advancing knowledge and understanding about human symbolic interaction. Presenting the latest studies and findings by leading communications scholars, the journal extends the boundaries of a rapidly expanding area of behavioral science.

Recent Issues include these articles:

On Linking Social Performance with Social Competence: Some Relations Between Communicative Style and Attributes of Interpersonal Attractiveness and Effectiveness DAVID R. BRANDT

The Role of the Press in Determining Voter Reactions to Presidential Primaries LEE B. BECKER and MAXWELL E. McCOMBS

Stigma Management in Normal-Stigmatized Interactions: Test of the Disclosure Hypothesis and a Model of Stigma Acceptance TERESA L. THOMPSON and DAVID R. SIEBOLD

The Palo Alto Group: Difficulties and Directions of the Interactional View for Human Communication Research CAROL WILDER

Television Use by Children and Adolescents ALAN M. RUBIN

Cognitive Switching: A Behavioral Trace of Human Information Processing for Television Newscasts THOMAS A. McCAIN and MARK G. ROSS

A Grammar of Conversation with a Quantitative Empirical Test ERNEST L. STECH

Attributional Confidence and Uncertainty in Initial Interaction GLEN W. CLATTERBUCK

Published four times a year. Founded 1974.
International Communication Assn.
Balcones Research Center
10,100 Burnet Road
Austin, TX 78758

COMMUNICATION FACTORS
AND ORGANIZATION GOALS

BOOKS AND DISSERTATIONS

Apter, Rita. *A Comparison of Selected Characteristics of Principals, Teachers, and Schools in Open and Closed Climate Intermediate Schools in Fairfax County, Virginia.* Ed.D. Dissertation, The George Washington University, 1976. DAI, Vol. 37, No. 8, p. 4973-A.

Studies open climate and closed climate schools, finding no significant differences when compared on variables of teacher age, teacher sex, teacher length of service, and principals' self-acceptance. FS.

Bailey, Judith. *A Study of the Relationships Between Selected Personal and Situation Variables and Principal Job Satisfaction.* Ed.D. Dissertation, Virginia Polytechnic Institute and State University, 1976. DAI, Vol. 37, No. 4, p. 1890-A.

Finds no significant relationship between type of school calendar (full-year versus nine-month) and job satisfaction of principals. A relationship was determined between the amount of salary received and principals' satisfaction with the compensation. T/C.

Balk, Walter L. *Improving Government Productivity: Some Policy Perspectives.* Beverly Hills, CA: Sage Publications, 1976.

Emphasizes the theoretical and conceptual aspects of productivity. Includes discussions of motivation, productivity measurement, and information systems. T/C.

Bandy, Lynn S. *Relationships of Perceived Administrative Styles of Selected Elementary School Principals to Predetermined Situational Variables.* Ed.D. Dissertation, The American University, 1977. DAI, Vol. 38, No. 2, p. 557-A.

Concludes that school setting, instructional type, size, or principal's sex were not good predictors of principal's administrative style. Female principals were perceived to be using more effective styles than male principals. FS.

Bartley, Mary L. R. *Political-Leadership Styles of School Superintendents.* Ed.D. Dissertation, Rutgers University, The State University of New Jersey, 1976. DAI, Vol. 37, No. 6, p. 3283-A.

Concludes that school superintendents tend to use consensus as means of gaining compliance. In teacher-administrative relations, board of education members perceived superintendents as using manipulation, while principals viewed superintendents as using coercion. FS.

Behrman, Edward H. *Teacher-Student Relations as a Predictor of Teachers' Job Satisfaction.* Ed.D. Dissertation, University of Pennsylvania, 1976. DAI, Vol. 37, No. 9, p. 5467-A.

Finds that perceived interpersonal relations with students, peers, and administrators were all significantly related with teacher job satisfaction. Teachers who perceived that they got along well with students had higher job satisfaction. FS.

Bennis, Warren G. *The Unconscious Conspiracy: Why Leaders Can't Lead.* New York: AMACOM, 1976.

Provides anecdotes and illustrations in the discussion of problems inherent to leadership in organizations. Problems discussed include inadequate information, conflict resolution, innovation, organizational structure, etc. T/C.

Blue, Terry W. *The Effect of Written and Oral Student Evaluative Feedback and Selected Teacher and Student Demographic and Descriptive Variables on the Attitudes and Ratings of Teachers and Students.* Ph.D. Dissertation, The Pennsylvania State University, 1976. DAI, Vol. 37, No. 6, p. 3284-A.

Determines that brief weekly evaluative discussions of teacher and student attitudes towards themselves, others, and the school environment were more influential on the participants than more intensive evaluations. Demographic variables and group processes variables, such as cohesiveness, peer liking, and leadership patterns, also influenced attitudes. FS.

Blumstein, Ted I. *X, Y, and Z Oriented Elementary School Principals' Attitudes Towards Participative Leadership Policies and Participative Leadership Expectations.* Ph.D. Dissertation, Fordham University, 1976. DAI, Vol. 37, No. 5, p. 2523-A.

Indicates that principals who viewed teachers as self-actualized and rational beings tended to involve teachers more in the decision-making process. Principals believed that teacher participation would improve morale, but were very reluctant to expand teacher influence and self-direction. FS.

Bonen, Richard C. *A Study of the Relationships Between Both the Cognitive Style of the Principal and the Principal-Faculty Cognitive Style Match and the Principal's Leadership Effectiveness as Perceived by the Staff.* Ed.D. Dissertation, St. John's University, 1977. DAI, Vol. 38, No. 2, p. 559-A.

States that a relationship exists between the cognitive style match and the staff's perception of the principal's leadership effectiveness. FS.

Bowers, David G. *Systems of Organization: Management of the Human Resource.* Ann Arbor: The University of Michigan Press, 1976.

A book about the ideas of Rensis Likert. Gives a comprehensive description of the participative management system, insights into "System 4" concepts and a chapter in which Likert responds to questions concerning his concepts. T/C.

Burgett, Kenneth J. *Administrative Practices as They Relate to Teacher Morale in Class II School Districts in Montana.* Ed.D. Dissertation, Montana State University, 1976. DAI, Vol. 37, No. 9, p. 5469-A.

Predicts teacher morale by the use of the Purdue Teacher Opinionaire; and finds that a high level of agreement between school boards and superintendents results in lower teacher morale. FS.

Burke, Matthew. *A Study of Decision Making in the Implementation of Regional Board Governance for the Elementary Schools in the Diocese of Brooklyn, New York.* Ph.D. Dissertation, Fordham University, 1976. DAI, Vol. 37, No. 5, p. 2526-A.

Finds that the decision to reorganize elementary school structure gave little attention to the degree of management and control to be exercised or individual and total performance expected. However, the extent of participation by the change agents was proportionate to the extent of information available. T/C.

Buxton, Mary M. *A Study of the Job Satisfaction of Elementary Teachers in Open-Space and Traditional Schools.* Ed.D. Dissertation, Ball State University, 1976. DAI, Vol. 37, No. 10, p. 6256-A.

Reports no significant difference in job satisfaction between teachers in open-space schools and teachers in traditional schools. FS.

Caplow, Theodore, *How to Run Any Organization.* New York: Holt, Rinehart and Winston, 1976.

Synthesizes the empirical research on organizational effectiveness and translates it into suggestions for the practicing manager. Topics covered include communication, productivity, morale, and change. T/C.

Carrell, Michael R. *A Longitudinal Assessment of Employee Perceptions of Equitable Treatment in a Field Setting.* DBA Dissertation, University of Kentucky, 1976. DAI, Vol. 38, No. 2, p. 888-A.

Concludes that pay increases did not substantially increase job satisfaction. Employee receiving pay increases reported no higher perceptions of equitable treatment, while those not receiving increases reported a decrease in perceptions of equitable treatment. FS.

Cerullo, Nicholas J. *Staff Responses and Their Impact Upon the Implementation of Curriculum Innovations Within the Formal and Informal Organizational Settings.* Ed.D. Dissertation, Columbia University Teachers College, 1976. DAI, Vol. 37, No. 9, p. 5556-A.

Notes that the formal organizational structure provided few opportunities for the informal structure to participate in decision-making; and the informal organization made few attempts to affect the decision-making process. FS.

Chaplain, Oscar S., Jr. *A Comparison of Selected Characteristics of Principals, Teachers, and Schools in Open and Closed Climate Elementary Schools in Fairfax County, Virginia.* Ed.D. Dissertation, The George Washington University, 1976. DAI, Vol. 37, No. 4, p. 1898-A.

Examines various factors relating to the openness of twenty-five selected schools and concludes that open climate schools tend to have older, more experienced principals who have positive attitudes towards themselves and others, positive self-acceptance, and are self-confident. Teacher and organizational characteristics have minimal effects on openness. FS.

Clegg, S. *Power Rule and Domination: A Critical and Empirical Understanding of Power in Sociological Theory and Organizational Life.* Boston: Rutledge and Kegan Paul, 1975.

Analyzes power and authority at a structural and a phenomenological level through the use of tape recorded discussions. FS.

Cox, Raymond R. *A Study of the Perceptions of Teachers, Principals and School Board Members About the Real and Ideal Behaviors of Public School Superintendents in Nebraska Class III School Districts.* Ed.D. Dissertation, The University of Nebraska—Lincoln, 1976. DAI, Vol. 37, No. 7, p. 4009-A.

Finds significant differences among teachers, principals, and school board members as to their perceptions of the real and ideal leadership behavior of school superintendents. The interaction of role, sex, and school district was not found to be significant. FS.

Curtis, Gary L. *Correlates of Effective Decision-Making in Critical Incidents in Public School Systems.* Ed.D. Dissertation, University of Missouri, 1976. DAI, Vol. 38, No. 2, p. 563-A.

Reports that the team approach in decison-making resulted in more satisfactory solutions than those formulated by a single person. FS.

Dachanuluknukul, Sumala. *A Study of the Organizational Climate of Elementary Schools in the Province of Sukhothai, Thailand.* Ph.D. Dissertation, North Texas State University, 1976. DAI, Vol. 37, No. 12, p. 7430-A.

Reports a direct relationship between the size of organization and "closed" climate. Principals tend to perceive open school climates more frequently than teachers. FS.

Dobbins, Joel B. *The Relationships Between School Climate and Teacher Attitudes and Behavior in Managing their Classrooms.* Ph.D. Dissertation, The University of Texas—Austin, 1976. DAI, Vol. 37, No. 12, p. 7631-A.

Suggests that there is no relationship between school organizational climate and teacher behavior. Support was also provided for earlier studies indicating that smaller schools have a more open climate. FS.

Dodge, Calvert R. *Communication Factors Associated with Reduced Recidivism of Paroled Youths in Colorado.* Ph.D. Dissertation, University of Denver, 1971. DAI, Vol. 37, No. 5, p. 2493-A.

Reports no significant differences between juvenile recidivists and non-recidivists in communication patterns between delinquent youths and their counselors. FS.

Dunagan, Frances A. *A Study of the Relationship Between Nursing Education Administrative Climate and Nursing Teacher Morale as Perceived by Teachers of Nursing.* Ed.D. Dissertation, University of Southern Mississippi, 1976. DAI, Vol. 37, No. 9, p. 5479-A.

Reports a significant relationship between administrative climate and nursing teacher morale. Salary and occupational status were major variables in nursing teacher morale. FS.

Emery, Fred and Einar Thorsrud. *Democracy at Work.* Leiden: Humanities Press, 1976.

Reports four studies conducted in Norway during the 1960's which attempt to increase worker satisfaction by increasing worker participation in management. Includes a discussion of union and management's role in the democratization process. Offers specific strategies for producing such changes. FS.

Faris, John P. *A Study of the Determinants of Job Satisfaction.* DBA Dissertation, The George Washington University, 1976. DAI, Vol. 37, No. 10, p. 6600-A.

Indicates that job satisfaction, perceived success, and life satisfaction appear to be highly intercorrelated. Life satisfaction is considered the final measure against which the other two variables are measured. FS.

Fatehi-Sedeh, Kamal. *The Relationships Between Perceived Pay Satisfaction, Perceived Autonomy Satisfaction and Job Satisfaction of Managers.* Ph.D. Dissertation, The Louisiana State University and Agricultural and Mechanical College, 1976. DAI, Vol. 37, No. 11, p. 7195-A.

Finds an inverse relationship between intrinsic job satisfaction and extrinsic job satisfaction, suggesting the possibility of trade-offs between intrinsic and extrinsic rewards. FS.

Fear, David E. *Technical Communication.* Glenview, IL: Scott, Foresman, and Company, 1977.

Designed for students heading for technical careers involving writing and speaking. Covers basic areas such as plan formulation, organization, revision, illustration, and argumentation. Also includes discussions of oral presentation, group discussion, telephone conversations, and dealing with "red tape." Reference chapters include: grammar, punctuation, word usage, and research papers. P/D.

Finley, Earl R. *Self Perceptions and Subordinate Perceptions of the Leadership Behavior of Prestigious High School Principals in Missouri.* Ed.D. Dissertation, University of Missouri—Columbia, 1976. DAI, Vol. 37, No. 9, p. 5482-A.

Indicates there were no significant differences between principals and subordinates on perceptions of the principal's leadership behavior, but there were differences among the subordinates. FS.

Folkins, Larry D. *A Study of Teacher Morale in Secondary Schools.* Ed.D. Dissertation, University of Missouri—Columbia, 1976. DAI, Vol. 37, No. 9, p. 5483-A.

Finds that teacher morale was directly influenced by monetary rewards and personal, frequent contact between administrators and staff. FS.

Gibbon, John. *The Relationship Between the Leadership Style of Principals and the Organizational Climate in Secondary Schools in the Republic of South Africa.* Ed.D. Dissertation, University of Virginia, 1976. DAI, Vol. 36, No. 4, p. 1907-A.

Notes significant relationship between organizational climate and leadership style in South African secondary schools. The age, sex, and professional experience of principals, languages used and sex composition of students were not considered significant predictors of leadership style and organizational climate. FS.

Glickman, Carl D. *An Investigation of the Relationship Between Teachers' Perception of Organizational Climate and Students' Perception of Classroom Climate.* Ed.D. Dissertation, University of Virginia, 1976. DAI, Vol. 37, No. 5, p. 2534-A.

Concludes that teachers have a significant influence on classroom climate, either by allowing the school climate to permeate the classroom or to block it out completely. Teachers who held negative perceptions of their principal's behavior were found to have students who held positive perceptions of their teacher's behavior. FS.

Hedrick, Stanley H. *Leadership Behavior and Organizational Climate as Related to Department Chairpersons.* Ph.D. Dissertation, University of Maryland, 1976. DAI, Vol. 37, No. 6, p. 3500-A.

States that college administrators tend to agree among themselves as to role-expectations and need-dispositions while subordinates tend not to agree on some variables. Use of the Leader Behavior Description Questionnaire is questioned unless students become more knowledgeable of leadership behavior. FS.

Henderson, Lester F. *Elementary Teacher Satisfaction and Morale and Perceived Participation in Decision-Making.* Ed.D. Dissertation, University of Arkansas, 1976. DAI, Vol. 37, No. 5, p. 2535-A.

Reports that teachers who perceived that they had high participation in school decision-making have higher morale than teachers who perceived that they had low participation in school decision-making. In addition, teachers participating in school decision-making exhibited more positive attitudes towards their principals. FS.

Henry, David R. *Decision-Making in the Truman Administration.* Ph.D. Dissertation, Indiana University, 1976. DAI, Vol. 37, No. 8, p. 4699-A.

Examines methods used by President Truman in the decision-making process and finds that initial defects were later rectified by a more aggressive communication style. T/C.

Hsieh, Wen-Chuyan. *A Comparative Study of Relationships Between Principals' Leadership Style and Teachers' Job Satisfaction in the Republic of China and the State of Iowa.* Ph.D. Dissertation, The University of Iowa, 1976. DAI, Vol. 37, No. 5, p. 2540-A.

Finds that personal and normative leadership dimensions are positively correlated with teacher job satisfaction in both Chinese and American schools. Chinese teachers are less satisfied than American teachers in fifteen out of sixteen aspects of job satisfaction as measured by the Minnesota Satisfaction Questionnaire. FS.

Jackson, Thomas E. *The Leadership Behavior and Role Expectations of Elementary School Principals as Perceived by Elementary School Secretaries, Building Representatives, and Principals.* Ph.D. Dissertation, The University of Michigan, 1976. DAI, Vol. 37, No. 6, p. 3303-A.

Concludes that the perceived and expected leadership role of elementary school principals differed significantly when secretaries, building representatives, and principals were compared to each other. No difference was found in the perceptions of inner-city and outer-city subjects. FS.

Jenks, Carl F. *A Comparison of First-Level and Second-Level Supervisors' Perceptions of Organizational Effectiveness.* Ph.D. Dissertation, Purdue University, 1976. DAI, Vol. 37, No. 8, p. 5225-A.

Finds a significant difference in perceptions by managers and supervisors of overall organizational effectiveness. Supervisors emphasized productivity of the individual work unit, while managers stressed organizational stability. FS.

Johnson, Sandra F. *An Attempt to Change School Climate and Productivity Through the Use of FIRO-B.* Ph.D. Dissertation, University of Kansas, 1976. DAI, Vol. 38, No. 2, p. 572-A.

Concludes that self-awareness and knowledge of interpersonal needs is not sufficient for improving organizational climate or productivity perceptions; and recommends facilitators trained in human relations and communication skills to improve organizational climate. FS.

Keadle, Maynard E. *A Study of the Relationships Between the Perceptions of Teachers of the Organizational Climate and Selected Cognitive and*

Non-Cognitive Variables Associated with Elementary Students. Ph.D. Dissertation, University of Maryland, 1976. DAI, Vol. 37, No. 6, p. 3307-A.

Finds that there is no relationship between "open" and "closed" climates in elementary schools and student achievement, student self-perception, classroom behavior, and students' perception of their teachers' feelings towards them. FS.

Keffer, Wayne M. *Job Satisfaction of Field Staff of the Virginia Polytechnic Institute and State University Extension Division.* Ph.D. Dissertation, The Ohio State University, 1976. DAI, Vol. 37, No. 8, p. 4781-A.

Reports significant relationships between overall job satisfaction and both job satisfiers (motivation factors) and job dissatisfiers (hygiene factors). Motivation factors were more strongly related to job satisfaction than hygiene factors. FS.

Kilpatrick, Sheila R. *An Exploratory Study of the Communication Climate of Two Naval Ships.* Ph.D. Dissertation, University of Colorado—Boulder, 1976. DAI, Vol. 37, No. 12, p. 7386-A.

Finds that effectiveness was directly related to climate. The more effective naval ship was found to have the better communications climate. FS.

Kirchoff, William J. *A Comparison of Teacher Perceptions of the Leader Behavior of Principals in Operating Lutheran Elementary Schools with Principals in Recently Closed Lutheran Elementary Schools.* Ed.D. Dissertation, Northern Illinois University, 1976. DAI, Vol. 37, No. 12, p. 7441-A.

Finds that teachers in operating schools rated principals higher than did teachers in recently closed schools. FS.

Lagios, Socrates A. *A Formal Plan for a Principal to Get Feedback from Faculty to Improve Leadership Behavior.* Ed.D. Dissertation, Boston College, 1977. DAI, Vol. 38, No. 3, p. 1153-A.

Concludes that teachers considered their principal to be more closed in attitude than he perceived himself to be. Previous findings that female teachers had higher morale than male teachers were not supported. FS.

Lake, Jevoner F. *An Investigation of Selected Characteristics of Principals, Teachers, and Schools Within Two Dimensions of Organizational Climate in the Public Schools of Caroline County, Maryland.* Ed.D. Dissertation, The George Washington University, 1977. DAI, Vol. 38, No. 3, p. 1153-A.

Determines that the principal's age, experience, self-acceptance, and perceptions of self-acceptance were not school climate indicators, while principal's educational levels were indicators. Teacher age and experience were not indicators, but teacher sex was an indicator. FS.

Lefton, R. E. *et al. Effective Motivation Through Performance Appraisal: Dimensional Appraisal Strategies.* New York: Wiley and Sons, 1977.

Presents the Dimensional Model of Subordinate Appraisal Behavior and the Dimensional Model of Superior Appraisal Behavior. Presents a step-by-step method for doing effective appraisals, explains the skills needed to do them, and shows how to adopt the method so it can be individualized for each subordinate. P/D.

Leszczynska, Mary E. *A Study of the Effects of Organizational Structure on Organizational Climate in Private Institutions for Dependent, Neglected Children.* DSW Dissertation, The Catholic University of America, 1977. DAI, Vol. 38, No. 2, p. 1025-A.

Confirms that size and staffing in social institutions are significantly related to organizational climate. FS.

Lewis, Kenneth R. *A Comparison of Selected Individual Characteristics with Employee-Reported Job Satisfaction and Perceived Organizational Climate.* Ed.D. Dissertation, The George Washington University, 1976. DAI, Vol. 37, No. 9, p. 5531-A.

Concludes that the perceived organizational climate for rewards and promotions was lower for clerks and secretaries than for supervisors and technical specialists. FS.

Lichtenfeld, Robert V. *A Comparison of the Effects and Determinants of the Executive Professional Leadership of Public and Independent Elementary School Principals.* Ed.D. Dissertation, Columbia University Teachers College, 1977. DAI, Vol. 38, No. 1, p. 51-A.

Reports that similar administrative skills are necessary to provide effective educational leadership in both public and private schools. FS.

Manning, Renfro C. *The Satisfiers and Dissatisfiers of Virginia Superintendents of Schools.* Ed.D. Dissertation, University of Virginia, 1976. DAI, Vol. 37, No. 7, p. 4028-A.

Notes that school superintendents view interpersonal relations with teachers and the community as a dissatisfier, although interpersonal relations with school boards was reported as a satisfying aspect of their job. FS.

Manuie, Mohamed A. *A Study of Teacher-Principal Perceptions of the Organizational Climate in Selected Schools in Riyadh, Saudi Arabia.* Ph.D. Dissertation, The University of Oklahoma, 1976. DAI, Vol. 37, No. 5, p. 2548-A.

Finds that Saudi schools tend to be characterized by weak leadership and poor morale. Communication between Saudi and non-Saudi teachers was satisfactory; interaction and communication among teachers in the lower socioeconomic areas was less extensive. FS.

March, James G. and Johan P. Olsen. *Ambiguity and Choice in Organizations.* Bergen, Norway: Universitesforlaget, 1976.

Devoted to research and theory on what the authors term the "garbage can" theory of decision making. The theory posits that decision making is largely irrational and ritualistic. Reports natural setting and participant observation studies in support of the theory. The research was conducted in educational institutions. FS.

Marco, Jerome M. *The Difference Between Selected Characteristics of Principals, Teachers, and Schools Within Two Dimensions of Organizational Climate in the Public Schools of Frederick County, Maryland.* Ed.D. Dissertation, The George Washington University, 1977. DAI, Vol. 38, No. 3, p. 1157-A.

Finds no significant differences in principal characteristics in open and closed climates. Teachers' experience was found to be related to the degree of openness in schools. FS.

McCalla, Jimmy R. *The Relationship of Teacher Morale to the Racial Composition of the Student Bodies in Selected Mississippi High Schools.* Ed.D. Dissertation, Mississippi State University, 1976. DAI, Vol. 37, No. 7, p. 4030-A.

Finds that teachers in schools where the racial balance was approximately equal scored significantly higher in rapport with students than teachers in schools where there was a greater dispority between the races. Morale among the teachers was significantly higher in schools where non-Caucasians were a large majority of the students. FS.

Mead, Nehemiah. *The Leadership Behavior of Jamaican High School Principals: Perceptions and Expectations of Teachers and Principals.* Ed.D. Dissertation, Andrews University, 1976. DAI, Vol. 37, No. 12, p. 7448-A.

Reports that preferred leadership behavior of principals included a high degree of initiative and delegation of reponsibility to subordinates. FS.

Mermoud, Charles F. *Teacher Effectiveness as Perceived by Peers and Principals and the Influence of Teacher Self-Concept and School Climate.* Ed.D. Dissertation, University of Kansas, 1976. DAI, Vol. 38, No. 2, p. 576-A.

Finds no significant relationships among organizational climate, self-concept, and teacher effectiveness. FS.

Meyers, Claude A. *Morale and Values Among Teachers.* Ph.D. Dissertation, University of Oregon, 1977. DAI, Vol. 38, No. 3, p. 1160-A.

Concludes that teachers in parochial schools have higher degrees of self-lessness and morale than their public school counterparts. FS.

Milburn, Corinne M. *The Relationship Between Men and Women Secondary Teachers' Perceptions of Ideal and Real Leader Behavior of the Woman*

Secondary Principal in Public Schools. Ed.D. Dissertation, University of South Dakota, 1976. DAI, Vol. 37, No. 10, p. 6392-A.

Analyzes teacher perception as to leader behavior of female school principals, finding no significant differences between male and female teacher views. FS.

Mitchell, Roy I. *A Study to Determine the Extent to Which Selected School Community Members are Involved in the Participatory Management Process.* Ed.D. Dissertation, Florida Atlantic University, 1977. DAI, Vol. 38, No. 1, p. 55-A.

Observes that administrators believe students and staff to be involved in participatory management to a greater extent than perceived by the same students and staff. Recommends that schools provide ways for all members to become integral parts of the decision-making process. FS.

Mullinix, Jess R., Jr. *The Characterizations of Effective Organizations Among Institutions Providing Long-Term Geriatric Care.* DBA Dissertation, The University of Oklahoma, 1976. DAI, Vol. 37, No. 12, p. 7843-A.

Determines that the nursing home administrator, involved in planning, communications, and problem-solving, had a key role in organizational effectiveness, and the quality of patient care. Employee perception of the administrator as being able to plan, communicate, and solve problems resulted in a more effective organization. FS.

Neveaux, Mark J. *The Decision-Making Role of a Building Principal in Regard to Administrative Decentralization.* Ed.D. Dissertation, The University of Michigan, 1976. DAI, Vol. 37, No. 10, p. 6191-A.

Investigates the role of building principals in two decentralized school districts, and shows that such decentralization has resulted in an improvement in the flexibility, speed, and quality of decision-making. FS.

Nicholson, Jeanne B. *Perceptions of Organizational Goals and Effectiveness: A Study of Four Metropolitan Washington Women's Commissions.* Ph.D. Dissertation, The Johns Hopkins University, 1976. DAI, Vol. 36, No. 4, p. 2398-A.

Studies the relationships among organizational goals, role conflict between commissioners and staff members, and organizational effectiveness. While indicating the need for further study, the author concludes that existing organizational assessment techniques (operations research, systems analysis, and policy analysis) are inadequate for understanding citizen's commissions. FS.

Nontasak, Suriyan. *The Leadership Behavior of the Provincial School Superintendents in Thailand as Perceived by Provincial High School Principals.* Ed.D. Dissertation, Mississippi State University, 1976. DAI, Vol. 37, No. 7, p. 4034-A.

Finds that no significant differences exist among superintendents in terms of desirable leadership behavior as perceived by high school principals when classified according to the superintendents' sex, age, level of education, or type of education. FS.

Ozigbo, Stephen O. *Dogmatism, Pupil Control Ideology, and Perceptions of School Organizational Climate on the Part of Secondary School Teachers Attending Selected Evening Graduate Classes at the University of Oklahoma during the Spring of 1976.* Ph.D. Dissertation, The University of Oklahoma, 1976. DAI, Vol. 37, No. 8, p. 3021-A.

Finds significant relationships among teacher dogmatism, pupil control ideology, and teacher perception of school climate. FS.

Page, Bill D. *The Influence of School Administrators' Management Style and Organizational Climate Upon Successful Implementation of Change as Perceived by Staff.* Ph.D. Dissertation, Saint Louis University, 1976. DAI, Vol. 36, No. 4, p. 1923-A.

Reports that neither organizational climate nor school administrators' management style were significantly related to the success of change efforts. No significant relationship was found between perceived managerial style and organizational climate. FS.

Perkins, Bobby R. *The Perceptions of Mississippi Public School Principals and Superintendents of Team Management.* Ed.D. Dissertation, Mississippi State University, 1976. DAI, Vol. 37, No. 12, p. 7458-A.

States that the team management approach to the administration of public schools was not considered effective in the schools studied. Significant differences were found between the *ideal* team management approach and the *real* team management approach currently in use. FS.

Perkins, Mark L. *A Canonical Correlational Analysis of the Relationships Among School Climate, Teacher Morale, and Educationally-Relevant Performances of Fourth Grade Students.* Ph.D. Dissertation, University of Georgia, 1976. DAI, Vol. 37, No. 7, p. 4309-A.

Finds a positive relationship between teachers' perceptions of school environment and educationally-related performance of elementary students. A similar relationship exists between students' perceptions and their educationally-related performance. FS.

Perry, Carol M. *The Relationship Between Teacher Morale and the Principal's Attempts to Improve Teacher Performance.* Ed.D. Dissertation, Mississippi State University, 1976. DAI, Vol. 37, No. 7, p. 4038-A.

Finds that teacher morale and rapport with principal are positively correlated with the principal's effectiveness in the improvement of teacher performance. FS.

Perry, Henry B. *Physician Assistants: An Empirical Analysis of Their General Characteristics, Job Performances, and Job Satisfaction.* Johns Hopkins University, Baltimore, Maryland, September 1976, 370 p.

Discusses various aspects of job satisfaction and job performance of physician assistants. Indicates that the strongest correlates of both job satisfaction and job performance was the degree of physician supervisory support and amount of responsibility for patient care. FS.

Powell, Gary N. *Attitude Toward Work-Related Change and Organizational Climate.* Ph.D. Dissertation, University of Massachusetts, 1976. DAI, Vol. 36, No. 4, p. 2293-A.

Maintains that there is no significant relationship between attitude toward change and each dimension of organizational climate as tested by the 1965 revision of the organizational climate description questionnaire. It was concluded that this revision is inappropriate for the measurement of organizational climate, particularly in health-care organizations. FS.

Powell, Lee E. *The Differences Between Selected Characteristics of Principals, Teachers, and Schools within Two Dimensions of Organizational Climate in the Public Schools of Carroll County, Maryland.* Ed.D. Dissertation, The George Washington University, 1976. DAI, Vol. 37, No. 8, p. 4760-A.

Finds little difference between more-open schools and less-open schools in terms of principal characteristics, principals' concept of self-acceptance, and selected characteristics of teachers. FS.

Powers, Neill M. *Congruence of Leadership Styles, Teacher Loyalty to Principal, and Teacher Job Satisfaction.* Ed.D. Dissertation, The University of North Carolina—Chapel Hill, 1976. DAI, Vol. 37, No. 8, p. 4761-A.

Concludes that congruence of superintendents' and principals' leadership styles resulted in greater teacher loyalty and job satisfaction. Leadership style of principals was more influential than style of superintendents. FS.

Quinn, Kathryn I. *Self-Perceptions of Leadership Behaviors and Decisionmaking Orientations of Men and Women Elementary School Principals in Chicago Public Schools.* Ph.D. Dissertation, University of Illinois—Urbana-Champaign, 1976. DAI, Vol. 37, No. 10, p. 6199-A.

Indicates differences between male and female elementary school principals in self-perceptions of their administrative behavior. These differences were most significant in instructional leadership and in the assumptions held about the decisionmaking role of teachers. FS.

Randolph, Robert. *Effect of Morale on Risk Behavior of Elementary School Administrators.* Ph.D. Dissertation, Purdue University, 1976. DAI, Vol. 37, No. 8, p. 4761-A.

Finds that overall morale levels do not affect risk behaviors of school administrators, noting the tendency for risk-taking to decrease with longevity. FS.

Raspa, Salvatore L. *An Investigation of Selected Characteristics of Principals, Teachers, and Schools in Open and Closed Climate Public*

Elementary and Secondary Schools in St. Mary's County, Maryland. Ed.D. Dissertation, The George Washington University, 1976. DAI, Vol. 37, No. 9, p. 5507-A.

Notes that younger, less-experienced principals tended to be in open-climate schools. No relationship was found between type of climate and personal characteristics of principals or teachers. FS.

Reely, Robert H., Jr. *An Analysis of the Relationships Between Job Satisfaction/Enrichment Factors and Demographic Variables for United States Air Force Military Education Faculty.* Ed.D. Dissertation, Auburn University, 1976. DAI, Vol. 37, No. 7, p. 4041-A.

Finds a negative relationship between military rank and overall job satisfaction. Positive relationships existed between the number of faculty members supervised and job satisfaction. Intrinsic job satisfaction was found to contribute more to overall job satisfaction than extrinsic job satisfaction. FS.

Remmert, Richard L. *The Relationships Among Teacher Characteristics, Why Teachers Stay on the Job, and Organizational Climate in the School.* Ed.D. Dissertation, University of Illinois—Urbana-Champaign, 1976. DAI, Vol. 37, No. 10, p. 6200-A.

Analyzes the interactions of the reasons teachers remain on the job and organizational climate. The perception of organizational climate by teachers who remained on the job for various reasons differed significantly from those who remained on the job for no apparent reason. The former group perceived the school climate to be more group interactive-collaborative. FS.

Rings, Robert L. *A Comparative Analysis of Selected Organizational Communication Variables in a Public Utility Company.* Ph.D. Dissertation, Ohio University, 1976. DAI, Vol. 37, No. 11, p. 6823-A.

Determines that supervisors play a key role as facilitators of two-way communicative behavior and role definition. Supervisors initiate communicative efforts to maintain basic job satisfaction in subordinates, while being receptive and responsive to subordinate initiated communication. FS.

Roberts, Carl E. *Principal Leadership Characteristics as Predictors of Teacher Job Motivation Factors.* Ed.D. Dissertation, University of Northern Colorado, 1977. DAI, Vol. 38, No. 2, p. 581-A.

Concludes that leadership characteristics of principals has no relationship to principal's ability to perceive teacher job motivation. Teachers ranked challenging work and interpersonal relations as most important job motivation factors, while principals perceived the primary factors to be good wages and task recognition. FS.

Rogers, Robert E. *An Investigation of Factors Related to Job Satisfaction and Dissatisfaction of Teachers in School Districts with Differing Labor*

Climates. Ph.D. Dissertation, Saint Louis University, 1976. DAI, Vol. 37, No. 12, p. 7461-A.

Notes differences in job satisfaction between school districts with labor strife and districts with labor harmony. Concludes that there is a need to stress meaningful work opportunities for teachers in both types of districts to avoid job dissatisfaction. FS.

Rohr, Stephen M. *An Investigation of the Differences Between Selected Characteristics of Principals, Teachers, and Elementary Schools Within Two Categories of Organizational Climate in the Public Schools of Frederick County, Maryland.* Ed.D. Dissertation, The George Washington University, 1977. DAI, Vol. 38, No. 3, p. 1166-A.

Finds no significant differences in principal and teacher characteristics in open and closed organizational climates. FS.

Rundle, Fred W. *School Size and Perceived Satisfaction with Leadership.* Ed.D. Dissertation, University of Georgia, 1976. DAI, Vol. 37, No. 7, p. 4044-A.

Concludes that school size does not affect subordinates' perceived satisfaction with formal leadership. FS.

Schafer, Susan D. *The Motivation Process.* Cambridge, MA: Winthrop Publishers, 1977.

Presents an introduction to theory and research on motivation designed for practitioners. Topics covered include models of motivation, incentives, punishment, and motivation of groups. Each of the chapters includes objectives, glossary, and a transcript of a panel discussion between managers concerning the particular topic. P/D.

Schoppert, Gail D. *The Development of a Model for Participatory Goal Setting in Private Educational Institutions.* Ed.D. Dissertation, University of North Carolina—Greensboro, 1976. DAI, Vol. 37, No. 5, p. 2565-A.

Develops a typology in which organizational goals are classified as manifest (stated and intended), hidden (unstated but intended), public relations (stated but unintended), and latent (unstated and unintended). A model for participatory goal setting in private schools and colleges is developed. T/C.

Schou, Andrew J. *Leadership Style: Flexibility and the Contingency Theory.* Ph.D. Dissertation, The Florida State University, 1976. DAI, Vol. 37, No. 7, p. 4478-A.

Reports that subordinate managers perceived superiors as flexible in leadership style and able to alter style to the nature of the problem. Subordinates, however, did not indicate the same degree of satisfaction at all levels of flexibility. FS.

Sheldon, Gary H. *Effect of Organizational Climates on School-Related Discussions Involving the Elementary Principal.* Ed.D. Dissertation, Drake University, 1976. DAI, Vol. 37, No. 11, p. 6889-A.

Notes that principals in "open" organizational climate schools participated in more school-related discussions than principals in "closed" organizational climate schools. Discussion in "open" schools tended to take place in more informal areas (lounges, halls, etc.). FS.

Shulman, Gary M. *A Theoretical and Empirical Study of the Communication Climate of University Departments,* Ph.D. Dissertation, Purdue University, 1976. DAI, Vol. 38, No. 2, p. 943-B.

University departments differ in faculty perceptions of downward communication. The size of the department significantly affects faculty perceptions of influence. Communication climate is composed of perceptions of downward communication, familiarity, and influence. FS.

Smith, Gerald B. *A Comparative Study of School Climate As Perceived by Selected Students, Teachers, and Administrators in Junior High Schools.* Ed.D. Dissertation, The University of Tulsa, 1977. DAI, Vol. 38, No. 3, p. 1170-A.

Shows that the greater the distance between respondents and the administrator in a hierarchical structure, the less positive the perception of school climate. High socio-economic levels tended to produce the most positive perceptions of school climate. FS.

Smith Robert A. *A Study of the Perceptions of Superintendents, Teachers, and School Board Members About the Expected Performance of Nebraska Public School Superintendents in Ten Functional Task Categories.* Ed.D. Dissertation, The University of Nebraska—Lincoln, 1976. DAI, Vol. 38, No. 1, p. 61-A.

Concludes that perceptions about the expected performance of school superintendents vary according to role, group membership, and school district size. FS.

Smith, Stuart M. *The Relationship of Organization and Organization Sub-Unit Climate on Job Satisfaction.* Ph.D. Dissertation, University of Pittsburg, 1976. DAI, Vol. 37, No. 9, p. 6065-A.

Concludes that "bureau climate," the work atmosphere within the organizational sub-unit, had a greater influence upon job satisfaction than "agency climate," overall organizational climate. FS.

Stanfield, David P. *Characteristics of Successful Elementary School Principals.* Ed.D. Dissertation, East Texas State University, 1977. DAI, Vol. 38, No. 3, p. 1170-A.

Determines that intracommunication within the school and intercommunication between the school and community are strongly related to the success of elementary school principals. FS.

Steele, Fritz and Stephen Jenks. *The Feel of the Work Place: Understanding and Improving Organizational Climate.* Reading, MA: Addison-Wesley, 1977.

A book about organizational climate: what influences it, what the consequences are, and how it can be changed. Analyzes leadership, communication patterns, physical structures, and group norms. Suggests activities for diagnosing and implementing changes in climate. P/D.

Steinhauer, Marcia B. *Technology Transfer Within a Government Organization: A Study of the Innovation Process in Florida's Social Services.* Ph.D. Dissertation, The University of Florida, 1975. DAI, Vol. 37, No. 7, p. 4615-A.

Reports that the adoption and implementation of an innovative mechanism by a complex and decentralized governmental organization had limited success due largely to an emphasis on the administrative aspects of the program and hierarchical conflict within the organization. FS.

Stevens, Dixon G. *The Leader Behavior of Selected New York State Community College Presidents as Perceived by Trustees, Administrators and Faculty Leaders.* Ed.D. Dissertation, State University of New York—Albany, 1976. DAI, Vol. 37, No. 10, p. 6230-A.

Finds that community college presidents are perceived as having difficulty integrating the needs of the individual with the needs of the institution. This difference in roles is assumed to be dysfunctional to the proper running of the schools. FS.

Streker, Irmtraud U. *A Comparison of the Effects of Job Redesign With and Without Employee Participation.* Ph.D. Dissertation, Yale University, 1976. DAI, Vol. 37, No. 7, p. 3661-B.

A method emphasizing employee participation in job redesign has positive effects on employee satisfaction with various aspects of their job. FS.

Struzziery, Joanne M. *School Climate and Racial Attitudes: A Case Study of White Secondary Students' Attitudes Toward a Voluntary Busing Program.* Ed.D. Dissertation, Boston University School of Education, 1977. DAI, Vol. 37, No. 12, p. 7677-A.

Indicates that school climate variables can affect racial attitudes in areas where voluntary school desegregation is taking place. More positive attitudes towards voluntary busing were found among students in schools where principals shared such attitudes. FS.

Sumrall, Charlotte C. H. *A Study of the Relationship Between the Leadership Behavior of Instructional Supervisors and the Job Satisfaction of Teachers in Texas.* Ed.D. Dissertation, University of Houston, 1976. DAI, Vol. 37, No. 5, p. 2571-A.

Suggests that Texas schools create open organizational climates conducive to the establishment of supportive relationships. FS.

Vegso, Raymond W. *Organizational Characteristics that Influence Innovative Behavior.* Ph.D. Dissertation, University of Cincinnati, 1976. DAI, Vol. 37, No. 6, p. 3761-A.

Uses the organizational components of freedom, inducements, and communication, and finds moderate support for hypothesis that management innovation is significantly correlated with organizational climate. FS.

Vick, Theodore E. *A Study of the Relationship Between the Principal's Management Style and School Climate.* Ph.D. Dissertation, University of California—Riverside, 1975. DAI, Vol. 38, No. 1, p. 65-A.

Determines that elementary school principals with teacher-centered management styles tended to have schools with open climates. No significant correlation, however, was achieved between innovativeness and climate. FS.

Warnemunde, Dennis E. *Organizational Communication in the University: A Descriptive Study of the Communication Behavior of Department Chairmen.* Ph.D. Dissertation, University of Colorado, 1976. DAI, Vol. 37, No. 4, p. 1876-A.

Indicates that primary communication flow is upward from subordinates to the chairmen, as opposed to the downward flow in other formal organizations. Such communications were informational, rather than decisional, in nature. Characteristics of "successful" and "less successful" chairmen were examined, with "successful" chairmen more frequently involved in the informational process. FS.

Weinberg, Martha. *Managing the State.* Cambridge, MA: MIT Press, 1977.

Presents a case study of Massachusett's Governor Frances Sargent's management of four state agencies. Explicates a rational model and a crisis model of decision making. Discusses the decision making process characteristic of this governor. FS.

Wells, Charlie. *An Investigation of the Relationship Between Faculty Involvement in Policy Formulation and Faculty Morale.* Ed.D. Dissertation, Viriginia Polytechnic Institute and State University, 1976. DAI, Vol. 37, No. 6, p. 3335-A.

Concludes that faculty morale varies directly with perceptions of faculty involvement in university policy formulation. FS.

Whiting, Bruce G. *The Relationships Between Three Supervisor Performance Variables and Leadership Success Criteria in a Formal Organization.* DBA Dissertation, The George Washington University, 1976. DAI, Vol. 37, No. 6, p. 3763-A.

Finds a positive relationship between accuracy of the perception of leadership and success criteria, as measured by productivity and group status. No positive relationship was found between knowledge of leader skills or willingness to engage in leadership behavior, and productivity and group status. FS.

Zerla, Alan F. *Relationships of Organizational Climate, the Change Agent Style of the Principal, and the Occurrence of Selected Educational Innovations in Tennessee Public High Schools.* Ph.D. Dissertation, George Peabody College for Teachers, 1976. DAI, Vol. 37, No. 8, p. 4777-A.

Reports no significant relationship among organizational climate, change agent style of principals and the occurrence of educational innovations. Finds no support for the theory that schools react successfully to stress when the principal's change strategies are congruent with faculty's compliance patterns. FS.

Zibilich, Foster. *A Study of the Effectiveness of Classroom Observation Procedures on the Improvement of Faculty Morale in Selected Catholic Schools.* Ed.D. Dissertation, University of Southern Mississippi, 1976. DAI, Vol. 37, No. 9, p. 5525-A.

Reports that morale changes improved after principals took part in a classroom observation improvement course. Greatest positive morale changes occurred among female teachers and those over 40 years of age. FS.

ARTICLES, PAPERS, AND U.S. GOVERNMENT PUBLICATIONS

Acker, D. D. "Professional Aspects of Contemporary Management," *ASME Papers*, No. 76-WA, Mgt 8, Meeting of December 5, 1976, 5 p. Defense Systems Management School, Fort Belvoir, VA.

Contends that "proactive management" is supplanting traditional "reactive management." Ties in concept of change in all society leading to demand for adaptive management. A study of professional standards reveals some areas of need. T/C.

Adams, Randolph K. "An Analysis of Existing Ethical Guidelines and the Development of a Proposed Code of Ethics for Managers," September 1976, 181 p. Report No. GSM/SM/765-1.

Develops a proposed universal code of ethics for managers in response to public demand for a clearer picture of the ethical responsibilities of today's leaders. FS.

Arvey, R. D. and H. D. Dewhirst. "Goal Setting Attributes, Personality Variables and Job Satisfaction," *Journal of Vocational Behavior*, Vol. 9, No. 2, October 1976, pp. 179-189.

Positive relationships were found between goal setting attributes and job satisfaction. Individual needs (e.g., need for achievement, autonomy, and affiliation) did not moderate this relationship. FS.

Ashbaugh, Dennis M. and Larry J. Godfrey. "The Impact of the SAC Missile Management Working Group on Missile Combat Crew Member Attitudes," Air Force Insititute of Technology, Wright-Patterson AFB, OH, School of Systems and Logistics, September 1976, 199 p. Report No. SLSR-14-76B.

Discusses missile combat crew members' attitudes toward their job to determine the effect of the Missile Management Working Group (MMWG). MMWG was implemented to increase job satisfaction, thereby improving volunteer and retention rates. FS.

Badawy, M. K. "Applying Management by Objectives to R & D Labs," *Research Management*, Vol. 19, No. 6, November 1976, pp. 35-40.

Explains how employee awareness of "where they stand" relates to effective performance on the job. Participation and involvement, followed by feedback from upper levels, is shown applicable to all organizations. (18 references). T/C.

Baird, L. S. "Relationship of Performance to Satisfaction in Stimulating and Nonstimulating Jobs," *Journal of Applied Psychology*, Vol. 61, No. 6, December 1976, pp. 721-727.

Work satisfaction is correlated with job performance only when the job is not a stimulating one. FS.

Bennis, W. "Leadership: A Beleaguered Species?" *Organizational Dynamics*, Vol. 5, No. 1, Summer 1976, pp. 3-16.

The role of the leader is changing. To cope with these changes the leader must a) manage, not lead, b) cop-out, c) lead through limits and by diminuendo, and d) "sweep and dust." Seven guidelines for leaders in directing the process of change are proposed. P/D.

Berman, Sorrell. "The Use of Insight in Management Decisions," Naval Postgraduate School, Monterey, CA, September 1976, 54 p.

Presents a case for the acceptance of insight as the key element in effective decision making. By developing a basic model of the environment in which the manager functions, insight is viewed as the basis for the effective manager's art. T/C.

Bluestone, Irving. "Implementing Quality-of-Worklife Programs," *Management Review*, Vol. 66, No. 7, July 1977, pp. 43-47.

Warns organizations that attempts to improve the quality of worklife simply to increase productivity are doomed to failure. Emphasis must be on creating a climate of satisfaction and the opportunity for human development. If the intent is genuine, both management and employees will benefit. P/D.

Booher, Harold R. "Symposium Proceedings: Invitational Conference on Status of Job Performance Aids Technology, February 23-25, 1977," Navy Personnel Research and Development Center, San Diego, CA, May 1977, 108 p. Report No. NPRDC-TR-77-33.

Yields information dealing with the maintenance, evaluation and training of job performance aids (JPA). Includes seven papers assessing the state-of-the-art in JPA. New directions for information transfer research and JPA/Job-oriented training impact on personnel systems are covered in the papers. P/D.

Branson, Phillip A. and Walter R. Peacock, Jr. "A Study of Job Satisfaction of Air Force Civilian Employees," Air Force Institute of Technology, Wright-Patterson AFB, OH, School of Systems and Logistics, September 1976, 117 p. Report No. SLSR-26-76B.

Analyzes the determinants of job satisfaction for United States Air Force civilian employees through a survey conducted by the Air Force Management Improvement Group (AFMIG). The primary technique used is the Monitored Automatic Interaction Detection Multivariate (MAID-M) program. Conclusions revealed that the major determinants of job satisfaction of Air Force civilian employees are job related factors, such as job challenge, freedom, personal growth, and job preparation for greater responsibility. FS.

Brief, A. P., R. J. Aldag, and R. A. Wallden. "Correlates of Supervisory Style Among Policemen," *Criminal Justice and Behavior*, Vol. 3, No. 3, September 1976, pp. 263-271.

Initiating structure positively correlates with faith in people, experienced responsibility for work, general job satisfaction, job involvement, internal work motivation, and organizational commitment. It correlates negatively with defensive posture. Consideration correlated positively with organizational commitment. FS.

Brief, A. P., J. Munro, and R. Aldag. "Correctional Employees' Reactions to Job Characteristics: A Data-Based Argument for Job Enlargement," *Journal of Criminal Justice*, Vol. 4, No. 3, Fall 1976, pp. 223-230.

Correction employees responded more positively to a job offering them skill variety, autonomy, task identity, and feedback than they did to a job perceived as dull and monotonous. FS.

Briggs, Channing. "The Essence of Staff Growth—or the New S.A.S.S.", *NASPA*, Vol. 13, No. 3, Winter 1976, pp. 57-60.

Discusses the self-actualization and self-growth of staff members within an organizational setting. Staff aspirations and the various factors which determine their satisfaction or frustrations are considered. P/D.

Carrell, Michael R. and John E. Dittrich. "Employment Perceptions of Fair Treatment," *Personnel Journal*, Vol. 55, No. 10, October 1976, pp. 523-524.

Demonstrates how employees who feel they receive fair treatment by their organization and their supervisors are more compelled to stay with an organization and be more effective employees than employees who feel they are treated unfairly. FS.

Child, J. "Participation, Organization, and Social Cohesion," *Human Relations*, Vol. 29, No. 5, May 1976, pp. 429-451.

Discusses problems associated with employee demands for participation in decision-making. Issues related to organizational growth, bureaucratization and decentralization are examined. P/D.

Cummings, L. L. and Chris J. Berger. "Organization Structure: How Does It Influence Attitudes and Performance?" *Management Review*, Vol. 66, No. 2, pp. 40-43.

Findings drawn from 50 studies over the past 10 years indicate that: satisfaction increases as individuals move up in an organization, individuals who are higher up in the organization are happier, there are no important differences in satisfaction levels of line and staff individuals and managers' satisfaction increases with amount of subordinates supervised. Other variables are also discussed. T/C.

Cummings, T. G. and J. Bigelow. "Satisfaction, Job Involvement and Intrinsic Motivation: An Extension of Lawler and Hall's Factor Analysis," *Journal of Applied Psychology*, Vol. 61, No. 4, August 1976, pp. 523-525.

Results support Lawler and Hall's conclusion that job attitudes of satisfaction, job involvement, and intrinsic motivation are conceptually distinct and empirically independent. FS.

Downey, H. K., J. E. Sheridan, and J. W. Slocum. "The Path-Goal Theory of Leadership: A Longitudinal Analysis," *Organizational Behavior and Human Performance*, Volume 16, No. 1, June 1976, pp. 156-176.

Weak support is found for House's path-goal theory of leadership effectiveness. Data suggests the need for considering moderator variables other than task structure. FS.

Downs, Cal W. and Michael D. Hazen. "A Factor Analytic Study of Communication Satisfaction," *The Journal of Business Communication*, Vol. 14, No. 3, Spring, 1977, pp. 63-74.

The multidimensionality of communication satisfaction was explored. A self-designed questionnaire was administered to 4 organizations in order to compare the factor structure derived from each. Eight factors were identified that were quite stabile across organizations. FS.

Drake, Bruce and Terence Mitchell. "The Effects of Vertical and Horizontal Power on Individual Motivation and Satisfaction," *Academy of Management Journal*, Vol. 20, No. 4, 1977, pp. 573-591.

Examines the effects of both vertical and horizontal power on participants. The results indicate that both power dimenisons are important for understanding people's reactions to participation in the decision process. FS.

Dubin, Robert and Joseph Champoux. "Central Life Interests and Job Satisfaction," *Organizational Behavior and Human Performance*, Vol. 18, No. 2, 1977, pp. 366-377.

The perceptual set of the individual worker regarding the centrality of work as a life interest is shown to be related to a measure of job satisfaction. FS.

Dunham, Randall. "Reactions to Job Characteristics: Moderating Effects of the Organization," *Academy of Management Journal*, Vol. 20, No. 1, 1977, pp. 42-65.

Canonical analysis established a significant relationship between task design and effective response measures for 784 middle level executives. Of particular significance are environmental elements which cause the worker to focus on task design. FS.

Edmunds, Stahrl. "Unifying Concepts in Social Responsibility," *Academy of Management Review*, Vol. 2, No. 1, 1977, pp. 38-45.

Social responsibility is having an impact upon business which can deal with it in alternative ways. Information disclosure and participative decision structure are aspects of the alternatives. T/C.

Elsasser, Theodore E. "Development of Executive Success," Naval Postgraduate School, Monterey, CA, September 1976, 187 p. Report No. NPS-54C176096.

Discusses various aspects of executive development and success. Executive effectiveness is defined through the eyes of an individual whose goals are to rise through the hierarchy and attain executive success. Also discusses the function of executives and the qualities that distinguish successful executives from mediocre ones. T/C.

Falcione, Raymond L., James C. McCroskey, and John A. Daly. "Job Satisfaction as a Function of Employees' Communication Apprehension, Self-Esteem, and Perceptions of Their Immediate Supervisors," in *Communication Yearbook I*, Brent D. Rubin ed., Austin, TX: International Communication Association, pp. 363-375.

Results indicate that subordinate satisfaction with immediate supervision is closely associated with perception of supervisor communication behavior, credibility, attractiveness, and attitude homophily, and to a lesser extent with oral communication apprehension and self-esteem. FS.

Faunce, William A. "Work, Status, and Self Esteem," Michigan State University, East Lansing, MI, August 1976, 284 p. Contract No. DL-91-26-74-24.

Presents a case for explaining the relationship between occupational achievement or lack of achievement to self esteem through the self investment theory. This theory explains how work conditions affect motivation, productivity, job satisfaction, and how working life can be improved. T/C.

Feldman, D. C. "A Practical Program for Employee Socialization," *Organizational Dynamics*, Vol. 5, No. 2, August 1976, pp. 64-80.

Three stages of organizational adjustment are identified (getting in, breaking in and settling in). Socialization Programs influence job satisfaction but not productivity or motivation. Suggestions are made for effectively devising and maintaining a socialization program. P/D.

Forbes, Benjamin J. *et al.* "Organizational Policy Decisions as a Function of Individual Differences and Task Design: Monitoring Tasks," Akron University, OH, Dept. of Psychology, August 1976, 205 p. Report No. TR-9 Contract N00014-75-C-0985.

Presents two visual monitoring tasks, one requiring low levels of task related abilities and the other requiring higher levels of task related abilities. Both performance and satisfaction were related to individual differences in ability as well as selected personality and preference measures. Congruence between task demands and individual abilities was found to be highly significant in determining these relationships. LS.

Franklin, J. L. "Relations Among Four Social-Psychological Aspects of Organizations," *Administrative Science Quarterly,* Vol. 20, No. 3, September 1975, pp. 422-433.

Examined a model describing causal relations among four factors in organizational functioning. The major links found were from organizational climate to managerial leadership, from managerial leadership to peer leadership, and from peer leadership to group process. FS.

Gemmill, Gary and Donald DeSalvia. "The Promotion Beliefs of Managers as a Factor in Career Progress: An Exploratory Study," *Sloan Management Review,* Vol. 18, No. 2, Winter 1977, pp. 75-81.

Identifies factors leading to promotions in large, complex organizations. Although many discussions lead participants to believe that "politics" and public image are primary ones, the study reported on suggests that folklore may be misleading. FS.

Gleason, James M., F. James Seaman, and Edwin P. Hollander. "Emergent Leadership Processes as a Function of Task Structure and Machiavellianism," State University of New York—Buffalo, NY, November 1976, 21 p. Report No. TR-3 Contract N00014-76-C-0754.

Discusses various aspects of leadership processes, using sixteen groups in an experiment involving a model-building task. Half were given explicit procedural instructions (High Structure) and half were not (Low Structure). On the Machiavellianism Scale, medium machs were more likely to be rated leaders than High or Low Machs. Low structure increased emergent leadership, while high structure was related to group members' satisfaction. LS.

Goodman, Paul and Johannes Pennings. "Toward a Framework of Organizational Effectiveness," Carnegie-Mellon University, Pittsburgh, PA, Graduate School of Industrial Administration, September, 1976, Report No. TR-3, Contract N00014-75-C-0973.

Reviews five original papers on organizational effectiveness presented at a workshop at Carnegie-Mellon University in 1976. T/C.

Gordon, George G. and Bonnie E. Goldberg. "Is There a Climate for Success?" *Management Review,* Vol. 66, No. 5, May 1977, pp. 24-28.

Discusses how companies differ in climates, successful companies' climates, and how to change climates. Findings suggest successful companies have managers who communicate expectations clearly and provide compensation that is competitive and performance related. P/D.

Gould, Bruce R. "Review of an Air Force Job Satisfaction Research Project: Status Report Through September 1976," Air Force Human Resources Laboratory, Brooks AFB, TX, December 1976, 34 p. Report No. AFHRL-TR-76-75.

Presents the status of a long-term comprehensive job satisfaction research project in its fifth year. The ultimate goal of the project is full utilization of personnel. Research findings are presented on the dimensions of job satisfaction operating in the Air Force work environment and on job attitudes and performance. T/C.

Green, Stephen G. and Delbert M. Nebeker. "The Effects of Situational Factors and Leadership Style on Leader Behavior," *Organizational Behavior and Human Performance*, Vol. 19, No. 2, 1977, pp. 368-377.

Fiedler's hypothesis that relationship—motivated and task-motivated persons differ in responses and leadership situations was supported in the experiment. LS.

Greenberg, J. and G. Leventhal. "Equity and the Use of Overreward to Motivate Performance," *Journal of Personality and Social Psychology*, Vol. 34, No. 2, August 1976, pp. 179-190.

Subjects who attempted to raise workers' performance gave higher rewards to members of failing groups than to members of successful groups. Subjects who attempted to motivate better performance gave higher rewards to lazy workers than to well-motivated workers. LS.

Gunderson, E. K. and Saul B. Sells. "Organizational Stresses and Health," Naval Health Research Center, San Diego, CA, October 1973, 15 p. Report No. 73-59.

Describes a research program which investigated the importance of environment factors, organizational stress, and individual characteristics in job satisfaction and organizational effectiveness. A set of descriptors of naval organizations is related to job satisfaction, individual and group effectiveness, and health. FS.

Gyllenhammar, Pehr G. "How Volvo Adapts Work to People," *Harvard Business Review*, Vol. 55, No. 4, July-August 1977, pp. 102-113.

Discusses how job satisfaction and productivity can be increased by using work teams instead of assembly lines. Describes how change was introduced and implemented in various plants, Volvo's philosophy and guidelines, and the need for different managerial styles. P/D.

Hackman, J. Richard. "Improving the Quality of Work Life: Work Design," Bethany, CT, June 1975, 125 p. Contract L-74-77.

Advances understanding about work redesign as an approach to personal and organizational change. Discusses activation, motivation-hygiene, and job characteristic theories of work design. Presents a job characteristics model of work motivation to explain how job redesign can increase productivity and employee satisfaction. Discusses the importance of individual differences in skills and growth needs, organizational structure, interpersonal relationships, and technology to work system redesign success. T/C.

Hackman, J. Richard, L. Pearce, and Jane Caminis. "Effects of Changes in Job Characteristics on Work Attitudes and Behavior: A Naturally-Occurring Quasi-Experiment," Yale University, New Haven, CT, School of Organization and Management, December 1976, 30 p. Report No. TR-13 Contract N00014-75-C-0269.

Discusses various aspects of the effects of changes in the motivational properties of jobs on behaviors and work attitudes. Results showed that growth satisfaction, internal motivation, and general satisfaction were directly affected by changes in job characteristics. Satisfaction with work context was not affected. FS.

Hall, Hardy L. and Dale R. Baker. "An Overview of the Upward Mobility Assessment Center for the Bureau of Engraving and Printing," Civil Service Commission, Washington, D.C. Personnel Research and Development Center, August 1975, 41 p.

Discusses the effectiveness of the assessment center process that was applied as one of the evaluation instruments for selecting participants for the Bureau of Engraving and Printing's Upward Mobility Program. Results produced a wide range of candidate scores, making possible counseling and feedback to all of the candidates. Findings show favorable responses to the total assessment center process. FS.

Hamner, W. C. and E. P. Hamner. "Behavior Modification on the Bottom Line," *Organizational Dynamics*, Vol. 4, No. 4, Spring 1976, pp. 2-21.

Behavior modification techniques emphasizing the use of both positive reinforcement and verbal feedback by managers can improve employee performance. T/C.

Hansen, Gary B. *et al.* "Manpower Advisory Service in the Workplace: A Missing Link in National Manpower Policy, Volume I," Utah State University, Logan UT, Economic Research Center, March, 1976, 246 p.

Reports a study which examines U.S. employer's training and management problems. A resource consulting service was established in this project, focusing on improving training approaches, personnel systems, and management practices of public agencies and private firms. FS.

Harris, Thomas O. and Robert E. Scott. "Model Personnel Manual," Kansas State College of Pittsburg, Department of Vocational-Technical Education, 1975, 66 p.

Presents a model for assisting supervisors in personnel policies and procedures. This manual indicates how policies are to be administered and outlines various aspects of employer-employee relationships. The use of this manual is expected to increase designation of line of authority and planning changes. P/D.

Hazelwood, Leo *et al.* "Executive Aids for Crisis Management," CACI Inc. Federal, Arlington, VA, April 1977, 77 p. Contract N00014-77-C-0135.

Presents documented research on developing a prototype executive aid for crisis management. Highlights of the research are included, presenting the best solutions for potential crises. T/C.

Hespe, G. and T. Wall. "The Demand for Participation Among Employees," *Human Relations*, Vol. 29, No. 5, May 1976, pp. 411-428.

Suggests that participation will be more meaningful to workers when those to be affected participate in decisions concerning the practices to be adopted in their own workplace. T/C.

Hilgendorf, E. L. and B. L. Linden. "Workers' Experience of Participation: The Case of British Rail," *Human Relations*, Vol. 29, No. 5, May 1976, pp. 471-505.

Job experience and the opportunity to be involved in various kinds of decision-making affect workers' attitudes toward participation. FS.

Ivancevich, John M. "Different Goal Setting Treatments and Their Effects on Performance and Job Satisfaction," *Academy of Management Journal*, Vol. 20, No. 3, September, 1977, pp. 406-419.

Two hundred technicians and supervisors from seven parts manufacturing plants participated in a field experiment to determine how different methods of setting goals affected their satisfaction and performance. Formal goal setting, participation, and assigned goal setting are superior to "do your best." FS.

————. "Effects of Goal Setting on Performance and Job Satisfaction," *Journal of Applied Psychology*, Vol. 61, No. 5, October 1976, pp. 605-612.

Participative and assigned goal setting were both more effected than no-training goal setting in improving performance and satisfaction after nine months. However, this effect disappeared within 12 months. FS.

Jago, A. G. and V. H. Vroom. "Hierarchical Level and Leadership Style," *Organizational Behavior and Human Performance*, Vol. 18, No. 1, February 1977, pp. 131-145.

Found a greater propensity for use of participative managerial methods at higher organizational levels. FS.

Joslin, Edward O. "Career Mangement: How to Make It Work," *Personnel*, Vol. 54, No. 4, July-August 1977, pp. 65-72.

A new methodology is presented where an individual's personal attributes, and their degree of expertise are listed, and compared to attributes required for various jobs. This listing can aid personnel in career management—employment, training, performance review, promotions, and counseling. P/D.

Karmel, B. and D. Egan. "Managerial Performance: A New Look at Underlying Dimensionality," *Organizational Behavior and Human Performance*, Vol. 15, No. 2, April 1976, pp. 322-334.

Four dimensions of managerial performance (perceived managerial competence, activity level, role centrality, and purposefulness) were obtained from an analysis of data supplied by practicing managers. LS.

Katerberg, Ralph Jr., Jeanne B. Herman, and Charles L. Hulin. "Organizational and Individual Characteristics, Organizational Climate, and Job Attitudes: A Multivariate Investigation of Responses at Individual and Group Levels of Analysis," University of Illinois—Urbana-Champaign, Department of Psychology, February 1977, 82 p. Report No. TR-77 Contract N00014-75-C-0904.

Describes a field study which investigated demographic and organizational position items; questionnaire included an organizational climate measure and a job attitude instrument. Results showed that climate was more predictable than were job attitudes. In view of work on organizational climate, these results suggest that climate is a set of shared perceptions at some level above that of the individual. FS.

Katzell, Raymond A. *et al.* "Work, Productivity, and Job Satisfaction: An Evaluation of Policy-Related Research," New York University, NY, January 1975, 435 p. Grant No. NSF-SSH73-07939-A01.

Discusses various aspects about how work affects the productivity and job satisfaction of workers. Emphasis is placed on determining if and how job satisfaction and productivity combined may be promoted by changing control, job enrichment, and compensation. Attention is focused on policy makers and their tactics and the strategies of taking action. FS.

Kaufman, Harold E. and Louis H. Bluhm. "Leadership Structures in 3 Small City-Centered Communities. Technical Bulletin 78," Mississippi State College, MS, 1976, 16 p. ERIC ED 134-370.

The leadership hierarchies of 3 Mississippi communities with single population centers of around 20,000 in 1970 were compared in terms of 3 dimensions—complexity, coordination, and openness. Leadership groups were compared by age, schooling, occupation, and race. It was found that there was a high correlation between coordination and complexity of participation. FS.

Kavanagh, M. J. and M. Halpern. "The Impact of Job Level and Sex Differences on the Relationship Between Life and Job Satisfaction," *Academy of Management Journal*, Vol. 20, No. 1, March 1977, pp. 66-73.

Job and life satisfaction are positively related for both males and females regardless of job level. FS.

Knoop, Robert and Robert O'Reilly. "Participative Decision-Making in Curriculum," *High School Journal*, Vol. 59, No. 4, January 1976, pp. 153-158.

Paper examines practices in decision-making in light of the maxim: Individuals who are affected by decisions should partake in making these decisions. FS.

Koch, James L. "Effects of Feedback on Job Attitudes and Work Behavior: A Field Experiment," Oregon University, Eugene, Department of Management, October 1976, 46 p. Report No. TR-6 Contract N00014-76-C-0164.

Examines various aspects of feedback on work behavior and job attitudes of sewing machine operators. Results indicated that increased feedback improved group cohesion and goal commitment of the operators. FS.

Komaki, Judi, William Waddell, and M. George Pearce. "The Applied Behavior Analysis Approach and Individual Employees," *Organizational Behavior and Human Performance*, Vol. 19, No. 2, 1977, pp. 337-352.

Employee in two small businesses participated in experiments involving time-off with pay, feedback, and self-recording. Their performance improved. FS.

Kostick, May M. and Robert Pearse. "The Dynamics of Productive Compatibility," *Management Review*, Vol. 66, No. 6, June 1977, pp. 48-54.

To accept change gracefully and achieve maximum job efficiency, an organization's employees' various needs must be met, assert the authors. Through a system of testing personality traits and group awareness training, these needs can be dealt with. The personality tests and their analysis are included. P/D.

Krivonos, Paul D. "The Relationship of Intrinsic-Extrinsic Motivation and Communication Climate in Organizations," paper presented at the Annual Meeting of the Western Speech Communication Association, San Francisco, CA, November 1976, 26 p. ERIC ED 131 512.

Reports on a study of 65 supervisory-managerial personnel from two large manufacturing companies. Subjects were given an intrinsic/extrinsic motivation scale and a communication-climate questionnaire. Partially supports hypothesis that those who are intrinsically motivated perceive communication climate as being more ideal than those who are extrinsically motivated. FS.

Lauderdale, Michael L. "Review of Management by Objectives," Texas University—Austin. Center for Social Work Research, October 1975, 29 p.

Discusses Management by Objective (MBO) as a program concerned with the goals of the organization and its specific work objectives rather than with task definition of human needs. Organizational steps that should be initiated at the executive management level are discussed.

Lawler, Edward E. "Improving the Quality of Work Life: Reward Systems," Lawler (Edward E.) III, Pinckney, MI, June 1975, 130 p. Contract No. L-74-78.

Examines the relationship between reward systems, the quality of work life, and organizational effectiveness. Discusses characteristics of different reward systems and the advantages and disadvantages of different performance based pay systems in different organizational settings. T/C.

————. "New Approaches to Pay: Innovations That Work," *Personnel*, Vol. 53, No. 5, September-October 1976.

Suggest improvements over traditional methods of pay administration. Cafeteria-style fringe benefits programs, lump-sum salary increases, skill evaluation pay plans and employee participation in pay decisions, are discussed. Emphasizes that the pay system is an important motivator and helps organizational effectiveness if used in harmony with the total organizational system. P/D.

———— et al. "Job Choice and Post Decision Dissonance," *Organizational Behavior and Human Performance*, Vol. 13, No. 1, February 1975, pp. 133-145.

Attitudes toward firm attractiveness determine job choice behavior, and job choice behavior influences post employment attitudes about firm attractiveness in the direction predicted by dissonance theory. LS.

Likert, Rensis and M. Scott Fisher. "MBGO: Putting Some Team Spirit into MBO," *Personnel*, Vol. 54, No. 1, January-February 1977, pp. 40-47.

Author asserts that management by group objectives (MBGO) is superior to MBO. Explains how it works, it's differences from MBO and it's similarity to Systems 4 management. Higher motivation to reach objectives, more loyalty to co-workers and superiors and better teamwork and coordination are some advantages over MBO. P/D.

Longest, Beaufort B. "Job Satisfaction for Registered Nurses in the Hospital Setting," Georgia State University—Atlanta. Institute of Health Administration, 1974, 7 p.

Discusses the role of job satisfaction in relation to productivity of nurses. Ten factors were identified in relation to job satisfaction, based on Herzberg's previous research. Results indicate that the ranking of job satisfaction factors may be beneficial to nursing administrators who deal with the problems of productivity, turnover, and absenteeism. FS.

MacEachron, Ann E. "Two Interactive Perspectives on the Relationship Between Job Level and Job Satisfaction," *Organizational Behavior and Human Performance*, Vol. 19, No. 2, 1977, pp. 226-246.

Asymmetrical and Symmetrical models were applied to this field study of 70 women in a hospital nursing staff. The asymmetrical was the best predictor. The primary significant correlation was between job level and satisfaction with pay. FS.

Mainstone, Larry E. "The Impact of Selected Individual Difference and Organizational Variables on Expectancy Theory Cognitions and Performance for Salaried Employees," Michigan State University, East Lansing, MI, Department of Management, 1976, 179 p. Contract DL-91-26-75-32.

Examines the impact of twelve individual differences and organization variables upon six expectancy theory cognitions. FS.

Mansperger, Thomas E. "Motivation of Program Managers," Defense Systems Management School, Ft. Belvoir, VA, May 1976, 43 p.

Discusses the inherent motivation of program management positions. Motivation was found to be significant in promoting excellent performance. Nearly all respondents of the survey indicated strong growth needs, but feedback from the job itself did not always aid the manager's perception of his/her performance effectiveness. FS.

Marcus, Alfred C. *et al.* "Administrative Leadership in a Sample of Successful Schools from the National Evaluation of the Emergency School Aid Act," paper presented at the Annual Meeting of the American Educational Research Association, San Francisco, CA, April 1976, 37 p. ERIC ED 125 123.

Examines the relationship between administrative leadership and schools' success in raising achievement. Analysis of the survey data showed that schools where principals emphasized the importance of selecting basic instructional materials and made more decisions in the instructional area showed achievement gains in the subject area of reading and math. FS.

McAlindon, Harold R. "Developing Organizations in which the Self-Actualizing Executive Flourishes," *Personnel*, Vol. 54, No. 3, May-June 1977, pp. 22-29.

Discusses how a self-actualizing executive will make an organization more profitable. Outlines how an organization can become actualizing and gives guidelines for human research managers on how to achieve this. P/D.

McKillip, Richard H. and Cynthia L. Clark. "Biographical Data and Job Performance," Civil Service Commission, Washington, D.C., Personnel Research and Development Center, August 1974, 18 p.

Summarizes research findings concerning the use of biographical data in predicting job performance. Studies and relates biodata that covers a wide range of human characteristics. Discusses difficulties in using biodata in Federal examining. Generalizations cannot be made across occupations about predictors of success in several kinds of jobs. Conclusions are that the research, although valuable, is a long-term, high-risk effort. T/C.

Merryman, Craig and Ester Shani. "Growth and Satisfaction of Employees in Organizations," *Personnel Journal*, Vol. 55, No. 10, October 1976, pp. 492-494.

Findings show that when an organization's size, efficiency and profits increase, employees' job satisfaction, and effective interpersonal communication decrease. FS.

Michael, Stephen R. "The Contingency Manager: Doing What Comes Naturally," *Management Review*, Vol. 66, No. 11, November 1976, pp. 20-31.

Author advises managers to use a contingency approach in deciding upon what management practice (i.e., Systems 4, job enrichment, transactional analysis, etc.) to use. Proposes that the problem and the total situation be taken into account. P/D.

Miles, R. H. and W. D. Perreault. "Organizational Role Conflict: Its Antecedents and Consequences," *Organizational Behavior and Human Performance*, Vol. 17, No. 1, October 1976, pp. 19-44.

Tested and defined a model of role conflict in terms of antecedents and consequences. Antecedents included objective role requirements and the characteristics of the role set. Consequences included job related tensions and satisfaction, perceived effectiveness and attitudes toward role senders. FS.

Mitchell, Terence R. "Expectancy and Expected Value: Decision Models for Organizations," Washington University, Seattle Department of Psychology, January 1976, 48 p. Report No. TR-75-77 Contract N00014-67-A-0103-0032.

Reviews the basic concepts of the development of Expectancy Theory and Expected Value Models, the areas of decision making leadership attitudes and motivation and social power support. These models also provide insights into the questions of organizational design and communication. T/C.

Moreau, David. "When War Breaks Out in the Company," *Management Review*, Vol. 66, No. 3, March 1977, pp. 35-36.

Names six common situations which often cause conflict among executives: staff takeover, over-promotion, generation gap, new arrivals, company crises, and personal dislike. The author advises that these conflicts can be avoided through sound administration and communication. P/D.

Morse, J. J. "Sense of Competence and Individual Managerial Performance," *Psychological Reports*, Vol. 38, No. 3, June 1976, pp. 1195-1198.

Significant and positive relationships between managers' sense of competence (set of psychological feelings of confidence an individual has about his/her abilities to master the external environment) and three measures of managerial performance are found. FS.

Motowidlo, Stephen J. *et al.* "Motivation, Satisfaction and Morale in Army Careers: A Review of Theory and Measurement," Personnel Decisions Inc. Minneapolis, MN, December 1976, 209 p. Contract DAHC19-73-C-0025.

Review and relates to each other the major concepts and theories that differentiate and define motivation, satisfaction, and morale. Discusses those theories and instruments most likely to be usefully applied in the context of the Army. A number of practical implications for action are derived from the theories. T/C.

Mowday, Richard T. "Leader Characteristics and Methods of Upward Influence in Organizational Decision Situations," Oregon University, March 1977, 19 p. Report No. TR-12 Contract N00014-76-C-0164.

Discusses the exercise of power in organizations. Using a sample of elementary school principals, consistent relationships were found between several methods of influence and the principals' needs for power and achievement and their years of supervisory experience. FS.

Muchinsky, Paul. "Organizational Communication: Relationships to Organizational Climate and Job Satisfaction," *Academy of Management Journal*, Vol. 20, No. 4, Dec. 1977, pp. 592-607.

Data collected from 695 employees of a public utility indicates that certain dimensions of organizational communication were related to climate and satisfaction. FS.

Nadler, D., P. Mirvis, and C. Cammann. "The On-Going Feedback System: Experimenting with a New Managerial Tool," *Organizational Dynamics*, Vol. 4, No. 4, Spring 1976, pp. 63-80.

An on-going feedback system is a useful management tool, the effectiveness of which is constrained by the knowledge, skill, and motivation of users. Describes the implementation of one such system. P/D.

Nebeker, Delbert M. and Melvin C. Moy. "Work Performance: A New Approach to Expectancy Theory Predictions," Navy Personnel Research and Development Center, San Diego, CA, September 1976, 52 p. Report No. NPRDC-TR-76TQ-47.

Discusses and tests a new conceptualization of Vroom's (1964) expectancy model. This new model predicts that an individual chooses from among levels of performance rather than from among levels of effort to exert. A questionnaire was administered to employees of a bank operation measuring several performance levels and their affect on work outcomes. FS.

Nord, Walter R. "Dreams of Humanization and the Realities of Power," paper presented at the Annual Meeting of the American Psychological Association, Washington, D.C., September 1976, 17 p. ERIC ED 132 649.

Humanization in organizations has not been easy to achieve because of the role that power plays. In humanized organizations, members are treated justly, are engaged in meaningful work, encouraged to develop their potential, and are treated as ends rather than as means. The author presents four postulates that relate to power and indicates why humanization has not taken place. P/D.

Odiorne, George S. "MBO in the 1980's: Will it Survive? *Management Review*, Vol. 66, No. 7, July 1977, pp. 39-42.

Asserts that organizations which have failed with MBO is a result of their: reluctance to shift away from an autocratic power base, refusal to make advance commitments, and deficiency in MBO technique. Determines a need for quality training in MBO since it will be greatly needed in the future. P/D.

O'Reilly, Charles A. "Personality-Job Fit: Implications for Individual Attitudes and Performance," *Organizational Behavior and Human Performance*, Vol. 18, No. 1, February 1977, pp. 36-46.

Two indices of work orientation (expressive and instrumental) interact with job type (challenging or nonchallenging) to affect job performance and attitudes. FS.

————. The Intentional Distortion of Information in Organizational Communication: A Laboratory and Field Approach, Ph.D. Dissertation, University of California, Berkeley, 1976. DAI, Vol. 37, No. 9, p. 4741-B.

A bias exists toward screening certain types of information from upward transmission. Low trust in the receiver of a message leads to more suppression by senders of information that reflects unfavorably on the sender's performance. A measure of information distortion is significantly and inversely associated with job satisfaction and both individual and group performance. LS.

Organ, Dennis. "Inferences About Trends in Labor Force Satisfaction: A Causal-Correlation Analysis," *Academy of Management Journal*, Vol. 20, No. 4, 1977, pp. 510-519.

Analysis of five causal models reveals a stable pattern of job attitudes for the period 1945-1976. The data was based on samples of 38,000 manufacturing organizations. FS.

Owens, Robert G. and Edward Lewis. "Managing Participation in Organizational Decisions," *Group & Organization Studies*, Vol. 1, No. 1, March 1976, pp. 56-66.

Suggests a three part schema for classifying teachers' attitudes towards problems which normally arise in a school system. Based upon these concepts, the authors developed and tested a technique for assessing teachers' views as a source of data to guide principals and superintendents in deciding whom to involve in dealing with problems. T/C.

Payne, R. L., S. Fineman, and T. D. Wall. "Organizational Climate and Job Satisfaction," *Organizational Behavior and Human Performance*, Vol. 16, No. 1, June 1976, pp. 45-62.

Eight conceptual types of climate and satisfaction are summarized via a facet analysis of the concepts of organizational climate and job satisfaction. T/C.

Pennings, J. M. "Dimensions of Organizational Influence and Their Effectiveness Correlates," *Administrative Science Quarterly*, Vol. 21, No. 4, December 1976, pp. 688-699.

Organizational effectiveness was related to an individual's level of influence, decentralized participation, and autonomy. FS.

——— and Paul S. Goodman. "A Framework of Organizational Effectiveness," paper presented at the Annual Meeting of the American Sociological Association, New York, NY, August-September 1976, and the Annual Meeting of the American Psychological Association, Washington, D.C., September 1976, 26 p. ERIC ED 132 672.

Examines the nature of complex organizations and describes a new conceptual framework for considering organizational effectiveness. Organizations are viewed as open systems with distinct but interdependent subsystems and as political areas consisting of internal and external constituencies that negotiate a complex set of constraints, goals, and referents. T/C.

Peterson, Dwight G. and John W. Vogt, Jr. "The Interaction of Job-Related Variables with Leader Dimension in Air Force System Program Officers," Air Force Institute of Technology, Wright-Patterson AFB, OH, School of Systems and Logistics, September 1976, 106 p. Report No. SLSR-9-76B.

Discusses various aspects of leader behavior, identifying initating structure, and consideration as two dimensions related to variables of job satisfaction, organizational climate, organizational size, and hierarchical level. FS.

Pinder, C. C. "Additivity Versus Nonadditivity of Intrinsic and Extrinsic Incentives: Implications for Work Motivation, Performance and Attitudes," *Journal of Applied Psychology*, Vol. 61, No. 6, December 1976, pp. 693-700.

Found that intrinsic and extrinsic incentives are not additive in determining organizational attidues and behaviors. LS.

Powers, Thomas E. "Selecting Presentation Modes According to Personnel Characteristics and the Nature of Job Tasks Part I. Job Tasks," Maryland University, Baltimore County, Baltimore MD, January 1977, 157 p. N00014-74-C-1067.

Discusses the generic behaviors involved in technical job task performance. A description of civilian and military efforts in developing behavioral outlines of job performance and performing job task analyses is included. FS.

Reeley, Richard Harold, Jr. "An Analysis of the Relationships Between Job Satisfaction/Enrichment Factors and Demographic Variables for United States Air Force Professional Military Education Faculty," Air Force Institute of Technology, Wright-Patterson AFB, OH, August 1976, 131 p. Report No. AFIT-CI-7T-10.

Focuses upon an application of job motivation/satisfaction theory to the faculty of the United States Air Force Air University. Subjects were measured with the Air University Facility Motivation Survey. The instrument presented and defined 15 job factors. Scales to measure both an individual's satisfaction with the perceived importance of each factor, and six job enrichment factors, and selected demographic variables were also included. FS.

Reinkober, Thomas E. "Technology and Its Impact on the Employee," Defense Systems Management School, Ft. Belvoir, VA, May 1976, 24 p.

Discusses the effects of technology on the employee in terms of job satisfaction and alienation. Results indicated that the technological impact on the employee has been one of alienation. Efforts are being made to accept innovativeness in order to establish a more satisfying job. FS.

Retondi, T. "Organizational Identification: Issues and Implications," *Organizational Behavior and Human Performance*, Vol. 13, No. 1, February 1975, pp. 95-109.

A negative relationship between organization identification and both creativity and effectiveness was found suggesting that behaviors related to organizational identification may produce dysfunctional as well as functional outcomes. FS.

Ripley, Randall B. "CETA Prime Sponsor Management Decisions and Program Goal Achievement," Ohio State University Columbus, June 1977, 133 p. Contract DL-2-39-75-10.

Discusses the relation of Comprehensive Employment and Training Act (CETA) management decisions at the sponsor level to local program goal achievement. Reviews the various management decisions and the conditions which promote maximum goal achievement. P/D.

Roach, John M. "Managing Psychological Man," *Management Review*, Vol. 66, No. 6, June 1977, pp. 27-40.

In an interview, Dr. Harry Levinson, Industrial psychologist, states that the theories of Maslow, Herzberg, and McGregor are too generalized to use in dealing with individuals. Claims that managers need to understand motivation theories. Offers guidelines for effective leadership. P/D.

Roach, John M. "Why Volvo Abolished the Assemby Line," *Management Review*, Vol. 66, No. 9, September 1977, pp. 48-52.

Pehr G. Gyllenhammar, president of Volvo, explains his people-oriented philosophy of work, how workers should be treated in an organization, the implications for managers, and how to unlock worker potential. P/D.

Robinson, Thomas E. "Crises Offer Opportunities," *Journal of Educational Communication*, Vol. 1, No. 3, November-December, 1975, pp. 4-7.

Advises that conflict in the schools calls for more effective utilization of personnel and other resources. Administrators should reestablish a strong working relationship with teachers, by teaching classes themselves occasionally to keep in touch with the instructional program, and nurture a community atmosphere in their schools. P/D.

Rogers, D. L. and J. Molner. "Organizational Antecedents of Role Conflict and Ambiguity in Top Level Administrators," *Administrative Science Quarterly*, Vol. 21, No. 4, December 1976, pp. 598-610.

Interorganizational variables account for the largest amount of variance in role conflict while intraorganizational variables account for the largest amounts of variance in role ambiguity. LS.

Rosow, Jerome. "Solving the Human Equation in the Productivity Puzzle," *Management Review*, Vol. 66, No. 8, August 1977, pp. 40-43.

Author claims that productivity is too often viewed from a technical, scientific viewpoint, while the human factor of productivity is ignored. Productivity and the quality of working life for people can both be improved. By accentuating positive behaviors in individuals, which the author outlines, this goal can be attained. Ten concepts to follow in this plan are also detailed. P/D.

Rubinstein, Sidney P. "Participative Problem Solving: How to Increase Organizational Effectiveness," *Personnel*, Vol. 54, No. 1, January-February 1977, pp. 30-39.

Participative problem solving is discussed as a method which can: increase productivity; deal with unemployment in a counterinflationary way; increase motivation and job satisfaction; and respond to pressure to change from EPA and OSHA. Successful illustrations from government and industry are given. P/D.

Sakkal, George. "Executive Planning Process Guidance Manual," Maryland Department of State Planning, Baltimore, November 1975, 128 p.

Deals primarily with fundamental aspects of executive plan preparation, thereby attempting to improve the quality of decision-making and communication within and among state government agencies. Discusses the function of the executive planning process in Maryland as that which relates future goals to immediate policy and budgetary issues. Presents a directory of data resources and elaborations on various planning methodologies and procedures. P/D.

Schmid, John R. and Richard K. Hovey. "Utility Theory in Military Personnel Management," B-K Dynamics Inc., Rockville, MD, July 1976, 87 p. Contract N00014-72-C-0526.

Discusses the criteria used for evaluating changes as an important element of personnel policy testing and decision making with computer simulation models. Presents two Delphi experiments and a Broadcast experiment that were conducted to solicit the opinions of Navy experts regarding productivity of an average enlisted man in terms of utility to the Navy through the years. FS.

Schmitt, Neal, Bryan Coyle, and Bruce Saari. "Types of Task Information Feedback in Multiple-Cue Probability Learning," *Organizational Behavior and Human Performance*, Vol. 18, No. 2, 1977, pp. 316-328.

Subjects' achievement, consistency, and matching were evaluated in a 2 x 4 x 4 design. Results indicate that outcome feedback produces lower consistency but slightly better matching than no outcome feedback. LS.

Schou, Andrew J. and Robert J. Biersner. "Leadership-Style Flexibility," Naval Submarine Medical Research Lab., Groton, CT, May 1977, 257 p. Report No. NSMRL-852.

Discusses various aspects of leadership style. Two groups of managers completed a questionnaire concerning their satisfaction with leadership and the perceptions of the leadership styles used by their managers. Study's purpose was to view leadership flexibility as a function of 1) the situation, 2) the nature of the problem, 3) performance evaluations of subordinates, 4) subordinate satisfaction,and 5) LPC scores. FS.

Schriesheim, C. A., R. House, and S. Kerr. "Leader Initiating Structure: A Reconciliation of Discrepant Research Results and Some Empirical Tests," *Organizational Behavior and Human Performance*, Vol. 15, No. 2, April 1976, pp. 297-321.

Examines and resolves some differences in the various definitions and conceptualizations of leader initiating structure. FS.

Schriesheim, C. A. and C. J. Murphy. "Relationships Between Leader Behavior and Subordinate Satisfaction and Performance: A Test of Some Situational Moderators," *Journal of Applied Psychology*, Vol. 61, No. 5, October 1976, pp. 634-641.

Leader structure is related to satisfaction in larger work units and consideration is related to satisfaction in smaller units, In low stress jobs consideration enhances satisfaction and performance but in high stress jobs structure is helpful. High structure has dysfunctional effects only when accompanied by low consideration. FS.

Schuler, R. S. "Participation with Supervisor and Subordinate Authoritarianism: A Path-Goal Theory Reconciliation," *Administrative Science Quarterly*, Vol. 21, No. 2, June 1976, pp. 320-325.

Found participation to be satisfying to low authoritarian subordinates regardless of the degree of task repetitiveness but satisfying to high authoritarian subordinates only when tasks were low in repetitiveness. Highly repetitive tasks were less conducive to ego involvement than low repetitive tasks. FS.

Schuler, Randall S. "Role Conflict and Ambiguity as a Function of the Task-Structure-Technology Interaction," *Organizational Behavior and Human Performance*, Vol. 20, No. 1, 1977, pp. 66-74.

This research analyzed the task-structure-technology interaction as a predictor of perceived role ambiguity and conflict. The results suggest that research on ambiguity and conflict should consider the influence of structure and technology as well as task. FS.

————. "Role Perceptions, Satisfaction and Performance Moderated by Organizational Level and Participation in Decision-Making," *Academy of Management Journal*, Vol. 20, No. 1, 1977, pp. 159-165.

Multiple linear regression model was used to investigate the relationships. Participation in decision-making was found to have a significant interaction with satisfaction. FS.

————. "The Effects of Role Perceptions on Employee Satisfaction and Performance Moderated by Employee Ability," *Organizational Behavior and Human Performance*, Vol. 18, No. 1, 1977, pp. 98-107.

Role ambiguity and role conflict are negatively related to employee satisfaction and performance. FS.

———— and Howard H. Greenbaum. "The Influence of Role Perceptions on the Communication-Outcome Relationships," paper presented at the National Annual Meeting of the Academy of Management, Orlando, FL, August 1977, 24 p.

Relates four types of communications to outcome variables of worker satisfaction, performance, and involvement. Finds that informative and integrative communications had positive relationships with outcome variables while regulatory and distortive communications were negatively related to the same variables. Indicates that results support a vicious cycle interpretation of the communications-role perceptions-outcome sequence. FS.

Scott, W. E. "The Effects of Extrinsic Reward on 'Intrinsic Motivation'," *Organizational Behavior and Human Performance*, Vol. 15, No. 1, February 1976, pp. 117-129.

Reviews studies of intrinsic motivation and finds that there is no acceptable evidence that extrinsic reinforcers inevitably disrupt behavior maintained by other, but perhaps less obvious, reinforcing events. Notes that the meaning of "intrinsic motivation" remains obscure. A reinforcement analysis is proposed as more fruitful. T/C.

Scoville, Paul A. "A Test of Herzberg's Two Factor Theory of Job Satisfaction," Air Force Institute of Technology, Wright-Patterson AFB, OH, School of Engineering, June 1976, 100 p. Report No. GSM/SM/76S-23.

Tests the basic premise of Herzberg's theory that motivators and hygiene factors lead to job satisfaction and dissatisfaction, respectively. Three hundred and one responses to a questionnaire from students enrolled in the Air Force Institute of Technology's School of Engineering and Systems Logistics, were analyzed using the Automatic Interaction Detection algorithm and Spearman rank order correlation. Significant relationships were found between several variables that contradicted Herzberg's two-factor theory. FS.

Seeborg, Irmtraud S. "The Influence of Employee Participation in Job Redesign," Yale University, New Haven, CT, School of Organization and Management, December 1976, 29 p. Report No. TR-12 Contract N00014-75-C-0269.

Describes a study on job redesign. In a 2½ day simulation, five groups of individuals worked with identical job designs, then their jobs were redesigned through employee participation or by the supervisor. Results showed that supervisors concentrated on vertically loading the jobs, whereas employees were interested with social aspects of the work. Under employee participation, employee satisfaction improved. LS.

Seyboh, J. W. "Work Satisfaction as a Function of the Person-Environment Interaction," *Organizational Behavior and Human Performance*, Vol. 17, No. 1, October 1976, pp. 66-75.

More organizational inducements (pay, job, variety, task complexity) are required to satisfy well educated employees than are needed to satisfy less well educated individuals. FS.

Silverman, Gerald G. "Attitudes of Research and Development Professional Federal Employees Toward Nature Systems and Operative Goals: A Study of Scientists, Engineers and Managers at a Federal Installation," Army Electronics Command, Fort Monmouth NJ, January, 1977, 83 p., Report No. ECOM-HFE-1-77.

Discusses organizational goals of professionals in a research and development organization, focusing on the impact of motivation in productivity. This project establishes a starting point for additional studies into employee concepts and their relationships to employee motivation and job satisfaction. FS.

Singhal, S. "Need-Gratification, Absenteeism and Its Other Correlates," *Journal of Industrial Relations*, Vol. 2, No. 3, January 1976, pp. 351-361.

Participation in the organization leads to reduced absenteeism. Absenteeism was also affected by interpersonal perception, interpersonal communication and group cohesiveness as well as by personal correlates (number of dependents, other sources of income, length of service, unionization, and anxiety). FS.

Singhal, S. "Need Gratification and the Perception of Job Incentive," *Indian Journal of Social Work*, Vol. 37, No. 1, April 1976, pp. 73-79.

Safety was found to be the most important need. Important job incentives included opportunity for promotion and training and good working conditions. FS.

Sinha, J. B. "The Authoritative Leadership: A Style of Effective Management," *Indian Journal of Industrial Relations*, Vol. 2, No. 3, January 1976, pp. 381-389.

Contrasts three leadership styles. Proposes a continuum from authoritarian to participative. Suggests a middle position is optimal (labeled authoritative leadership) for the transition to democratic management. T/C.

Slovic, Paul, Baruch Fischhoff, and Sarah Lichtenstein. "Behavioral Decision Theory," Decisions and Designs Inc., Mclean, VA, September 1976, 97 p. Contract N00014-76-C-0074.

Presents an overview of research that has been conducted in the working environment. The focus of this report is on work integrating research with attention to how people make decisions. T/C.

Smith Frank J., Kenneth D. Scott, and Charles Hulin. "Trends in Job Related Attitudes of Managerial and Professional Employees," *Academy of Management Journal*, Vol. 20, No. 3, 1977, pp. 454-460.

Data about job satisfaction was kept on the same group of managers for a period of 4 years. The results show the job satisfaction of this group of managers declining. This was true for all tenure groups for all facets of job satisfaction except financial reward. FS.

Srivastava, A. K. "Money as a Motivating Force: A Critical Evaluation," *Psychological Studies*, Vol. 19, No. 2, July 1974, pp. 93-98.

Money, in itself, is a secondary motive for working efficiently. Other job characteristics are just as important. T/C.

Stahl, Michael J. "Innovation and Productivity in Research and Development: Some Associated Individual and Organizational Variables," Air Force Institute of Technology, Wright-Patterson AFB, OH, May 1976, 282 p. Report No. AFIT-TR-76-10.

Explores the relationships of organizational variables with innovation and productivity of scientists and engineers in R&D laboratories. Rewards for innovation and communication on technical matters with other scientists/engineers within the work group were significantly involved in the relationships found between organizational variables and innovation and productivity. Levels of participation in goal setting and group leader's level of empathy were also consistently related to level of productivity. FS.

Steers, Richard M. *et al.* "The Influence of Job Scope on the Personality-Turnover Relationship," Oregon University, Eugene, December 1976, 31 p. Report No. TR-8 Contract N00014-76-C-0164.

Examines the influence of job scope on the relationship between selected personality characteristics of employees and turnover. No direct relationships were found between personality characteristics and turnover for the combined sample of employees on high and low scope jobs. Results found that the correlations between turnover and the needs for achievement and affiliation found among employees on high and low scope jobs were significantly different. FS.

————. "The Motivational Properties of Tasks," Oregon University, Eugene Graduate School of Management and Business, September 1976, 34 p. Report No. TR-7 Contract N00014-76-C-0164.

Discusses six conceptual models of the motivational properties of tasks in terms of its specificity and scope in explaining motivational procedures related to task design. T/C.

————. "The Role of Achievement Motivation in Job Design," Oregon University, Eugene Department of Management, December 1976, 24 p. Report No. TR-10 Contract No. N00014-76-C-0164.

Examines the effects of job scope and need for achievement on management commitment and performance. Results supported the following hypotheses: 1) high scope jobs would be associated with increased organizational commitment irrespective of need for achievement, and 2) high scope jobs would be related to increased performance only for high need achievement subjects and not low need achievement subjects. FS.

Stewart, Charles T. Jr. "Jobs, Occupations, Careers," George Washington University, Washington, D.C. Graduate School of Arts and Sciences, June 1976, 23 p. Report No. TR-1281 Contract N00014-75-C-0610.

Suggests that the reward-structure of the Navy should recognize differences in motivation and therefore in the effectiveness of alternative incentives. Some incentives that are mentioned are pay, training opportunities, and promotion. Pay is a high motivation for job-seekers and those unlikely to reenlist; occupation-oriented pesonnel are more motivated by training opportunities; and career-minded personnel are more motivated by training and promotion. T/C.

Stone, Eugene F. "Some Personality Correlates of Perceptions of and Reactions to Task Characteristics," Oregon University, March 1977, 31 p. Report No. TR-11 Contract N00014-76-C-0164.

Reviews the theories related to task characteristics. Results showed that both reactions to and perceptions of characteristics were influenced by measured individual differences variables. LS.

Strauss, George. "Improving the Quality of Work Life: Managerial Practices," Berkeley, CA, June 1975, 127 p. Contract L-74-84.

Concerns the role that management plays in determining the Quality of Work Life (QWL) through their daily contacts with members of the work force. Manager consideration, facilitation, promotion of cohesive groups, and reward systems are discussed as they relate to QWL. Stresses participation as a way of improving QWL by increaseing the employee's control over his job. T/C.

Thompson, Paul H. and Gene W. Dalton. "Are R&D Organizations Obsolete?" *Harvard Business Review,* Vol. 54, No. 6, November-December 1976, pp. 105-116.

Findings indicate that organizational obsolescence, not individual obsolescence, result in low motivation in individuals. Authors identify four career development stages and discuss their application to prevent obsolescence. Recommendations are offered to managers to avoid conflicts. FS.

Umstot, D. D., C. H. Bell, and T. R. Mitchell. "Effect of Job Enrichment and Task Goals on Satisfaction and Productivity: Implications for Job Design," *Journal of Applied Psychology,* Vol. 61, No. 4, August 1976, pp. 379-394.

Job enrichment had a substantial impact on job satisfaction but little effect on productivity. Goal setting had a major impact on productivity and a less substantial impact on satisfaction. FS.

—————. "Goal Setting and Job Enrichment: An Integrative Approach to Job Design," Air Force Insititute of Technology, Wright-Patterson AFB, OH, School of Systems and Logistics, April 1977, 50 p. Report No. AFIT-LS-2-77.

Reviews the empirical literature relating job enrichment and goal setting. Describes how these two factors aid productivity and job satisfaction. Organizational characteristics are reviewed with a set of hypothesized relationships. T/C.

Viall, Charles C. "Factors Contributing Toward Diverging Definitions of the Effective Project Manager," Defense Systems Management School, Ft. Belvoir, VA, May 1976, 34 p.

Analyzes various aspects on the determination of the effective program manager. Research indicated nine specific areas as sustaining factors in the definition of the effective program manager. Productivity and effectiveness of the program manager is outlined. T/C.

Vogt, Molly T. "Conflict Management As An Integral Part of Planning in the University, avail. School of Health Related Professions, University of Pittsburgh, Pittsburgh, PA, 1976, 18 p. ERIC ED 127 886.

Rapidly changing societal norms and values have affected the organizational structure of educational institutions. Presents a conceptual planning process in the university. T/C.

Vroom, Victor H. "The Social Structure of Decision Making," Yale University, New Haven, CT, School of Organization and Management, May 1977, 11 p. Contract N00014-76-C-0024.

Provides a general perspective of research areas in leadership. Some of these areas are: new methods for studying leadership, leader behavior, perceptual differences in leadership style, organizational structure and leadership style, and leadership development and training. T/C.

Vrooman, Roger M. "An Analysis of Factors Associated with the Job Satisfaction and Career Intent of Air Force Personnel with Less Than Six Years of Service," Air Force Institute of Technology, Wright-Patterson AFB, OH, School of Engineering, December 1976, 189 p. Report No. GOR/SM/76D-13.

Reviews the variables related to job satisfaction and career intent. Factors associated were found to be personal growth satisfaction, personnel standing satisfaction, job challenge, and future preparation for positions with greater responsibility. FS.

Weihrich, Heinz. "MBO-Quo vadis?" *Management Review*, Vol. 66, No. 1, January 1977, pp. 43-44.

Suggests an open-systems approach to MBO—where the external environment is integrated with the organization's activities and plans. Provides six steps to use as a model to implement a comprehensive MBO system. P/D.

Wergin, Jon F. "The Evaluation of Organizational Policy Making: A Political Model," *Review of Educational Research*, Vol. 46 , No. 1, Winter 1976, pp. 75-115.

Discusses how evaluation research can be more effective if policy formation is included in its scope. The areas discussed in this article deal specifically with organizational policy. The relationship between policy formation and evaluation research are examined and a framework for evaluating policy is presented. T/C.

Whitehill, Arthur M. Jr. "Maintenance Factors: The Neglected Side of Worker Motivation," *Personnel Journal*, Vol. 55, No. 10, October 1976, pp. 516-519, 526.

Presents a case for a closer look at maintenance factors in Herzberg's two dimensional theory of job satisfaction and motivation. Points out the managers should devote more attention to lower level security and safety needs rather than emphasizing the higher level "motivators". P/D.

Wilde. David M. "Information Needs for Decision Making by Program Management Office Personnel," Defense Systems Management School, Ft. Belvoir, VA, November 1975, 42 p.

Examines the need for decision-making information by program management office (PMO) personnel. Defines a management framework which can reduce costs within the program office. Compares an individual's personality and job requirements to the decision-making process. Implications show that adjusting program office information needs to meet the information needs of individual decision-makers will result in a reduction of program costs. T/C.

Zagoria, Sam. "An Evaluation of the Nassau County Project," Labor-Management Relations Service, Washington, D.C., July 1975, 23 p. Contract DL-74-82.

Discusses the Nassau County, NY, Multi-Municipal Labor-Management Productivity Project. The objective of this project was to achieve and improve the productivity among the 25,000 workers in Nassau County, by developing procedures advancing productivity and unifying job descriptions. FS.

Zaleznik, Abraham. "Managers and Leaders: Are They Different?" *Harvard Business Review*, Vol. 55, No. 3, 1977, pp. 67-78.

Bueaucratic organizations, in which managers flourish, may be inimical to the growth of leaders. A person may not be able to be both a manager and a leader. P/D.

Zenger, John. "Increasing Productivity: How Behavioral Scientists Can Help," *Personnel Journal*, Vol. 55, No. 10, October, 1976, pp. 513-526.

Discusses how productivity can be increased by applying behavioral research findngs to ten areas. They are: executive attitudes, managerial behavior, supervisory skills, job design, work group norms, compensation, nonmonetary reward systems, communication and feedback, technological interface, and labor-mangement relations. T/C.

(No author; alphabetized by title)

"Decision Making in Educational Organizations," National Institute of Education (DHEW), Washington, D.C., May 1975, 28 p. ERIC ED 131 551.

Summarizes the views expressed by participants in a conference on decision-making in educational organizations. Deals with decision-making under conditions of goal ambiguity and suggests directions and priorities for future research. T/C.

"Training Program in Gerontology and Voluntarism. Retired Senior Volunteer Program—Foster Grandparent Program," Utah University, Salt Lake City, Rocky Mountain Gerontology Center, 1974, 64 p.

Documents a series of 14 workshops for personnel involved in volunteer programs for elderly persons. A summary of workshop participants' responses to questions concerning the factors motivating participation by the elderly in volunteer programs and techniques for interviewing volunteers is included. Results of tests administered to training session participants are summarized. Papers on motivation and on a 'no-fault' approach to problem solving are included. T/C.

SEE ALSO

Interpersonal Variables: Arams, Bernardin & Alvares, Bodden & Leonard, Burlem, Caplow, Constantin, Dansereau & Graen & Haga, Dipboye, Dolgoff, Dubin & Champeux & Porter, Gillerman, Harris & Scott Herold & Greeler, Kavanagh, Kennedy, Nesberg & Spurr, Schneider, Shapira, Oldham & Hackman & Pearce, Rosen & Jerdee, Weigand, Zaleznik
Intragroup Variables: Baird & Weinberg, Dowling, Hackman, Morley & Silver, Rickards, Schlenker & Miller, Vallacher & Seymour & Gunderson
Intergroup Variables: Akinbode & Clark, Hurst *et al.*, Moller, Schermerhorn
Skill Improvement and Training: Argyris, Barker, Burstiner, Carroll & Anthony, Cooper *et al.*, Danish *et al.*, "Final Training Program Report," "Guidelines for Staff Development," "Integration of Services is a Process, Not a Product," Slezak, Strauss & Hartem & Kempher, Van Cleve
System Analysis: Bailey, Brannen *et al.*, Bowey, Carlson, Cook, Herbst, Heichberger, Infelise, Jacobson, Lachenmeyer, Lambright, "Manual for Applying Management by Objectives to Human Services Programs," "Management Information Study of Nursing Education, Santa Clara County, California," Munitz & Russell, Nielson & Kimberly, Patten, Pugh & Hinings, Reid, Roberts & O'Reilly, Roeber, Schaub, Schuelke, Spector & Hayes & Crain, "Social Planning and Decision Making in Washoe County, Nevada, Volume 1," Tichy & Hornstein, Wheeler & Petrie, Zagoria
Research Methodology: Alexander *et al.*, Bolyard, Duffy, Felsinger, Fiks *et al.*, Jones & James, Mitchell & Moudgill, Selvidge, "SESA Productivity Measurement System: Measuring the Productivity of the State Employment Source Agencies," Stumpff & Chevalier, Young, Zytowski
Texts, Anthologies, Reviews, and General Bibliographies: Allen, Baird, Balachandran, Bernstein, Bowen, Bowers, Castetter, Cohen, David, DiSalvo, Duncan, Gilmer & Deci, Grooms, Gruneberg, Hackman & Suttle, Hall, Douglas T., Hall, Richard H., Harlem, Heirs & Pehrson, Huseman & Logue & Freshley, Ingalls, Johnson, Landy & Trumbo, Levinson, Lillico, London, Maccoby, Oaks, Rabinowitz & Hall, Reitz, Richardson & Baldwin, Roskey, Rothman & Erlich & Teresa, Scott & Mitchell, Schroeder & Adams, Simon, Shonyo (2), Steers, Steiner, Sutermeister, Taylor *et al.*, Wofford & Gerloff & Cummins

SKILL IMPROVEMENT AND TRAINING IN
ORGANIZATIONAL COMMUNICATION

BOOKS AND DISSERTATIONS

Allman, Jack F. *Critical Issues in the Orientation of New School Board Members with a Multi-Media Presentation.* Ed.D. Dissertation, University of Arkansas, 1976. DAI, Vol. 37, No. 5, p. 2519-A.

Indicates that the orientation process of new school board members is inadequate, with the greatest amount of information coming from the school administrators. Board of Education incumbents' input in the orientation process was minimal. FS.

Anderson, Ronald. *Selecting Media for Instruction.* Florence, KY: Van Nostrand, 1976.

Covers print, video, and computer media. Chapters include media selection, developmental testing, guidelines for visuals, still visuals, moving visuals, audio, printed materials, physical objects, and computers. P/D.

Anglin, Richard D. *Changes in Open-Mindedness and Self-Concept in College Freshmen as a Result of Human Communication Training.* Ph.D. Dissertation, The University of Oklahoma, 1976. DAI, Vol. 37, No. 5, p. 2659-A.

Finds that college students who received four weeks of communication training experienced more openness and more positive self-concept changes than students receiving no training. FS.

Barber, James A. *A Study of Changes in the Building Principal's Leader Behavior Perceived by Superordinates, Subordinates, and Selves That Result from Instructional Planning, Monitoring and Feedback Processes.* Ed.D. Dissertation, University of Kentucky, 1975. DAI, Vol. 37, No. 9, p. 5466-A.

Reports significant differences between the perceptions of school superintendents and teachers towards principals who completed in-service training sessions involving planning, monitoring, and feedback processes. FS.

Bartel, Carl. *Instructional Analysis and Material Development.* Chicago, IL: American Technical Society, 1977.

Covers preparation, selection, application, and development of educational materials for training instructors. P/D.

Bateman, Charles F. *The Effect of Selected In-Service Activities Upon the Organizational Climate in an Elementary School.* Ed.D. Dissertation, University of Virginia, 1976. DAI, Vol. 37, No. 7, p. 4001-A.

Reports a significant improvement in organizational climate after in-service training designed to change organizational climate was administered to elementary school teachers. FS.

Brannen, Dalton E. *An Analysis of Training Needs of Lower and Middle Management Personnel.* Ph.D. Dissertation, The University of Mississippi, 1976. DAI, Vol. 37, No. 11, p. 7194-A.

Observes that management training is most needed in the areas of people management skills and top management skills. Little concern was indicated for training in social, legal, or ethical responsibilities. FS.

Bryngleson, James D. *Staff Development: Increasing Teacher Interaction Skills Through Consultation Strategies.* Ed.D. Dissertation, University of Northern Colorado, 1976. DAI, Vol. 37, No. 7, p. 4294-A.

Concludes that a one-semester consultation program using constructs from transactional analysis, teacher effectiveness training, and values clarification resulted in higher levels of teacher empathy and human interaction skills. FS.

Buchholz, Steven W. *The Effects of Training in Managing Interpersonal Relationships on the Perceptions of Social Style: An Empirical Study.* Ph.D. Dissertation, The University of Nebraska—Lincoln, 1976. DAI, Vol. 38, No. 1, p. 23-A.

Indicates that participation in a two-day management course improved a subject's behavior in interpersonal communication encounters. LS.

Bunning, Richard L. *Skills and Knowledges for Adult Educators: A Delphi Study.* Ph.D. Dissertation, Arizona State University, 1976. DAI, Vol. 37, No. 10, p. 6216-A.

Reports that the "skill of communicating" was considered a significant skill in adult educators. FS.

Burke, Beverley A. *The Effect of Teaching Communication Skills to Teachers in an Elementary Bureau of Indian Affairs School.* Ph.D. Dissertation, The University of Oklahoma, 1976, DAI, Vol. 37, No. 12, p. 7627-A.

Finds that a ten-week program of teaching communications skills increased active listening skills and empathy. FS.

Chiosso, Edward T. *A High School Curriculum in Interpersonal Relations: A Deliberate Psychological Education Intervention.* Ph.D. Dissertation, University of Minnesota, 1976. DAI, Vol. 37, No. 6, p. 3372-A.

Notes that a seven-phase high school curriculum emphasizing the active, responsible learning of role-taking skills resulted in the gaining of valuable interpersonal skill by students. FS.

Coleman, Susan D. *A Training Program to Raise Teacher Trainees' Level of Functioning in the Communication of Empathic Understanding.* Ph.D.

Dissertation, University of Illinois—Urbana-Champaign, 1976. DAI, Vol. 37, No. 10, p. 6415-A.

Discusses the effectiveness of a special training program designed to raise the level of functioning in the communication of empathic understanding, noting that results were significantly superior to the use of written instructions. LS.

Davison, Kathryn M. *Simulation Versus Case Study Strategy for Developing Pre-Service Teacher Verbal Communication Competency.* Ph.D. Dissertation, The Ohio State University, 1976. DAI, Vol. 37, No. 11, p. 6994-A.

States that a simulation strategy was feasible for developing teacher verbal communication abilities. More positive relationships between teachers and students were found in the case study approach. LS.

Day, Peter, R. *Methods of Learning Communication Skills.* New York: Pergamon Press, 1977.

Applies to the training situation. Discusses the practical implications of communication theories as well as the methods for teaching them. Topics covered include learning processes, teaching methods, interviewing, simulations, and group exercises. Designed for special workers. P/D.

Doyle, Michael and David Straus. *How to Make Meetings Work: The New Interaction Method.* Wyden, 1976.

Presents a method which the authors claim is the "First up-to-date method for running meetings since Robert's Rules of Order." It is a "how to" guide which could be used in training. P/D.

Easley, Ann H. *Evaluation of a Modular Methodology for Developing Teacher Communication.* Ed.D. Dissertation, Auburn University, 1976. DAI, Vol. 37, No. 11, p. 7084-A.

Concludes that special facilitative training for developing teacher communication did not result in skills being applied to classroom. LS.

Egan, Gerard. *Interpersonal Living: A Skills/Contract Approach to Human-Relations Training in Groups.* Monterey, CA: Brooks/Cole Publishing Company, 1976.

Assumes that many group experiences require people to use skills they may not already have. To remedy this, the book includes such topics as self-disclosure, concreteness in communication, expression of feelings, listening, genuineness and respect, confrontation, and changing interpersonal behavior.

Egan, Kieran. *Structural Communication.* Belmont, CA: Fearon Publishers, Inc., 1976.

Presents a new methodology for improving communication (especially in discussion groups) based on Skinner's and Brunner's ideas. Can be useful in training activities. P/D.

Elliott, Teresa G. *An Experimental Study of the Effects of Presenting an Intercultural Communication Unit in the Basic Speech Course.* Ph.D. Dissertation, University of Maryland, 1976. DAI, Vol. 37, No. 11, p. 6837-A.

Observes no difference in student attitudes whether taught by lecture, simulation, and videotape. However, all three methods resulted in more changes than in a control group not exposed to the three methods. LS.

Griffin, John A., Jr. *The Effect of a Marathon Sensitivity Training on the Individual Behavior of Principals and Teachers and on the Organizational Climate of Selected Schools.* Ph.D. Dissertation, University of Pittsburgh, 1976. DAI, Vol. 37, No. 7, p. 4016-A.

Finds that an intensive small group experience (T-Group marathon) produced behavioral changes in the participants. Elementary and junior high school participants, female participants, and participants with less than ten years of experience showed a greater frequency of behavioral changes. FS.

Hargreaves, J. *Good Communications—What Every Manager Needs to Know.* New York: Wiley and Sons, 1977.

Examines the stucture of communication and its flow vertically and horizontally. Answers the questions, "Why bother to communicate?" Gives some checkpoints for success, and deals briefly with some of the techniques geared to practicing managers. P/D.

Hart, Andrew A. and James A. Reinking. *Writing for Career-Education Students.* New York: St. Martin's Press, 1977.

Discusses both the basic elements of writing and the complex forms of business writing. Topics covered include letters, memorandums, proposals, progress reports, and investigative reports. T/C.

Hemphill, Norma J. *Evaluating the Effectiveness of Communications Training for Special Education Support Personnel.* Ph.D. Dissertation, University of Kansas, 1976. DAI, Vol. 38, No. 2, p. 728-A.

Concludes that participants in a one-semester graduate course in communications significantly improved various specific skills, such as paraphrasing and evaluator reponses. LS.

Hopkins, Mitchell L. *The Effect of Effectiveness Communication Skill Development on Teacher Self-Report.* Ed.D. Dissertation, Drake University, 1976. DAI, Vol. 37, No. 10, p. 6419-A.

Determines that an Effectiveness Communications program, modeled after a similar program developed by Gordon and lasting twelve weeks, had no significant effect on the level of teachers' self-concepts. LS.

Hubbord, Nettie L. F. *An Investigation of Incident Case and In-Depth Case Method of Instruction in Selected Business Communications Classes.* Ed.D. Dissertation, Arizona State University, 1976. DAI, Vol. 37, No. 10, p. 6602-A.

Studies two methods of construction in business communications classes, and finds no significant differences between the Incident Case Method and the In-Depth Case Method when measured on an objective test. However, when measured on a subjective instrument, the Incident Case Method was preferred by students. LS.

Jones, John E. and J. William Pfeiffer. *The 1977 Handbook for Group Facilitators.* La Jolla, CA: University Associates, 1977.

This is the sixth volume in a series of annual guides aimed for practitioners and trainers. Includes a series of group exercises as well as a series of questionnaires, all designed for human relations training. Also contains bibliographies on nonverbal communication and small group training, reviews of recent literature on assertiveness training and organizational development, and brief discussions of conceptual and substantive issues. P/D.

Kirkpatrick, Donald L. *How to Plan and Conduct Business Meetings.* Chicago, IL: Dartnell, 1977.

Covers such topics as leadership, questions, controlling meetings, meeting evaluations, and sales meetings. Includes self-report forms and handouts. Primarily for training. P/D.

Madden, F. Mel. *The Effect of Human Relations Training on Group Leaders' Decisions and Members' Satisfaction.* Ed.D. Dissertation, The University of North Dakota, 1976. DAI, Vol. 38, No. 1, p. 52-A.

Concludes that leaders who had the benefit of a group discussion and who received human relations training made significantly more accurate decisions than leaders who acted alone and had received no training. LS.

Main, Charles D. *Modifying Teacher and Student Expectancies: Effects of Training Problem High School Students in Communication Skills.* Ph.D. Dissertation, The University of New Mexico, 1976. DAI, Vol. 37, No. 5, p. 2639-A.

Reports no significant differences between the "problem" high school student exposed to communication skills training and other students in a control group. Stresses the need for longitudinal studies to determine the long-range effects of this type of training. FS.

Malickson, David L. and John W. Nason. *Advertising—How to Write the Kind that Works.* New York: Scribners, 1977.

Emphasizes the pragmatic aspects of writing advertisements. Offers specific guidelines for the preparation of copies. Aimed for practitioners. P/D.

Maurer, Carolyn G. *The Effects of a Self-Instruction Program in Facilitation and Communication Skills for Elementary School Teachers.* Ph.D. Dissertation, The University of Florida, 1976. DAI, Vol. 37, No. 10, p. 6423-A.

Determines that a self-instruction program in facilitation and communication skills offered an effective method of training teachers in interpersonal skills. FS.

Maynard, William L. *The Effects of Specialized Training for Administrators and Teachers on the Improvement of School Climate.* Ed.D. Dissertation, University of Washington, 1976. DAI, Vol. 37, No. 7, p. 4030-A.

Reports that the amount of statistical change in the organizational climate was not great enough to indicate that certain specialized training of administrators was of practical value. FS.

Melrose, John. *Bucomco: A Business Simulation.* Chicago, IL: Science Research Associates, 1977.

Provides materials for simulating the communication activities of a large corporation. Provides students with opportunities to deal with such problems as information overload, lack of information, inaccurate data, performance evalution, authority delegation, etc. The accompanying instructor's guide is necessary for establishing the procedures and guidelines for the simulation. P/D.

Melton, Nancy J. N. *Perceptions of Identified Barriers to School Board Communication in Florida and Implications for Training.* Ph.D. Dissertation, The Florida State University, 1976. DAI, Vol. 37, No. 12, p. 7449-A.

Determines that an informal training program, consisting of reading and self help, was most valuable method for reducing barriers to communication into, through, and out of school systems. FS.

Nadler, Leonard and Zeace Nadler. *How to Improve Workshops and Conferences.* Houston, TX: Gulf Publishing Company, 1977.

Discusses procedures for facilitating the exchange of information in conferences and workshops. Topics discussed include conference activities, planning, and management. Primarily written for practitioners and trainers. P/D.

Ollier, Jule A. *Improvement in Communications by the Directorate, United States Dependents Schools, European Area, 1970-1975.* Ed.D. Dissertation, University of Southern California, 1976. DAI, Vol. 37, No. 9, p. 5505-A.

Concludes that instructional programs to improve communications within a government agency were effective, as judged by communication criteria derived from a statement of educational objectives of U.S. Dependents Schools, European Area. FS.

Pfeiffer, J. William and John E. Jones. *A Handbook of Stuctured Experiences for Human Relations Training.* Volume VI. La Jolla, CA: University Associates, 1977.

Presents a collection of twenty-three group exercises designed for utilization in human relations training. Some of the specific goals of these activities include leadership development, self-awareness, problem solving, and interpersonal awareness. Each activity specifies the amount of time required, materials needed, and its goals. P/D.

Roach, William L., Jr. *A Comparative Study of Two Models of Communications Skills Training.* Ph.D. Dissertation, The University of Mississippi, 1976. DAI, Vol. 37, No. 9, p. 5711-A.

Reports that the use of two communications skills training models, Ivey's Microcounseling Paradigm and Carkhuff's Systematic Human Relations Training Model, produced significant differences when compared with groups not exposed to the models. LS.

Robson, Donald L. *An Inventory of Perceived Management Skills of Practicing School Superintendents in Michigan.* Ph.D. Dissertation, Michigan State University, 1976. DAI, Vol. 37, No. 12, p. 7460-A.

Finds that school superintendents perceive themselves most proficient in planning skills, and most deficient in area of evaluation skills and decision-making skills. FS.

Rowzee, Jerry M. *The Effects of Communication Skill Training on Low Socio-Economic Level Underachieving Secondary Students' Facilitative Communication and Self-Concept Levels.* Ph.D. Dissertation, The University of Mississippi, 1976. DAI, Vol. 37, No. 11, p. 7048-A.

Determines that short-term facilitative communications training improved the communications skills of upward bound students. LS.

Shean, Jeannette M. *The Effect of Training in Creative Problem Solving on Divergent Thinking and Organizational Perceptions of Students of School Administration.* Ed.D. Dissertation, Northern Arizona University, 1977. DAI, Vol. 38, No. 2, p. 585-A.

Concludes that a fifteen hour training program in creative problem solving improved creative thinking ability, fluency, flexibility, and originality. Topics in the Training Program included principles of fact-finding, problem definition, deferred judgment, brainstorming, evaluation, and acceptance of ideas. LS.

Silvern, Leonard C. *How to Prepare Occupational Instruction.* Houston, TX: Gulf Publishing Company, 1977.

Covers such topics as instructional design, planning, curriculum development, and program analysis. Emphasis is on occupational training. P/D.

Steinmetz, Lawrence L. *The Art and Skill of Delegation,* Reading, MA: Addison-Wesley, 1976.

Aims to help individuals learn the "art" of delegating and to assist those who teach delegation in company training programs. Offers exercises at the end of each chapter to help understand material. P/D.

Stenzel, Anne K. and Helen M. Feeney. *Volunteer Training and Development: A Manual* (Revised Edition). New York: The Seabury Press, 1976.

Discusses methods for recruiting, training, and developing volunteer workers who need to develop decision-making and communication skills —and methods for training those who will supervise volunteers. P/D.

Terry, Mollie B. *An Experimental Study to Determine the Effects of Training in Listening Skills on Achievement In, and Attitudes Toward, A College Business Communication Course.* Ph.D. Dissertation, Georgia State University—School of Education, 1976. DAI, Vol. 37, No. 11, p. 6914-A.

Reports that training in listening skills did not affect learning retention or make a difference in student attitudes toward a business communications course. LS.

Wilson, Lee S. *Locus of Control as a Factor Affecting the Generation of Ideas in Real and Nominal Brainstorming Groups.* Ed.D. Dissertation, University of Virginia, 1976. DAI, Vol. 37, No. 7, p. 4057-A.

Finds no difference between the efforts of "nominal" brainstorming groups (combined efforts of individual brainstorming independently) and the efforts of "real" brainstorming groups (efforts of individuals functioning in a group setting), when the measure was the number of unique ideas generated. However, nominal groups were superior in the production of nonoverlapping ideas. LS.

ARTICLES, PAPERS, AND U.S. GOVERNMENT PUBLICATIONS

Agnew, Bill. "Training with Transactional Analysis," *Training Officer*, Vol. 12, No. 1, January 1976, pp. 3-5.

Discusses various forms of transactional analysis that can be used to improve trainer-trainee communication. Aspects of interaction process, training techniques, and interpersonal competence are examined. P/D.

Argyris, Chris. "Double Loop Learning in Organizations," *Harvard Business Review*, Vol. 55, No. 5, September-October 1977, pp. 115-125.

Argyris describes a method by which underlying assumptions, norms, and objectives can be openly questioned and challenged. This method decreases game-playing and ineffective communication which often serve to hide the organization's problems and lead to rigidity and deterioration. P/D.

Braby, Richard. "Training Requirements for the Naval Technical Information Presentation Program: A Needs Assessment," April 1977, 94 p. Government Report No. TAEG-TM-77-3.

Attempts to establish a dialogue between Naval Technical Information Presentation Program personnel (NTIPP) and Naval Education and

Training Command personnel regarding the design of technical manuals to better support training programs. P/D.

Brown, Dale K. "Evaluation of Navy Human Relations Training for Civilian and Military Supervisors and Managers—A Conceptual Framework and a Case Study," avail. Human Sciences Research Inc., Mclean, VA, May 1977, 69 p. U.S. Government Report No. HSR-RR-77/10-C1 Contract No. N00014-76-C-0163.

Presents a conceptual framework for studying the stages of development of race relations, equal opportunity, education, and training programs. Discusses the processes of personnel decisions made by supervisors and how they reflect EEO statistics. T/C.

Brunette, Douglas J. "Successful Workshop Training of Local Government Officials," *Training and Development Journal* Vol. 30, No. 4, April 76, pp. 24-27.

Reviews the Manpower Development Service of Utah State University, which designed workshop activities later adapted to the situations and needs of attending local government officials. P/D.

Buckner, Daniel W. "A Study on the Effectiveness of Transactional Analysis for Improving Organizational Performance," Naval Postgraduate School, Monterey, CA, September 1976, 74 p.

Compares the effectiveness of Transactional Analysis used in personnel training to conventional training, determining if Transactional Analysis training resulted in greater awareness of basic human needs. Results are included. FS.

Burstiner, Irving. "Development and Self-Evaluation of a Workshop in Creative Management," *College Student Journal,* Vol. 9, No. 4, December, 1975, pp. 315-318.

Describes an experiment utilizing administrators and supervisory personnel of a hospital who participated in a workshop in "Creative Management" theory. Participants received eight hours of training in creative thinking and problem-solving, leadership, group dynamics, and motivation. Comparisons of pre- and post-test rating revealed gains in both the Leadership and the Creative areas. FS.

Campbell, Samuel C. *et al.* "A-6E Systems Approach to Training. Phase I," Grumman Aerospace Corporation, Bethpage, NY, February 1977, 90 p. Contract N61339-75-C-0099.

Describes one of four Phase I programs, namely A-6E TRAM Instructional Systems Development (ISD) Program which was established to evaluate the application of a Systems Approach to Training (SAT) in Naval Aircraft Programs. This report discusses the Task Analysis, the selection of instructional media, and the role of the Subject Matter Expert (SME). P/D.

Carpenter, Dudley S. and James P. Herget. "Creating a Video-Tape Training Program," *Educational Broadcasting*, Vol. 9, No. 2, March-April 1976, pp. 15-32.

Discusses a training program created by the National Minority Purchasing Council to help minority business people understand and use sophisticated sales training methods to sell their products to large industries. P/D.

Carpenter, Kay F. and Jerome A. Kroth. "Effects of Videotaped Role Playing on Nurses' Therapeutic Communication Skills," *Journal of Continuing Education in Nursing*, Vol. 7, No. 2, March-April 1976, pp. 47-53.

Discusses research determining the effectiveness of videotape recorded (VTR) role playing as a teaching technique conducted on nurses attending continuing education classes in verbal and nonverbal therapeutic communication skills. VTR appears to be an effective technique. FS.

Carpenter-Huffman, Polly, "MODIA: Volume I. Overview of a Tool for Planning the Use of Air Force Training Resources," Rand Corporation, Santa Monica, CA, March 1977, 28 p. Report No. R-1700-AF-Vol-1 Contract F49620-77-C-0023.

Describes a Method of Designing Instructional Alternatives (MODIA). It is a system developed to help Air Training Command (ATC) plan technical courses. This report describes MODIA's rationale, structure, support requirements, and discusses the results of ATC's evaluation of its effectiveness as an aid to course planning. P/D.

Carroll, Archie B. and Ted F. Anthony. "An Overview of the Supervisor's Job," *Personnel Journal*, Vol. 55, No. 5, May 1976, pp. 228-231, 249-250.

Presents an overview of supervisory management for the new supervisor who wants an initial overview, and for the experienced supervisor, who wants to develop additional insights. P/D.

Cooper, Cary L. *et al* "Developing One's Potential: From West to East," *Group Organization Studies*, Vol. 1, No. 1, March 1976, pp. 43-55.

Examines the impact of sensitivity training on participants' self-actualization in the United Kingdom, Turkey, and Japan. The results suggest that as the economic and social conditions change and create a cultural environment more favorable to self-actualizing tendencies, individuals will respond more positively to educational innovations such as experimental learning groups. T/C.

Cooper, C. L. and D. Bowles. "Structured Exercise-Based Groups and the Psychological Conditions of Learning," *Interpersonal Development*, Vol. 5, No. 4, 1974-75, pp. 203-212.

Managers in structured exercise-based groups were found to have more negative changes on a variety of personality dimensions and to have a higher number of peer rated casualties than managers in unstructured experiential learning groups after training. LS.

Coulson, Robert. "Resolving Controversy in Education," paper presented at the Annual Meeting of the Elementary School Principals, Atlantic City, NJ, April 1976, 14 p. ERIC ED 123 741.

Experts from the American Arbitration Association conduct training programs in arbitration and negotiating advocacy to instruct potential negotiators in effective bargaining. A variety of films and pamphlets are used. P/D.

Crowley, Thomas and Allen E. Ivey. "Dimensions of Effective Interpersonal Communications Specifying Behavioral Components." *Journal of Counseling Psychology.* Vol. 23, No. 3, May 1976, pp. 267-271.

Teaching clients effective communication skills has become an important function of the counseling psychologist. This study examines language patterns of trainees in a communication skills program. Factor analysis suggests effective communication may be defined in terms of appropriately referred emotional expressiveness. Implications of their study for training are discussed. FS.

Dalton, Charles and Marie Dalton, "Personal Communications: The Space Factor," *Machine Design,* Vol. 48, No. 21, September 23, 1976, pp. 94-98.

Illustrates with verbal examples and photographs the importance of territoriality in business situations. Includes consideration of angle of approach, personality, race, and sex. Emphasizes importance to managers. T/C.

Danish, Steven J. *et al* "An Evaluation of Helping Skills Training: Effects of Helpers' Verbal Responses." *Journal of Counseling Psychology.* Vol. 23, No. 3, May 76, pp. 259-265.

Reviews the present and future utilization of paraprofessional manpower. Notes necessity for systematic training of such workers in their human service roles. The impact of a training program designed by Danish and Hauer for basic helping skills is evaluated. In particular, verbal responses used by human service workers is investigated. FS.

D'Augelli, Anthony R. and Steven J. Danish. "Evaluating Training Programs for Paraprofessionals and Nonprofessionals," *Journal of Counseling Psychology,* Vol. 23, No. 3, May 1976, pp. 247-253.

Offers three strategies for evaluating training programs for paraprofessional human service workers. The first concerns the assessment of the differential usefulness of selection versus training of helpers. The second focuses on factors producing effective training. The final strategy entails an evaluation of the impact of systematically trained helpers on helpees. T/C.

Davis, Kathleen L. and George M. Gazda. "Results of the 1973 Association of Teacher Education Human Relations Training Summer Workshop," *Education,* Vol. 96, No. 2, Winter 1975, pp. 184-189.

A systematic Human Relations Training Workshop is offered to members of the Association of Teacher Education to help them become more facilitative in their communications with students and peers. P/D.

DeGise, Robert F. "Writing: Don't Let the Mechanics Obscure the Message," *Supervisory Management,* Vol. 21, No. 4, April 1976, pp. 24-28.

Summarizes principles of effective business writing, with examples. Includes word choice, avoidance of rigid form, conciseness, and specificity. P/D.

Fair, Ernest W. "Make it Clear," *Supervision,* Vol. 39, No. 4, April 1977, p. 24.

Suggests 21 techniques for use in making instructions to employees "clear and sharp." Emphasis is placed on the sender, not the receiver, in the communication act. P/D.

Falcione, Raymond L. "Some Instructional Strategies in the Teaching of Organizational Communication," *The Journal of Business Communication,* Vol. 14, No. 2, pp. 21-34.

Outlines an instructional paradigm and discusses four instructional strategies: 1) case studies, 2) role playing, 3) field research, and 4) internships. T/C.

Fairnelli, Jean L. "Fine Tuning Employee Communications," *Public Relations Journal,* Vol. 33, No. 1, January 1977, pp. 22-23.

Recommends steps required to develop a communication plan or system for a business. Suggests questions which must have answers to allow a system to produce results. Reports several techniques presently used in established companies. P/D.

Fiedler, Decky and Lee Roy Beach. "On the Decision to be Assertive," avail. Washington University Seattle Department of Psychology, October 1976, 35 p. U.S. Government Report No. TR-76-5 Contract N00014-76-C-0193.

Examines the applicability of an Expectancy/Decision model to assertiveness in a nonclinical population. Results suggest that participants, irrespective of their scores on standard measures of assertiveness and anxiety, consider the consequences of being assertive when making a decision about how to behave. Results imply that training programs should focus on changing participants' perceptions of the risks involved in being assertive. LS.

Filson, James W. "Problems Solving for Managers," Defense Systems Management School, Ft. Belvoir, VA, May 1976, 28 p.

Discusses several techniques for problem solving by managers. This technique describes a step-by-step procedure for identifying the problem, a guide for the manager to use in solving the problem, and several role playing exercises for training. P/D.

Finlay, James L. "Student Role-Playing: Effective Way to Teach Management," *Balance Sheet*, Vol. 57, March 76, pp. 249, 251, 285.

Formulates guidelines for student role-playing; includes a case study to utilize role-playing techniques. P/D.

Foy, Nancy. "Action Learning Comes to Industry," *Harvard Business Review*, Vol. 55, No. 5, September-October 1977, pp. 158-168.

Action learning, explains the author, is a method where participants "learn by doing"—through finding a solution to a real company problem. The history and scope of action learning is detailed plus payoffs, comments from participants, and how to organize one's own program. P/D.

Greenberg, Lois *et al.* "Communication Skills for the Gerontological Practitioner. Gerontology Practitioner Training Manual," Pennsylvania State University, University Park, Gerontology Center, 1976, 78 p.

Discusses various aspects of the most effective method of communication—oral, written, or nonverbal, with the elderly patient. A training module is presented. P/D.

Guyot, James F. "Prescription Drugs and Placebos: A New Perspective on Management Training," *Personnel*, Vol. 54, No. 3, May-June 1977, pp. 67-72.

The author suggests that training produces a placebo effect—trainee's will improve simply because they are expected to, not because the training was actually effective. Examines the implications of this prospect. P/D.

Horan, Margaret Ann "Cross/Trans./Intercultural Communications Training: What It Is—What It Is Not," *Training and Development Journal*, Vol. 30, No. 11, November 1976, pp. 26-28, 30-31.

Describes intercultural communication training programs author-consultant held for U.S. business firms. Includes needs-attitudes survey made of trainees moving from one cultural area to another, especially those coming to the U.S.A. and later returning to other lands. FS.

Imberman, Woodruff "Letting the Employee Speak His Mind," *Personnel*, Vol. 53, No. 6, November 1976, p. 12-22.

Lists and explains procedures for using interviews to discover what employees really think. Warns against rash, unplanned activities to obtain upward communication for its own splash effect. Shows need for sincere involvement of top managers and first-line supervisors in a careful program. P/D.

Jandt, Fred E. and Mark Hare. "Instruction in Conflict Resolution," Speech Communication Association, Falls Church, VA, 1976, 32 p. ERIC ED 25-010.

Provides some of the major concepts and research findings emphasized in the study of communication and conflict resolution. Intended for teachers concerned with effective handling of conflict situations, it offers avenues to enhance conflict resolution skills. P/D

Kachur, Donald S. and Mary Ann Boyd. "Can Education Learn a Lesson From Employee Training in Business and Industry?" *Kappa Delta Pi Record*, Vol. 12, No. 1, October 1975, pp. 21-22.

The problems of in-service teacher education have caused some to turn to the private sector where successful training is taking place. The authors propose a careful look at what profit-making organizations are doing. P/D.

McVeigh, Eileen B. "Systems Approach to Information and Referral. Book V: Staff and Volunteer Training Methods for Information Giving and Referral: An Outline," United Way of Pinellas County, Inc., St. Petersburg, FL, 1974, 79 p. Grant DHEW-AOA-93-HD-75170.

Discusses various methods for systematizing staff training and employment in a volunteer-based information and referral service. Describes a three-phase staff development program in which staff levels reflect the service's client load. Presents a training model for paid and volunteer workers. P/D.

Mendoca, J.D. and T. Siess. "Counseling for Indecisiveness: Problem Solving and Anxiety Management Training," *Journal of Counseling Psychology*, Vol. 23, No. 4, July 1976, pp. 339-347.

In an experiment using college students, a combination of anxiety management training and problem solving training resulted in significantly greater gains than either method alone with respect to vocational exploratory behavior, awareness of career plans and problem solving behavior. LS.

Mezack, Michael III. "A Systematic Approach to Management Training Program Development," *NUEA Spectator*, Vol. 40, No. 23, March 1976, pp. 17-20.

Describes phases in the management training program development process, including needs assessment, program objectives, recommendations, implementation, requirements, resources, formative and summative evaluation, and feedback. P/D.

Nesbitt, M. W., D. W. Gill, and M. K. Lipecky. "Police Management Training on Factors Influencing DWI Arrests: Training State and Community Instructors," Valencia, PA, Aug. 1976, 97 p. Contract DOT-HS-501209.

Discusses a training program for individuals from local and state enforcement agencies to conduct Police Management Workshops as outlined in the National Highway Traffic Safety Administration curriculum package. P/D.

Penrose, John M. "A Survey of the Perceived Importance of Business Communication and Other Business Related Abilities," *The Journal of Business Communication*, Vol. 13, No. 2, Winter 1976, pp. 17-24.

Describes a survey concerned with the attitudes of local business leaders toward the importance of communication skills in business and discusses the education and business background of the survey respondents. FS.

Prentice, Lloyd. "Words, Pictures, Media: Communication in Educational Policies," Institute for Responsive Education, Boston, MA, 1976, 100 p. ERIC ED 133 797.

Presents a step-by-step system for planning and carrying out an effective communication campaign. Although the booklet emphasizes the planning processes, it also provides many specific practical tips on solving problems, identifying objectives, developing systematic strategy, budget planning, and evaluating a communication campaign. P/D.

Prophet, Wallace W. "The U.S. Army in the 1970s: Developments in Training and Manpower Technologies," Seville Research Corp., Pensacola, FL, 1977, 17 p. Report No. PP-77-01.

The Army has instituted a performance-based instructional program that employs criterion-referenced testing for evaluation. Training is organized on the basis of six principles: Active Skill Practice, Absolute Criterion, Functional Context, Individualization, Feedback, and Quality Control. P/D.

Sayers, P.H. "A Course for Managerial Development," *Training Officer*, Vol. 11, No. 12, December 1975, pp. 298-302.

Discusses attitude training, management development, training objectives, and course content. P/D.

Scott, Dru. "Productive Partnerships—Coupling MBO and TA," *Management Review*, Vol. 65, No. 11, November 1976, pp. 12-19.

Examines how management by objectives and transactional analysis are tools which are compatible and complementary. Through integration, productivity and profits can increase. P/D.

Slezak, Donald R. "Participatory Management—Shared Decision Making 'Putting It All Together,'" *Thrust for Education Leadership*, Vol. 5, No. 1, pp. 22-25.

Article focuses on six areas that the leader needs for building his leadership skills. P/D.

Stewart, Charles J. "Teaching Interviewing for Career Preparation," ERIC Clearinghouse; Speech Communication Association, Falls Church, VA, 1976, 40 p. ERIC ED 125 008.

Aids high school and college instructors in the preparation of informational and employment interviewing courses. Provides information on communication principles, suggested exercises on employment interviewing, and resume writing. P/D.

Stilwell, William E. and David A. Santoro. "A Training Model for the 1980's" *Personnel and Guidance Journal,* Vol. 54, No. 6, February 1976, pp. 323-326.

A learning development consultant model is presented as a prototype for counselor training in the future. T/C.

Stone, Gerald L. and Adrian Vance. "Instructions, Modeling and Rehearsal: Implications for Training," *Journal of Counseling Psychology,* Vol. 23, No. 3, May 1976, pp. 272-278.

Investigates effects of instructions, modeling, and rehearsal in training college students in empathic communication. Analysis of responses indicate that improvement in empathic communication occurs for all training groups. Specific instruction appears to be a critical factor in facilitating written performance. Modeling seems to be effective for the interview task. FS.

Strauss, Marvin D., Carol J. Harten, and Mark A. Kempner. "Training of Planning Personnel for Local and State Agencies," Cincinnati University, OH, 1975, 5 p.

Functioning of health systems agencies is considered in relation to the training of planning personnel for local and state units. Competencies that health planning personnel need to function effectively as planners and educators are noted, including technical orientation, managerial orientation, and humanistic orientation. P/D.

Wakefield, Beverly. "Perception and Communication," Speech Communication Association, Falls Church, VA, 1976, 32 p. ERIC ED 125-011.

Provides a summary of perception research and suggestions for practical application to improve student-teacher communication ability. The basic principles of perception included are: continuity, proximity, perceptual constancy, and figure-ground relationship. Applicable in training environments. T/C.

Warsylik, James E. *et al.* "Communication Training as Perceived by Training Personnel," *Communication Quarterly,* Vol. 24, No. 1, 1976, pp. 32-38.

Cites a study designed to quantify the nature and extent of in-house communications training and presents data collected from individuals who conduct such training. FS.

Wholey, Joseph S. and Alease M. Vaughn. "Directory of Evaluation Training Resources Relevant to the HRA Evaluation Training Design," avail. Urban Institute, Washington, DC, September 1976, 82 p. Contract PHS-HRA-230-75-0202.

Describes the training plan that HRA, working with the Urban Institute developed over the past year. The plan includes seven training modules, four which were pilot tested, planning evaluation, designing evaluation, data collection and analysis techniques, and evaluation techniques for managers. P/D.

Wilkinson, W. Roderick "Watch Your Language as You Train," *Supervision*, Vol. 39, No. 3, March 1977, p. 4-5.

Recommends that a manager plan conversations with subordinates as carefully as any other department operation to keep people ready for promotion. A personnel director form Scotland, the author offers several examples of how to do it. P/D.

Wittmer, Joe *et al.* "Race Relations Training with Correctional Officers," *Personnel and Guidance Journal,* Vol. 54, No. 6, February 1976, pp. 302-306.

Presents a model intended to assist correctional counselors and others in facilitating communication among prison guards of a different race from inmates, and, further, to illustrate how to train guards in the fundamentals of developing a helping relationship with inmates. T/C.

Yorks, Lyle "Managing Professional Relationships: I—Communication Skills; II—Influencing Skills," *Journal of Systems Management,* Vol. 28, No. 1, January 1977, p. 6-11; No. 3, and March 1977, p. 6-11.

Suggests I) how to insure getting heard with a proposal considering the great difference in communication styles (intuitor, thinker, feeler, and senser), and II) how to use an influencing model, rather than a adversary model, to win the commitment of others to work with change. P/D.

(No author; alphabetized by title)

"Developing Your Own Transactional Anaysis Training Program," *Training Officer,* Vol. 12, No. 1, January 1976, pp. 6, 8.

Discusses a four-phase program recently completed by the New York Telephone Company to improve its customer relations, through the development of a transactional analysis training program for its employees. P/D.

"Final Training Program Report. Arizona Department of Economic Security. Background Information," 1973, 27 p.

Documents the development of a staff orientation and training program to enhance the services integration efforts of the Arizona Department of Economic Security. Outlines the development of training objectives and of a four-phase orientation program to meet immediate needs. The training concepts were consistent with the department's policy on decentralization and were compatible with a commitment to management by objectives. P/D.

"Guidelines for Staff Development," avail. American Nurses' Association, Kansas City, MO, 1976, 15 p.

Outlines guidelines for the implementation, evaluation, and organization of educational programs for nursing personnel in health care agencies. The concepts presented are applicable to all agencies regardless of the size, location, and nature of the patient population. P/D.

"Integration of Services is a Process, Not a Product," San Jose State University, CA. Joint Center for Human Services Development, Vol. 77, No. 15, 160 p. SHR-0001 74/ES.

Establishes five objectives of the Training for the Integration of Services project which allows individuals to improve the processes by which they manage, plan, and integrate programs. Probabilities for the integration of individual, task, group, and organizational services are presented in the findings. P/D.

"National Project on Education for Management, Volume II," avail. Pennsylvania University, Philadelphia, May 1975, 188 p. Grant SRS-47-90040.

Outlines suggested courses to be undertaken by schools of social work and business in a study sponsored by the National Project on Education for Management of Social Welfare. Provides a proposed syllabus for a course on the management of conflict and change. Outlines educational objectives for management influence and leadership. Describes a general influence model which indicates that people will respond to an influencer/manager/change agent only when it will result in need satisfaction. P/D.

"Needs Assessment Training Package for the Utah State Department of Social Services. (The Designated Title XX Agency)," avail. Research Group, Inc., Atlanta, GA, November 1975, 73 p.

Presents training guidelines and materials for use in a two-day needs assessment training session for participants of the Utah State Department of Social Services needs assessment efforts. The manual presents a definition of needs assessment, including structured and unstructured surveys and interviews. P/D.

"Personnel Needs and Training for Biomedical and Behavioral Research, 1976 Report," National Research Council, Washington, DC, June 28, 1976, 252 p. Contract N01-OD-5-2109.

Reviews recommendations for federal training support levels in behavioral and biomedical fields. P/D.

"Teaching the Boss to Write," *Business Week*, No. 2455, October 25, 1976, p. 56, 58.

Points out that written reports in business are usually overlong and poorly done. Courses to teach executives to write are increasing in number. The complaint heard most often deals with the lack of purpose and conclusions in the reports. P/D.

SEE ALSO

Interpersonal Variables: Allen, Bell, "Developing Your Own Transactional Analysis Training Program," Entine, Rosenfeld & Civikly

Intragroup Variables: Purinton, Schindler-Rainman & Lippitt & Cole, Whitmore

Intergroup Variables: "Communicating During Negotiations/Strikes," Georges, "Employee Relations: Who Holds the Trump Card?," Hundley, Mauser, Maloney & Ekstrom & Lansdale

Communication Factors and Organizational Goals: Elsasser, Filson, Hall & Baker, Hansen *et al.,* Ivancevich, Joslin, Odiorne, Shelby, "Training Program in Gerontology & Voluntarism," Zenger

Media: Software & Hardware: Berkman, Braga, Bretz, Burns, Carlisle, Cathcart, Fears, Fisher, Max, Post & Price & Difeley, Schramm, Wells, Winfrey

Research Methodology: Ettlie, "Occupational Employment in Manufacturing Industries," Yelland

Texts, Anthologies, Reviews, and General Bibliographies: Brennan, Bowman & Branchaw, Finch & H. R. Jones & Litterer, Harris & Karp, J. E. Jones & Pfeiffer, Pickett & Laster, Vogel & Brooks

COMMUNICATION MEDIA IN ORGANIZATIONS: SOFTWARE AND HARDWARE

BOOKS AND DISSERTATIONS

Berman, William F. *Management By Objectives in Community College Student Personnel Departments: An Exploratory Study.* Ed.D. Dissertation, State University of New York—Albany, 1976. DAI, Vol. 37, No. 11, p. 6917-A.

Observes no significant differences in managerial effectiveness of community colleges using management by objectives. FS.

Bhandari, Labdhi P. R. *Communications for Social Marketing: A Methodology for Developing Communication Appeals for Family Planning Programs.* Ph.D. Dissertation, Columbia University, 1976. DAI, Vol. 37, No. 7, p. 4462-A.

Indicates a relationship between the recognition of value hierarchies of target populations and the success of the social program; and the need for communications designed to combat negative feelings towards proposed social programs. FS.

Boland, Richard J., Jr. *Protocols of Interaction in the Design of Information Systems: An Evaluation of the Role of the Systems Analyst in Determining Information Requirements.* Ph.D. Dissertation, Case Western Reserve University, 1976. DAI, Vol. 37, No. 12, p. 7837-A.

Examines two systems of analyst and user interaction in designing information systems, concluding that a high degree of analyst-user interaction is superior to the traditional approach wherein the analyst is more detached from the user. Teams using the first approach were found to have a higher level of conceptual agreement and a higher level of learning by both analyst and user. FS.

Brooks, Claire. *Practices and Perceptions in School-Media Relations in the Midwest.* Ph.D. Dissertation, Iowa State University, 1976. DAI, Vol. 37, No. 7, p. 4005-A.

Indicates that school superintendents, daily newspaper editors, and television news directors viewed finance-related news items as the most important items in school-media relations. Television news directors viewed school news items as less important than did school superintendents or newspaper editors. FS.

Burton, Phillip W. and Robert Miller. *Advertising Fundamentals*, 2nd edi-edition Columbus, OH: Grid, Inc., 1976.

An extensive (688 pages) coverage of the subject designed for college students. Topics discussed include: media planning, media research, marketing research findings, and creativity. P/D.

Carter, Meredith L. *Effects of a Management-by-Objectives System in Public Two-Year Community Colleges.* Ed.D. Dissertation, Ball State University, 1976. DAI, Vol. 37, No. 10, p. 6228-A.

Reports positive attitudes by administrators towards management-by-objectives, although some negative reactions were generated by time pressures, paperwork, and difficulty in setting objectives. FS.

Cerveny, Robert P. *The Effects of a Computerized Information System on Managerial Behavior and Attitudes: A Comparative Study of Corporate Risk Subscribers and Non Subscribers.* Ph.D. Dissertation, The University of Texas—Austin, 1976. DAI, Vol. 37, No. 5, p. 3007-A.

Notes that insurance companies using a computerized information retrieval system lowered their average cost-per-claim significantly after the advent of the retrieval system. FS.

Craft, Guy C. *Communications Network Systems in Selected Negro State Supported College and University Libraries.* Ph.D. Dissertation, Southern Illinois University, 1976. DAI, Vol. 37, No. 9, p. 5474-A.

Indicates that a majority of Negro college libraries favored membership in an automated communication network system, although such a system would require staff and organizational changes. FS.

Cureton, Robert D. *A Methodological Comparison of Telephone and Face-to-Face Interviewing for Political Public Opinion Polling.* Ph.D. Dissertation, Southern Illinois University, 1976. DAI, Vol. 37, No. 9, p. 5437-A.

Reports that telephone interviewing and face-to-face interviewing produced similar data, but the face-to-face method derived added information and a more positive response by the interviewees. FS.

Diran, Kevin M. *Human Acceptance of Management Information Systems in Colleges and Universities: A Case Study.* Ed.D. Dissertation, Columbia University Teachers College, 1977. DAI, Vol. 37, No. 12, p. 7560-A.

Analyzes failure of management information system in a large college. Finds failure attributable to assumptions that system would not alter human power structure, and that "obvious benefits" would engender support. Additional fault was found with the unattainable expectations promised by the system's proponents. FS.

Geary, William T. *An Examination of Expert-Client Interaction in Management Information Systems Design Activities Using a Role Theoretic Approach.* Ph.D. Dissertation, Northwestern University, 1976. DAI, Vol. 37, No. 11, p. 6815-A.

Discerns that perceived organizational support for management information systems is most important correlative with perceived success in the system. Little difference was found between groups involving project teams and groups relying on less structured teams. FS.

Gehrmann, Paul R. *A Study To Identify Contingent Functional Relationships Between An Organization's External Environment and Its Design of Effective Management Information Systems.* Ph.D. Dissertation, The University of Nebraska—Lincoln, 1976. DAI, Vol. 38, No. 1, p. 366-A.

Finds that the external environment plays an important role in management information system design, and the effective application of such design. FS.

Johnson, David C. *A Review of the Implementation of Management by Objectives in a Large Suburban School District.* Ph.D. Dissertation, Michigan State University, 1976. DAI, Vol. 37, No. 6, p. 3304-A.

Reports that administrators in a suburban school district view the management by objectives program as not having met its original objectives and interfering with their regular work routine. The program's failure is ascribed to a lack of organizational objectives, coordination, in-service preparation, and communications. FS.

Jump, Clifford O. *The Development of a Management Information System for Area Vocational Education Centers in Michigan as Demonstrated at the Calhoun Area Vocational Center.* Ph.D. Dissertation, Michigan State University, 1976. DAI, Vol. 37, No. 9, p. 5778-A.

Stresses the need for prior training of personnel involved in the development and implementation of management information systems. FS.

Kidane, Amdetsion. *The Adequacy of EXIR as an Information Storage and Retrieval System for Student Records.* DBA Dissertation, University of Colorado—Boulder, 1976. DAI, Vol. 37, No. 8, p. 5226-A.

Finds that EXIR (Executive Information Retrieval) is an inadequate method of storing and retrieving student records. Disadvantages include the need for numerous individual data-banks and the lack of clarity of some responses. FS.

Kroeber, Donald W. *An Empirical Study of the Current State of Information Systems Evolution.* Ph.D. Dissertation, University of Georgia, 1976. DAI, Vol. 37, No. 12, p. 7841-A.

Indicates a strong relationship between sophistication level and performance level of computer systems. Constructs a matrix involving the interaction of systems technology and performance; and appraises the current level of information systems evolution. FS.

Leach, James B. *The Development of an Operational Process Model for Developing a Policy Manual for State Boards of Education.* Ed.D. Dissertation, The University of Alabama, 1976. DAI, Vol. 37, No. 12, p. 7442-A.

Reports need for state boards of education to develop policy manuals, stressing the necessity for preliminary meetings and continuous policy drafting. T/C.

Lewis, Rodney J. *Administrative Perception of Management-By-Objectives Principles, Practices, and Plans in the Public School Systems Holding Membership in the Northern Illinois Cooperative in Education.* Ed.D. Dissertation, Northern Illinois University, 1976. DAI, Vol. 37, No. 8, p. 4753-A.

Notes that school superintendents and principals disagreed as to certain practices and plans of management-by-objectives while agreeing with the program's principles. Indicates that full implementation of the program cannot occur until such differences are reconciled. FS.

London, Keith R. *The People Side of Systems.* New York: McGraw-Hill, 1976.

Looks at people at work and the general problems and solutions of organizing computer systems development work. Describes methods for carrying out people oriented tasks, and discusses methods to improve communications within a project team and with the project leader. P/D.

Lyons, Arland W. *The Identification of Media Professionals in Selected Business and Industrial Concerns in Texas and the Media Competencies Needed by Such Professionals.* Ed.D. Dissertation, East Texas State University, 1976. DAI, Vol. 37, No. 11, p. 6910-A.

Discusses the role of media professionals in business and industry, noting their need for a comprehensive background in communications. FS.

McClurg, Ronald B. *An Exploratory Pilot Study of the Development and Utilization of Computer Assisted Management Information Systems in Public Higher Education.* Ph.D. Dissertation, Iowa State University, 1977. DAI, Vol. 38, No. 2, p. 662-A.

Concludes that computer assisted management information systems in public higher education are not being utilized to maximum potential. Institutions reported various problems in the operation of a "complete" system, including general financial constraints, hardware acquisition investments and personal policy conflicts. FS.

McIntosh, Donald W. *Techniques of Business Communication.* 2nd edition. Boston, MA: Holbrook Press, 1977.

Emphasizes communication skills. Includes introductory chapters on communication concepts. The letter writing chapters include format, organization, revision, tone, and persuasiveness. Also includes chapters on report writing and oral communication. P/D.

Mclean, E. R. and J. V. Soden. *Strategic Planning for MIS.* New York: Wiley and Sons, 1977.

Gives methods and procedures for system planning, installation, maintenance, and operation. Shows procedures for improved long-term planning. Explains processes for producing effective plans. Projects possible problems so that they may be avoided. P/D.

Murdick, Robert G. and Joel E. Ross. *Introduction to Management Information Systems.* Englewood Cliffs, NJ: Prentice-Hall, 1977.

Focuses on management. Presents an introduction to the area and illustrates many charts, tables, and diagrams to help the individual at the beginning level. P/D.

Phillips, Bonnie D. *Effective Business Communication.* New York: Van Nostrand Reinhold, 1977.

Includes chapters on listening and oral communication, but emphasizes written communication. Its chapters on writing skills include grammar, effectiveness, mechanics, and revisions. It also includes chapters on letter writing and report writing. P/D.

Reck, John D. *Systems Analysis and the Development of Management Information Systems in California Community Colleges.* Ph.D. Dissertation, University of Southern California, 1976. DAI, Vol. 37, No. 9, p. 5508-A.

Reports that a computer-based management information system designed to collect, store, organize, and retrieve data is an effective tool in community colleges. FS.

Roberts, Adrian R., Jr. *A Study of the Use of an Electronic Feedback System in the Decision-Making Process of Selected North Carolina School Districts.* Ed.D. Dissertation, Duke University, 1976. DAI, Vol. 37, No. 7, p. 4043-A.

Reports that an electronic feedback system, called Anonymous Audience Response System (AARS) was an aid in all phases of the decision-making process. The system was found to be more valuable in the final phases than in the initial phases of decision-making. FS.

Roman, Kenneth and Jane Mass. *How to Advertise.* New York: St. Martin's Press, 1976.

Provides a series of guidelines for effective advertising. In addition to marketing, the authors discuss media selection, media production, media planning, campaigns, and advertising testing. P/D.

Ryan, Edward J., Jr. *Management by Objectives in Perspective: A Comparative Study of Selected Federal Experience with the Fiscal Year 1975 Program.* DBA Dissertation, The George Washington University, 1976. DAI Vol. 37, No. 5, p. 3025-A.

Surveys federal involvement in mangement by objectives programs and is critical of the lack of success of such programs and the lack of commitment by various federal agencies to the programs, suggesting that extension of management by objectives in the federal government appears unlikely. FS.

Scaggs, Edward W. *A Study of the Effects of Management by Objectives on the Self Concept of Headstart Directors and Their Administrative*

Staff in the State of Missouri. Ph.D. Dissertation, Kansas State University, 1976. DAI, Vol. 37, No. 9, p. 5511-A.

Finds that the use of management-by-objectives had a significant effect on the self-concept of government agency directors. FS.

Schramm, Wilbur. *Big Media, Little Media: Tools and Technologies for Instruction.* Beverly Hills, CA: Sage Publications, 1977.

Covers both theoretical aspects of instruction and pragmatics of implementing instructional strategies. Topics include economics of instruction, instruction evaluation, nonformal education, and multi-media comparisons. Designed for practitioners in the area of educational media. P/D.

Shutt, Bruce T. *An Evaluation of the Indiana University Management Information System.* Ed.D. Dissertation, Indiana University, 1976. DAI, Vol. 37, No. 8, p. 4907-A.

Concludes that university top-management failed to assume responsibility for planning, guidance, and development of the management information system. FS.

Simpson, Kawanna J. *Error Acceptability in Written Business Communication as Perceived by Business Educators and by Business Communicators.* Ed.D. Dissertation, University of Kentucky, 1976. DAI, Vol. 38, No. 2, p. 600-A.

Finds no difference between perceptions of business educators and business communicators with regard to error acceptability in written business communication. Business educators, however, were less inclined to allow errors to be mailed. FS.

Smith, Harry R. *Decision Making in a Simulated Operating Environment: An Experimental Investigation of Computerized Data Inquiry Techniques.* Ph.D. Dissertation, University of Minnesota, 1975. DAI, Vol. 37, No. 6, p. 3759-A.

Examines various forms of database inquiry (basic, extended alphanumeric reformating, extended graphical reformating) and concludes that the extended forms are not associated with improved performance. Little differences were observed among the three treatments in terms of attitudes toward man-machine systems. LS.

Spiegler, Israel. *A Computer Aided Methodology for Bridging Analysis and Construction in the Design of Information Processing Systems.* Ph.D. Dissertation, University of California, Los Angeles, 1977. DAI, Vol. 37, No. 12, p. 7848-A.

Proposes a methodology for linking three conventional methods of building information processing systems (Information System Design and Optimization System, the Relational Model, and Data Base Management Systems) to accomplish a complete system development. Indicates that such a linkage would diminish difficulties as to cost, documentation, updating, and coordination. T/C.

Springer, Kenneth W. *Judgments of Selected Public School Administrators Regarding Expected Benefits Resulting from Management by Objectives Programs.* Ed.D. Dissertation, Ball State University, 1976. DAI, Vol. 37, No. 10, p. 6203-A.

Reports that implementation of a management-by-objectives program in Pennsylvania school districts did not insure the solution of administrative problems. Central office administrators were more supportive than lower-level administrators. FS.

Spurgat, Frederick A. *A Comparative Study of the Implementation and Use of Management Information Systems in a Federal Research Agency: Factors Affecting User Acceptance.* Ph.D. Dissertation, Northwestern University, 1976. DAI, Vol. 37, No. 7, p. 4483-A.

Notes that the use of management information systems (MIS) in a federal agency showed the interdependence of three groups: the administrative/functional group, the manager/client/user group, and the technical designer group. FS.

Terry, James P. *A Survey of Electronic Data Processing Usage in the Public School Districts in the State of Texas.* Ed.D. Dissertation, East Texas State University, 1976. DAI, Vol. 37, No. 5, p. 2573-A.

Finds that the larger the school district, the greater the use of electronic data processing in Texas school districts. Administrative applications of electronic data processing greatly outnumbered instructional applications. FS.

Troisi, Grace A. *Management by Objectives: A Study of the Implementation of a Management Process in an Inner City Public School District.* Ed.D. Dissertation, Columbia University Teachers College, 1976. DAI, Vol. 37, No. 10, p. 6206-A.

Maintains that the adaptation of management-by-objectives programs from business to school settings is far more complicated than indicated in earlier studies. Problems center around the school organizational structure, the authoritarian mode of school administration, and the excessive retraining needed. A seven-point program is presented to overcome these problems. FS.

Trotta, Maurice. *Handling Grievances: A Guide for Management and Labor.* Washington, DC: The Bureau of National Affairs, Inc., 1976.

Shows what causes grievances in the work places, how to avoid them, and how to settle them peacefully when they arise. Views grievances as rooted in human nature as it interacts with "company climate." P/D.

Ulanoff, Stanley M. *Advertising in America: An Introduction to Persuasive Communication.* New York: Hastings House, 1977.

Emphasis is on media evaluation and use. Includes topics such as copywriting, layout, organizational structure, and campaigns. P/D.

Vanzandt, Claire E. *The Effects of the Management by Objectives Account-ability Model on Student and Teacher Evaluations of a Selected School Guidance Program in Maine.* Ed.D. Dissertation, University of Maine, 1976. DAI, Vol. 37, No. 10, p. 6286-A.

Determines that a management-by-objectives accountability model of guidance services needs further research to assess its reliability and valid-ity; and stresses the need for communication during the evaluation phase of the program. FS.

Waller, Thomas C., Jr. *The Budgetary Control of the Development of Man-agement Information Systems.* Ph.D. Dissertation, University of Hous-ton, 1977. DAI, Vol. 38, No. 3, p. 1488-A.

Evaluates budgetary control of management information systems, em-phasizing need for close linkage between corporate and system develop-ment. FS.

Walstrom, John A. J. *An Investigation of Outcome Information in Manage-ment Information Systems for Higher Education.* Ph.D. Dissertation, The University of Nebraska—Lincoln, 1976. DAI, Vol. 38, No. 1, p. 66-A.

Reports that management information systems in universities were used for many purposes, including instructor evaluation and program evalua-tion. Such evaluations, however, were not generally conducted at regu-lar intervals. FS.

Wells, Walter. *Communications in Business.* Second Edition. Belmont, CA: Wadsworth Publishing Company, 1977.

Primarily discusses writing for business organizations. Includes chapters on letters, memos, style, sentences, paragraphs, job applications, report writing, and oral communication. Also includes recommended letter forms, common abbreviations, and glossary, as well as a grammar, spell-ing, and punctuation guide. P/D.

Winfrey, R. *Technical and Business Report Preparation.* Ames, IA: Iowa State University Press, 1976.

Includes discussions of report preparation, correspondence, table pre-sentation, laboratory reports, abbreviations, interviews, and verbal reports. P/D.

Wolfe, Michael N. *An Investigation into Computerized Personnel Manage-ment Information Systems: A Prescriptive Model.* Ph.D. Dissertation, University of Massachusetts, 1977. DAI, Vol. 38, No. 1, p 373-A.

Reports that computer use in the personnel function was directly related to company size. Corporate divisions reported a greater use of comput-erized information systems than did independent corporations. FS.

Worthington, James S. *An Analysis of the Readability of Footnotes to Financial Statements and Recommendations for Their Improvement.* Ph.D. Dissertation, University of Missouri—Columbia, 1976. DAI, Vol. 37, No. 9, p. 5906-A.

Indicates that financial statement footnotes are generally difficult to comprehend by the average investor; and recommends that footnotes consist of short sentences with understandable vocabulary geared to the audience. T/C.

ARTICLES, PAPERS, AND U.S. GOVERNMENT PUBLICATIONS

Alderson, John W. and Robert D. Hay. "The Effect of Order of Information in a Questionnaire Cover Letter," *The Journal of Business Communication*, Vol. 13, No. 2, Winter 1976, pp. 11-15.

Determines if a relationship exists between the order of information in a specific persuasive request letter situation and the effectiveness of the message. LS.

Alter, Steven L. "How Effective Managers Use Information Systems," *Harvard Business Review*, Vol. 54, No. 6, November-December 1976, pp. 97-104.

Demonstrates how managers can use computers to help them make decisions, support their decisions, and help communicate them. Explains and gives examples of the seven types of computer support systems. P/D.

Bagin, Don *et al.* "PR for School Board Members. A Guide for Members of Boards of Education and School Administrators to Improve and Strengthen School Information Programs," 1976, 74 p. ERIC ED 127-656.

A handbook designed to inform school boards of the need for effective communication and to offer suggestions for establishing constructive contact with public and school personnel. P/D.

Berkman, Dave. "Instructional Television: The Media Whose Future Has Passed?" *Educational Technology*, Vol. 16, No. 5, May 1976. pp. 39-44.

Presents reasons why television has never been an integral part of instruction, and why it will not be in the future. P/D.

Bretz, Rudy. "In-School Television and the New Technology," *Educational Technology*, Vol. 16, No. 5, May 1976, pp. 50-53.

Discusses how video and television technology has advanced and is being used in the schools as an example of educational innovation. P/D.

Burns, Richard W. "Instructional Television, Interaction and Learning Objectives," *Educational Technology*, Vol. 16, No. 5, May 1976, pp. 39-44.

Discusses some basic research questions for learning and television, including media and interaction objectives. T/C.

Carlisle, Robert D. B. "A Matter of Access," *Change*, Vol. 8, No. 5, June 1976. pp. 54-55.

Describes briefly the association of Godmark Communications Corporation (GCC) and the Association of Community College for Excellence in Systems and Services (ACCESS), and six community college districts across the country which will utilize Rapid Transmission Storage Mark I system to deliver videotaped courses to students at off-campus learning centers. P/D.

Carlson, Eric D. "Decision Support Systems: Personal Computing Services for Managers," *Management Review*, Vol. 66, No. 1, January 1977, pp. 4-11.

Discusses decision support systems (DSS), a new way to use computers to aid managers in retrieving, manipulating, and displaying information needed for decisions. Describes what components a DSS needs, the technical requirements, how managers can use them, and DSS's future. P/D.

Cathcart, William L. "The Exciting Future of Industrial Television," 1976, 7 p. ERIC ED 122-320.

Describes the kinds of jobs available in the industrial television field and discusses internship as an effective means for preparing students for a career in industrial television. Advocates that teachers assist interested students in adequate course preparation to meet the required needs of industrial television. P/D.

Cross, Edwin L. "Management Information System for the U.S. Army Satellite Communications Agency," Defense Systems Management School, Fort Belvoir, VA, May 1976, 44 p.

Reviews the potential benefits of implementing a central computerized Management Information System (MIS). Development of such a system is discussed. T/C.

Deutsch, Arnold R. "Does Your Company Practice Affirmative Action in Its Communications?" *Harvard Business Review*, Vol. 54, No. 6, November-December 1976, pp. 16+.

Points out how an organization loses credibility and alienates consumers, decision makers, and present and future employees when its communications (advertising, speeches, literature, in-house publications, letters) are discriminatory. Explains how changes can be made. P/D.

Fisher, Thomas J. *et al.* "Increasing Information-Seeking Behavior with a Model-Reinforced Videotape," *Journal of Counseling Psychology*, Vol. 23, No. 3, May 1976, pp. 234-237.

Studies the effects of a model-reinforced videotape in increasing vocational information-seeking behavior in an outreach, self-instruction-oriented career information resource center for college students. Results showed increased type and frequency of information-seeking behavior for students viewing the model videotape. FS.

Flory, Abram III. "The Computer in Public Personnel Administration—A Fifty State Study," Arizona Personnel Operations and Employment Relations, Phoenix, January 1976, 55 p.

Examines personnel functions in terms of computerization. Additional factors were examined that promoted, hindered, or had little effect upon computer applications. FS.

Grace, Gloria L. *et al.* "Navy Career Counseling Research: Evaluation of Multi-Media Career Counseling Materials," System Development Corp., Santa Monica, CA, September 1976, 168 p. Contract N00014-75-C-0311.

Evaluates the effectiveness of four multi-media presentations designed to support the Navy Career Counseling Program, and obtains additional data relative to the importance, adequacy, and flow of information relevant to objectives of the Navy Career Counseling program.

Herzlinger, Regina. "Why Data Systems in Nonprofit Organizations Fail," *Harvard Business Review*, Vol. 55, No. 1, January-February 1977, pp. 81-86.

Cites numerous examples of how nonprofit organizations, both governmental and private, misuse, underuse, or fail to use information and control systems. Consequently, they make uninformed decisions and are unable to evaluate performances, motivate employees, and protect themselves against fraud. Offers solutions and guidelines to prevent this.P/D.

Hills, James W. "Look It Up—Or Can You?" *Business Horizons*, Vol. 20, No. 2, April 1977, pp. 61-68.

Calls for business managers to find a comprehensive management communication index to help keep abreast of the field. It presents still another way to structure written communication. P/D.

Hoffman, Norbert. "Information Retrieval System Retrieved? An Alternative to Present Dial Access Systems," *Audio Visual Learning*, Vol. 14, No. 1, Spring 1976, pp. 9-14.

The expenses of a dial access information retrieval system (DAIRS) are weighed against its benefits. Problems of usage and efficacy for the student are outlined. A fully automated system is proposed, and its cost-saving features are pointed out. P/D.

Lunine, Leo R. "Procedure Writer as a Catalyst for Implementing Change," *Technical Communication*, Vol. 23, No. 4 (4th quarter) 1976, pp. 10-11.

Identifies one task of the corporate procedure writers as that of forcing change in an organization. The writer must interact with employees throughout the organization, doing much more than merely write. P/D.

Max, Robert R. "What's Your Communications 'IQ'?" *Supervisory Management*, Vol. 22, No. 4, April 1977, pp. 12-15.

Warns managers that the majority of the $70 billion expended annually on written messages alone gets wasted because readers miss the point. "Profile" the intended receiver and proofread the finished message are main recommendations. P/D.

McGough, Dixie P. "Tie-Line. Statewide Information and Referral Project," Georgia Department of Human Resources, Atlanta, GA, August 1975, 319 p. Grant 12-57655.

Presents the two-year experience of a statewide, telephone-accessed information and referral system called Tie-line that operated from a centralized location. Tie-line was perceived as an input system, but not as an output system. Results indicate that citizens from all over the state used Tie-line for access to a wide variety of services, with significant use by low income residents, but underutilization by the elderly. Includes recommendations for use of system. FS.

Post, T., Harold Price, and Gary Diffley. "A Guide for Selection Formats and Media for Presenting Maintenance Information," Biotechnology Inc., Falls Church, VA, November 1976, 57 p. Contract N000600-76-C-1373.

Discusses a method for selecting formats and media to use in presenting maintenance information. This method is recommended for program management personnel/equipment component engineers at the early stages of system development when TM decisions are made. P/D.

Puma, Michael. "Evaluation of the Status and Effectiveness of State and Local Human Services Information Systems. System Profile: Management and Social Services Information System (MSSIS)," Applied Management Sciences, Inc., Silver Spring, MD, 1976, 31 p. Contract DHEW-100-76-0010.

Describes the operational components and special features of the Wyoming MSSIS, supplying information on the hardware and software used, the role of data output, coordination and transfer activities, and staffing and training characteristics. FS.

Rizzo, William A. "Demonstration and Evaluation of a Microfiche-Based Audio/Visual System. Focus on the Trained Man," Orlando, FL, April 1977, 36 p. Contract TAEG-TM-77-2.

Discusses the cost effectiveness and feasibility of a microfiche-based audio/visual system. The study compares sound/microfiche programs to sound/slide programs. The use of sound/microfiche was preferred and recommended for further development. FS.

Schubeck, William. "Same Message, New Media," *American School and University*, Vol. 49, No. 3, November 1976, pp. 56, 58.

Describes how a video message display system similar to that used at airports to announce flight arrival and departure times replaced distracting public address announcements. P/D.

Spreitzer, Elmer A. "The Role of Informal Leaders Among Clients in a Comprehensive Rehabilitation Center," *Rehabilitation Counseling Bulletin*, Vol. 19, No. 3, March 1976, pp. 504-507.

Describes sources of informal peer influence among clients at an inpatient rehabilitation center. Findings show that the informal leaders among the clients had a positive influence that facilitated the rehabilitation process. Informal leaders, in some respects, functioned as "lay therapists" among their peers in reinforcing the therapeutic process. FS.

Sugarman, M. and James Neto. "A Systematized Approach to Using Jobseeker Information as a Means of Maintaining a Localized Job Search Information System," California State Employment Development Department, San Francisco, CA, July 1974, 250 p.

Reviews the various aspects of the Job Search Information System which was designed to increase job entry of Employment Service applicants. Results showed that more individuals found jobs through the direct participation of ES placements than through any other method. P/D.

Sylvia, Robert A. "TOSS: An Aerospace System That's GO for Manpower Planning," *Personnel*, Vol. 54, No. 1, January-February 1977, pp. 56-64.

Explains a computerized system that presents facts about a company's manpower. It reveals where people of various skills are, what they are doing, for how long, and where they will be needed in the future. TOSS's organization, application, capabilities, and efficiency are detailed. P/D.

Timm, Paul "The Bulletin Board: Economy and Effectiveness in Organizational Communication," *The Journal of Business Communication*, Vol. 13, No. 6, Winter 1976, pp. 37-44.

Deals with internal organizational communication, concentrating on the bulletin board as a valuable means of information dissemination. T/C.

Wuiff, J. Jepson and Michael Baker. "Human Service System Definition: The Preparation of a Feasibility Study Report," Human Ecology Institute, Wellesley, MA, January 1976, 177 p. Grant SRS-12-55947.

Presents guidelines for a system definition phase of human service system development, focusing on the production of a feasibility study report. The guide is intended for those who wish to install comprehensive integral human service systems that are responsive to the community. Disscusses the need for system definition and outlines a model of the development phase of a human services system. P/D.

(No author; alphabetized by title)

"Audiovisual Media Career Ladder, AFSCs 231xO, 231xOA, 231xOB, and 23192," Lackland AFB, TX, Air Force Occupational Measurement Center, March 1977, 66 p.

Discusses various aspects of the Audiovisual Media career ladder. It describes the administration and development of the instrument and includes summaries of tasks performed by airmen. Further study is recommended. P/D.

"Human Services Information System (HSIS) Project of Lancaster County. A Summary Statement: Volume XXIII," Human Services Information System Project of Lancaster County, PA, August 1974, 44 p.

Describes the five steps involved in the HSIS project. Expectations were that results could be used in the implementation of more efficient and effective arrangements for service agency operations. Summarizes key findings and recommendations of the HSIS project and describes the planning structure proposed to oversee future planning and implementation efforts. FS.

"Social Services Information System: Management Overview Manual," Colorado Department of Social Services, Denver Office of Information Systems, 1975, 54 p.

Provides an overview of the Social Services Information System (SSIS) of the Colorado Department of Social Services with an emphasis on the management and use of the system by local jurisdiction. Outlines management activities which contribute to a successful implementation of the system at the local level, including feedback to caseworkers concerning the system. P/D.

"Study of the Quality and Organization Structure of Information and Referral Services Presently Operating: Aggregate Report," Applied Management Sciences, Inc., Silver Spring, MD, August 1975, 72 p. Contract DHEW-OS-74-299.

Analyzes components of social service information and referral (I/R) systems, from the State agency on aging to the local I/R center, in an effort to assess the quality of the organizational structure of I/R services in terms of measurable benefits to the elderly. Four recommendations are proposed to the Administration on Aging. FS .

"TV that Competes with the Office Grapevine," *Business Week*, No. 2474, March 14, 1977, pp. 49, 51, 54.

Describes Ashland Oil Company's "CCTV newscasts" shown throughout eight facilities in order to send "factual accounts" of business activities to all employees. Top managers see advantages in dispelling mistaken rumors with this downward communication channel. P/D.

SEE ALSO

Intergroup Variables: Goble & Holiday, Roman & Mass, Ulanoff
Communication Factors and Organizational Goals: Schmid & Hovey
Skill Improvement and Training: Anderson, Bartel, Carpenter, D. S. & Herget, Carpenter, K. F. & Kroth, DeGise, Duffy & Miller & Staley, Hart & Reinking, McIntosh, McVeigh, Prentice, Silvern, "Teaching the Boss to Write," Wildberger & Hendershat
System Analysis: Kilgore, McLaughlin, Ramsgard
Texts, Anthologies, Reviews, and General Bibliographies: Bolch, et al., Hatch, Phillips

COMMUNICATION SYSTEM ANALYSIS
IN ORGANIZATIONS

BOOKS AND DISSERTATIONS

Alan, L. P. and A. J. Rowe, *Management Control and Decision Systems. Texts, Cases, and Readings.* New York: Wiley and Sons, 1977.

Discusses behavioral and technical aspects of control. Also discusses political realities of control and decision systems. Emphasizes behavioral and social environments in which controls may be applied, technical aspects of control systems and the political basis for control systems. Combines text, case histories, and readings. T/C.

Aragona, Louis. *The Functional Utilization of Information for Decision Making by Chief School Officers.* Ed.D. Dissertation, Columbia University Teachers College, 1976. DAI, Vol. 37, No. 9, p. 5463-A.

Notes that the "per pupil expenditure" status of a school district was not significantly related to information received by chief school officers relating to curriculum programs, costs, student achievement, and media use. FS.

Barker, Randolph T. *The Development and Implementation of a Communication Audit Related to Selected Systems Concepts.* Ph.D. Dissertation, The Florida State University, 1976. DAI, Vol. 37, No. 10, p. 6137-A.

Determines that barriers to communication flows exist between subsystems in a rural industrial plant, indicating that such barriers represent disruptions to production. FS.

Bonett, Herman R. *Information Processes in a State Legislative System: Kansas.* Ph.D. Dissertation, University of Kansas, 1976. DAI, Vol. 37, No. 8, p. 5322-A.

States that state legislators have greater difficulty in obtaining substantive information than procedural information. Major souces of substantive information were from outside the legislature. Verbal communication between peers was the principal method of the internal communication system. FS.

Bowey, Angela. *The Sociology of Organizations.* London: Hodder and Stroughton. 1976.

Adopts a cultural anthropological approach to the study of organizations. Concentrates on the human relations aspects of small organizations. Topics discussed include roles, systems theory, and relationships. T/C.

Brandt, Frederick A. *A Comparative Analysis of Management and Organizational Processes in Product and Service Organizations.* DBA

Dissertation, Arizona State University, 1976. DAI, Vol. 37, No. 7, p. 4463-A.

Reports that although product and service organizations have similar management and organizational systems, service managers were nearly unanimously dissatisfied with current practices, while product managers were much less dissatisfied. Variables included leadership, motivation, communication, decision-making, goal setting, and control. FS.

Brannen, Peter *et al. The Worker Directors: A Sociology of Participation.* Salem, NH: Hutchinson, 1976.

Provides a case study of the worker-director plan in the British Steel Corporation. Argues that worker participation in corporate management is not likely to result in significant social change. It is noted that workers and managers perceive the plan's purposes differently. P/D.

Burns, Tom R. and Walter Buckley. *Power and Control: Social Structures and Their Transformation.* Beverly Hills, CA: Sage Publications, Inc., 1976.

Presents ideas on social network theory; examining corporate interconnections through interlocking directorates; stability of structures, and case studies representing these. T/C.

Coburn, Dennis L. *The Relationship Between Organizational Climate and the Degree of Incongruence Between the Formal and Informal Communication Nets, Authority Structures and Goals in High Schools.* Ph.D. Dissertation, The University of Texas--Austin, 1976. DAI, Vol. 37, No. 5, p. 2734-A.

Finds that incongruence in the organizational dimension of formal and informal communication nets accounted for a significant portion of the variance in organizational climate. FS.

Coyle, R. G. *Management System Dynamics.* New York: Wiley and Sons, 1977.

Presents techniques of system dynamics. Examines the mechanisms in a company which can produce appropriate behavior when faced with change. Examines specific techniques for modeling change, as well as the analysis of modeling results. Explores the redesign of corporate policy. T/C.

Czander, William M. *The Relationship Between Organizational Climate and Bureaucracy of Community Health Service Delivery Organizations,* Ph.D. Dissertation, New York University, 1977. DAI, Vol. 38, No. 4, p. 1948-B.

As an organization increases in bureaucracy it moves from an open climate to a closed climate. Size is related to bureaucracy although it fails to affect the relationship between climate and bureaucracy. FS.

Duncan, Deirdre J. *A Study of Organizational Change: High School Budgeting.* Ph.D. Dissertation, The University of Manitoba Canada, 1976. DAI, Vol. 37, No. 11, p. 6867-A.

Determines that the success of organizational change depended on the presence of a skilled change agent who was either an outsider or had previous experience outside the system. The use of middle-level supervisors was important in the maintenance of communications links between administrators and teachers. FS.

Dunning, Christine M. *An Analysis of the Communication Structure of Three Police Organizations in Relation to Perceptions of the Department as Held by Its Members.* Ph.D. Dissertation, Michigan State University, 1976. DAI, Vol. 38, No. 1, p. 489-A.

Finds that lack of propinquity and lack of perceived ability to participate in decision and control processes negatively affected departmental communication. Communications tended to flow along the formal hierarchical structure. Job satisfaction correlated positively with horizontal and vertical communication satisfaction. FS.

Eich, Ritch K. *Organizational Communication Consulting: A Descriptive Study of Consultant Practices and Prescriptions.* Ph.D. Dissertation, The University of Michigan, 1977. DAI, Vol. 38, No. 3, p. 1118-A.

Examines the function of communication consultant and finds that this relatively new position is characterized by a lack of specific training. A need was indicated for supervised, practical organizational experience combined with classroom discussion. FS.

Gorodezky, Michael J. *Correlates of Management Information System Reporting Attitudes and Behavior.* Ph.D. Dissertation, The University of Michigan, 1976. DAI, Vol. 37, No. 6, p. 3908-A.

Reports no significant relationship between accurate input into management information systems (MIS) and the level of bureaucratization in the work setting. FS.

Hackathorn, Richard D. *Activity Analysis: A Methodology for the Discrete Process Modeling of Information Systems in Organizations with an Application to a Governmental Database.* Ph.D. Dissertation, University of California—Irvine, 1976. DAI, Vol. 37, No. 6, p. 3244-A.

Reports that the focusing upon the formalized information flows to a computerized database is an effective method of describing work flow activity. This methodology, called Activity Analysis, was found to be practical, useful, and potentially relevant to information systems theory. FS.

Herbst, P. G. *Alternative to Hierarchies.* Leiden Martinus Nijhoff Social Sciences Division of Humanities Press, 1976.

Discusses ways of decentralizing decision making in organizations. Emphasis is given to the process of diffusing such changes and their effect on worker satisfaction. T/C.

Kaye, Nancy L. *Assessing Communication Patterns and Attitudes of Special Education Management Personnel in a Technical Assistance Network.* Ph.D. Dissertation, The University of Michigan, 1976. DAI, Vol. 37, No. 10, p. 6403-A.

Finds that the development of an organizational communications system, called Statewide Technical Assistance Network in Special Education (STANSE), was a viable and worthwhile organizational innovation. FS.

Kilmann, Ralph. *Social Systems Design: Normative Theory and the MAPS Design.* New York: Elsevier North-Holland, 1977.

Argues that organizations should adopt control systems based on internal interaction. A system for doing this, MAPS—multivariate analysis, participation, and structure, is elaborated. The MAPS system is based on theories of humanistic psychology, statistics, and modeling. T/C.

Klein, Lisl. *A Social Scientist in Industry.* Gower Press, 1976.

Details experience in attempting to implement systematic programs of social scientific research in a large oil corporation, ESSO. Provides insight into the problems and possibilities of the role of "in-house" social scientist. P/D.

Koeing, Richard W., Jr. *A Longitudinal Analysis of the Relationship Between Participation, Feedback and Performance Efficiency in Organizational Planning.* Ph.D. Dissertation, Kent State University, 1976. DAI, Vol. 37, No. 10, p. 6804-A.

Determines that participation and feedback during planning are highly specialized and limited purpose activities. Potential negative effects exist for each, and extreme care and extensive effort are needed to achieve positive results. FS.

Kusterer, Kenneth C. *Knowledge on the Job: Workers' Know-How and Everyday Survival in the Workplace.* Ph.D. Dissertation, Washington University, 1976. DAI, Vol. 36, No. 4, p. 2445-A.

Finds that the solution of work problems requires the establishment of communal networks throughout the work organization. Although these networks are found to be effective means by which workers are able to reduce their own alienation, they are fragile and can be easily disrupted by management decisions affecting the division of labor. FS.

Lambright, W. Henry. *Adoption and Utilization of Urban Technology: A Decision-Making Study. Analysis and Conclusions,* New York: Syracuse Research Corporation, January 1977.

Analyzes the organizational problem-solving process model; suggests that innovation occurs over stages, depending upon the capacity of local entrepreneurs to recognize the barriers that inhibit technology. T/C.

Lipshitz, Raanan. *The Effectiveness of Third Party Process Interventions Into Simulated Organizations as a Function of the Consultant's Prestige and Style of Intervention.* Ph.D. Dissertation, Purdue University, 1976. DAI, Vol. 37, No. 8, p. 4201-B.

Intervention is more likely to succeed in those areas on which the intervention is focused. Teams using process analysis, with or without consultation, improved more in work process and cohesiveness than controls. Third party facilitation is ineffective. Prestige of consultant has no effect. LS.

Lundy, Susan R. *Communication in Common Cause.* Ph.D. Dissertation, The University of Iowa, 1976. DAI, Vol. 37, No. 5, p. 2497-A.

Finds that Common Cause, a voluntary organization recruited through the use of mass media, attracts two types of members, the minimally committed and the potential activist. Suggests that the types of communication used (impersonal—mass mailings, news coverage, or advertisements; and personal—knowledge of present members) caused this diversity of membership. FS.

Mazzaroppi, Loretta L. *A Study to Develop Generally Accepted Standards for Use in Conducting Organizational Communication Audits Within Industrial Organizations.* Ph.D. Dissertation, The Louisiana State University and Agricultural and Mechanical College, 1976. DAI, Vol. 37, No. 6, p. 3754.

Finds that majority of firms surveyed did not conduct formal internal communications audits, some feeling that the audit would be valueless, and others lacking knowledge required to conduct audits. FS.

Mclean, E. R. and J. V. Soder. *Strategic Planning for MIS.* New York: Wiley & Sons, 1977.

Gives methods and procedures for system planning, installation, maintenance, and operation. Shows procedures for improved long-term planning. Explains processes for producing effective plans. Projects possible problems so that they may be avoided. P/D.

Midgley, D. F. *Innovation and New Product Marketing.* New York: Wiley and Sons, 1977.

Collects information about consumer behavior from different disciplines, then formulates and presents a general theory of innovative behavior applicable to diverse market situations. Demonstrates how the theory can be applied, indicating which management techniques are relevant to new product management. T/C.

Mirvis, P. H. and David N. Berg, eds. *Failures in Organization Development and Change: Cases and Essays for Learning.* New York: Wiley & Sons, 1977.

Discusses the failure of organization development and change projects. Includes cases and essays covering a range of organization development activities by private and public sector organizations. Explores the conditions which breed failure in organization development, the failings of change efforts, and ways to foster learning from failures. T/C.

Nelson, Kenneth E. *A System Analysis of Information and Communication in Beef Marketing.* Ph.D. Dissertation, Oklahoma State University, 1976. DAI, Vol. 37, No. 9, p. 5962-A.

Uses simulation and linear programming to study beef marketing and finds that ineffective communications regarding prices and production hindered moves to a more efficient marketing system. LS.

Nichols, Theo and Peter Armstrong. *Workers Divided: A Study in Shopfloor Politics.* London: Fontana/Collins, 1976.

Reports a three year study of worker politics in a large English chemical industry. Mainly a descriptive analysis of why there was no worker militancy in the observed organizations, e.g. work stoppages, strikes, overtime opposition. FS.

Papageorgio, Peter E. *Towards Developing a Grounded Theory Relative to Imposed Compliance: A Study of Faculty Administrators' Written Communication Regarding an Affirmative Action Program.* Ph.D. Dissertation, University of Colorado, 1976. DAI, Vol. 36, No. 4, p. 1873-A.

Evaluates through the use of faculty written communications, the attitudes of the writers towards an affirmative action program. The author concludes that faculty administrators' dispositions tend to cluster in specific dimensions. FS.

Pasmore, William A. *Understanding Organizational Change: A Longitudinal Investigation of the Effects of Socio-Technical System, Job Redesign, and Survey Feedback Interventions on Organizational Task Accomplishment and Human Fulfillment.* Ph.D. Dissertation, Purdue University, 1976. DAI, Vol. 37, No. 10, p. 6609-A.

Analyzes the interaction of socio-technical system, job redesign, and survey feedback in university department, noting that a combined socio-technical system-survey feedback intervention worked equally as well as a job redesign-survey feedback intervention in the areas of employee attitudes and job perceptions. Productivity increased only in the socio-technical system-survey feedback intervention. FS.

Pugh, C. S. and C. R. Hinings. *Organizational Structure: Extensions and Replications,* Saxon House, 1976.

This survey of 82 firms focuses on organizational size, structure, and technology. Concludes that structure is a function of size as opposed to technology. FS.

Ramsgard, W. C. *Making Systems Work.* New York: Wiley and Sons, 1977.

Examines systems specialists and data operations, offers a program for identifying problems, and develops a plan for achieving an information structure. Supplies training programs for systems analysts and management. P/D.

Roeber, Joe. *Social Change at Work: The ICI Weekly Staff Agreement.* New York: Halsted Press. 1975.

A descriptive study of a large scale innovation in a major British chemical corporation. Emphasizes immense efforts and costs involved with such an undertaking. FS.

Sanders, Janet S. *Utilization of Lines of Communication Within the Administration of the University of Kansas Described by ECCO Analysis.* Ph.D. Dissertation, University of Kansas, 1976. DAI, Vol. 37, No. 8, p. 4705-A.

Reports that higher level administrators tend to know more information, know more accurate information, and relay more information than lower level administrators. Discovers several communication networks within the university. FS.

Smith, Theodore A. *Dynamic Business Strategy: The Art of Planning for Success.* New York: McGraw-Hill, 1977.

Emphasizes economic aspects of business operations. Topics include: information needs, decision making, and information feedback. P/D.

Spencer, Wallace H. *Presidential Communication: Information and Decision-Making.* Ph.D. Dissertation, University of Washington, 1977. DAI, Vol. 38, No. 3, p. 1631-A.

Finds that President's use of the information system available to him shapes his role and his relationships with the members of the system. FS.

Tate, Sean A. *Conflict and Communication Slippage in an Educational-Exchange System.* Ph.D. Dissertation, University of Pittsburgh, 1976. DAI, Vol. 38, No. 1, p. 64-A.

Reports inadequate communication between faculty and administrative personnel in a university foreign exchange student program. FS.

Torres, Scottie. *A Macroscopic Intrapolicy Approach to Supplying Information to Decision Makers.* Ed.D. Dissertation, University of Massachusetts, 1976. DAI, Vol. 37, No. 9, p. 5520.

Develops a three-step information collecting procedure for government agencies: 1) ascertaining the decision areas of concern; 2) selecting the appropriate information to be used; and 3) collecting and analyzing the information to determine baselines. FS.

Wigand, Rolf T. *Communication and Interorganizational Relationships Among Complex Organizations in Social Service Settings.* Ph.D. Dissertation, Michigan State University, 1976. DAI, Vol. 37, No. 9, p. 5413-A.

Finds that a preliminary path-analytic model of interorganizational relationships did not achieve satisfactory results. However, an expanded model incorporating variables as communication and goal attainment, was statistically significant. FS.

Yeager, Samuel J., III. *Upward Communication in a Large Organization.* DPA Dissertation, University of Georgia, 1976. DAI, Vol. 37, No. 8, p. 5347-A.

Finds that a subordinate's trust in immediate superior had impact on perceived accuracy of communication, directionality of communications, and overall satisfaction with communications. A desire for promotion and perceived supervisory influence had little impact on these aspects of communications. FS.

ARTICLES, PAPERS, AND U.S. GOVERNMENT PUBLICATIONS

Aldrich, Howard and Diane Herker. "Boundary Spanning Roles and Organization Structure," *Academy of Management Review*, Vol. 2, No. 2, pp. 217-229.

The creation, elaboration, and functions of boundary spanning roles are examined, with attention to environmental and technological sources of variation. T/C.

Allais, Philippe and Pierre Rodocenachi. "Research and Its Networks of Communications," *Research Management*, Vol. 20, No. 1, January 1977, pp. 39-42.

Emphasizes how research has become a vital part of the business it serves, explaining that research departments must now improve lateral communication within the organization it serves. Includes importance of informal communication channels. P/D.

Bacharach, Samuel B. and Michael Aiken. "Communication in Administrative Bureaucracies," *Academy of Management Journal*, Vol. 20, No. 3, September, 1977, pp. 365-377.

Data was collected by interviews and questionnaires from 44 local administrative bureaucracies in Belgian cities. Structural features such as size and shape seem to have little effect upon the frequency of department head communication, but they do appear to predict subordinate communication. FS.

Bagin, Don. "Key Communicators—An Authorized Grapevine," *Journal of Communicaiton*, Vol. 1, No. 1, July-August 1975, pp. 27-29.

Key communicators—community members who come in contact with many people and who are informal information sources—can be used by the schools as sources of feedback from the community and as information disseminators. T/C.

Bailey, John E. III. "Educational Organization Evaluation Model," February 1975, 22 p. ERIC ED 133 355.

Presents a model for evaluating an educational organization. Model is concerned with determining the needs of the community and judging the results of the organization in terms of those needs. Looks at the organization in terms of its ability to generate new solutions and to keep that process going. T/C.

Baker, H. Kent and Ronald H. Gorman. "Diagnosis: Key to O. D. Effectiveness," *Personnel Journal*, Vol. 55, No. 10, October 1976, pp. 506-510.

Stresses the importance of correct diagnosis through data gathering, feedback, and joint diagnosis as opposed to guesswork. A case study is used to illustrate the importance of proper diagnosis. P/D.

Bass, B. M. "A Systems Survey Research Feedback for Management and Organizational Development," *Journal of Applied Behavioral Science*, Vol. 12, No. 2, 1975, pp. 215-229.

Describes a survey instrument that gives individualized feedback to participating managers about the system of inputs, superior-subordinate relations and outputs which they and their subordinates perceive as operating in their workgroup situation. Some evidence indicates the survey is effective in producing change. Manipulative bosses are downgraded, while consultative superiors are favored. FS.

Blaesser, Willard W. "Organization Change Strategies to Facilitate Student Development Models," paper presented at the Annual Meeting of the American College Personnel Association, Chicago, IL, April 1976, 21 p. ERIC ED 131 367.

Defines "student development" as emphasizing processes whereby instructors and student affairs persons collaborate to facilitate cognitive-affective development. Discusses the application of principles and practices of Organizational Development. T/C.

Bowers, D. G. "Organizational Development: Promises, Performances, Possibilities," *Organizational Dynamics*, Vol. 4, No. 4, Spring 1976, pp. 50-62.

Discusses the history, characteristics and consequences of organizational development (OD). Observable effects of OD have generally been temporary and insubstantial from a cost-benefits standpoint. OD is viewed as a fad marked by three characteristics: superficiality, commercialism, and incorrect assumptions about the role of the consultant. T/C.

Burke, W. W. "Organizational Development in Transition," *Journal of Applied Behavioral Science*, Vol. 12, No. 1, 1976, pp. 22-43.

Describes changes within organizational development during the past 12 years. Makes a series of recommendations about future needs. P/D.

Carlson, Howard C. "Organizational Research and Organizational Change: GM's Approach," *Personnel*, Vol. 54, No. 4, July-August 1977, pp. 11-22.

Describes an experimental organizational change program which was designed to pull together the concepts and strategies of research as intervention, providing the framework for a total research program likely to reduce barriers to change. P/D.

Cook, John. "Organizational Development: An Available Management Strategy, Army War College Carlisle Barracks, PA, November, 1976, 32 p.

Describes the techniques and strategies to be used in organizational development, focusing on a manager's effort to utilize human resources so that participants are motivated to work toward organizational objectives as a way of achieving their own goals. P/D.

Frame, Robert M. and Fred Luthans. "Merging Personnel and OD: A Not-So-Odd Couple," *Personnel*, Vol. 54, No. 1, January-February 1977, pp. 12-22.

Presents a case for merging OD as a personnel department's function. Defines OD and discusses some common misconceptions about it. Details potential problems, weighs advantages and disadvantages, and offers strategies for an effective merger. P/D.

Friedlander, F. "OD Reaches Adolescence: An Explanation of Its Underlying Values," *Journal of Applied Behavioral Science*, Vol. 12, No. 1, 1976, pp. 7-21.

Describes three values (relationalism, pragmatism, and existentialism) which underlie OD. T/C.

George, William W. "Task Teams for Rapid Growth," *Harvard Business Review*, Vol. 55, No. 2, March-April 1977, pp. 71-80.

A case history of how Litton Microwave Cooking Division adapted to rapid growth through task team organization. The structure, responsibilities, leadership, and steps in team building plus its problems are detailed. P/D.

Goyer, Robert S. "Communicative Process as a Behavioral System: Research Implications for Organizational Communication," paper prepared for the special edition of "Communication Journal of the Communication Association of the Pacific" compiled for the C.A.P. Convention Kobe, Japan, June 1976, 9 p. ERIC ED 127 652.

Suggests that two words "communication" and "process" be viewed together as the goal-oriented combination of variables designed to produce a single communicative event. In an organizational setting, the assessment of this process, seen as a behavioral system, lends itself to the use of a systems approach. T/C.

Grunig, James E. "A Progress Report on a Multi-Systems Theory of Communication Behavior," 1976, 32 p. ERIC ED 127 619.

Presents a multi-system theory of communication behavior to explain communication behavior of individuals and organization-related systems and subsystems. Also attempts to extend the theory to communities, families, and social systems. T/C.

Gyllenhammar, Pehr G. "How Volvo Adapts Work to People," *Harvard Business Review*, Vol. 55, No. 3, 1977, pp. 102-113.

Volvo has encouraged employees to organize their work in teams in an attempt to overcome dissatisfaction, absenteeism, antagonism, and job-hopping. FS. CS.

Hanson, Mark. "School Governance and the Professional/Bureaucratic Interface: A Case Study of Educational Decision-Making," paper presented at the Annual Meeting of the American Educational Research Association, San Francisco, CA, April 1976, 32 p. ERIC ED 125 124.

Presents the Interacting Spheres Model to clarify the decision-making ramifications of professional employees working in bureaucratic organizations. The model suggests the presence of two interacting spheres of influence, with some decisions formally delegated to administrators and others informally assumed by teachers. FS.

Heichberger, Robert L. "Creating the Climate for Humanistic Change in the Elementary School with Principal as Change Agent," *Education*, Vol. 96, No. 2, Winter 1975, pp. 106-112.

Suggests that three necessary components are prerequisite to educational change. They are: dynamic leadership, a philosophical base, and a positive environment. The purpose of this paper is to discuss these components and indicate why and how they can be made available in a given elementary school situation. P/D.

Housel, Thomas J. "Communication Channels, Anonymity and the Reduction of Upward Communication Distortion: A Controlled Field Study," 1976, 26 p. ERIC ED 130 356.

Presents an experimental study of the effects of different channel communication methods (face-to-face, telephone, and written) on four levels of management. Results indicate that the channel used lead to significant differences in subjects' satisfaction with the channel, their satisfaction with the upward communication, and their perceptions of how openly they communicated. FS.

Infelise, Robert. "The Management Team: Turning Concept and Theory into Reality," *Thrust for Education Leadership*, Vol. 5, No. 2, November 1975, pp. 19-21.

Describes the District Management Team, designed to reorganize the existing school system in such a manner that it becomes more responsive to the needs of the entire district, including the community it serves and to all personnel within its organization. P/D.

Jacobson, Harvey K. "Toward an Economy of Information for Organizations in a Limited-Growth Environment," paper presented at the Annual

Meeting of the International Communication Association, Portland, OR, April 1976, 20 p. ERIC ED 123 690.

Outlines a framework designed to provide concepts beneficial to managers who wish to identify problems, conduct evaluations, and design solutions. The paper reviews and analyzes research literature, concentrating on economics of information, examines strategies for organizational adjustment, and proposes areas deserving the attention of researchers and managers. T/C.

Kilgore, Leonard L. "Adaptation of Business and Industrial Technology to Education," *Balance Sheet*, Vol. 57, March 1976, pp. 266-267, 280.

Six guidelines which industry and business follow are presented to help teachers adopt new techniques in their programs. These include areas of administrative principles, equipment, and staff utilization. P/D.

Krivonos, Paul D. "A Brief Background of the ICA (International Communication Association) Audit," 1975, 17 p. ERIC ED 120 834.

Notes that the ICA audit establishes an integrated communication audit system and a multi-method approach to the auditing of organizational communication. Attempts to examine the strengths and weaknesses of the audit system to provide clients of the ICA audit with a better understanding of the nature of their communication and to provide maps of the operational communication network. P/D.

—————. "Distortion of Subordinate to Superior Communication in Organizational Settings," 1976, 18 p. ERIC ED 122 318.

Concerned with message biasing of upward communication in organizational hierarchies. Analyzes this distortion in actual messages from subordinates to superiors in simulated situations to determine the effects of favorable and unfavorable situations on message content. FS.

Lachenmeyer, Charles W. "A System for the Analysis, Evaluation, and Design of Organizations, Work, and Jobs," Saint John's University, Jamaica, NJ, 1977, 115 p.

Reviews a theory of the design of organizations and jobs. The job analytic system includes the evaluation of the performance of workers, the structure of the job, and the relation of the job with the organization. T/C.

Lederman, Linda Costigan and Don Rogers. "Parallel Evolution in Science: The Historical Roots and Central Concepts of General Systems Theory; and 'General Systems Theory,' 'Modern Organizational Theory,' and Organizational Communication," paper presented at the Annual Meeting of the Eastern Communication Association, Philadelphia, PA, March 1976, 60 p. ERIC ED 127 653.

Focuses on general systems theory. Discusses the emergence and evolution of general systems theory, and relates some of the important features of general systems theory and of modern organizational theory to organizational communication theory. T/C.

Leonard, LaVerne. "Better Communications Unsnarl Production Tie-Ups," *Production Engineering*, Vol. 24, No. 1, January 1977, pp. 61-65.

Relates experiences of OD change agents in the Pullman and Harper buffing businesses. Describes the confrontation meetings. Encourages managers to try OD studies (Yale research agents). FS.

Luthans, Fred and Todd I. Stewart. "A General Contingency Theory of Management," *Academy of Management Review*, Vol. 2, No. 2, 1977, pp. 181-195.

A contingency theory is introduced as an overall framework that integrates the diverse process, quantitative and behavioral approaches to management; incorporates the environment; and bridges the gap between theory and practice. T/C.

Martino, Joseph P. "Managing Engineers by Objectives," *IEEE Transactions in Engineering Management*, Vol. EM-23, No. 4, November 1976, pp. 168-174.

Relates a manager's first-hand experience running a medium-size engineering organization. Includes some of the associated problems with solutions. FS.

Maude, Barry. "The Team Builders," *Industrial Management*, London, October 1976, pp. 29-31, 36.

Reviews experiences of a management consultant with firms which include Japan's Matsushita, Britain's Supreme Life Assurance, and the USA's Levi Strauss. P/D.

McLaughlin, M. W. "Evaluating Innovations: The Case for a New Paradigm," *Journal of Career Education*, Vol. 2, No. 3, Winter 1976, pp. 78-90.

Discusses the Rand Corporation Change Agent, a study which suggests institutional and process factors (local materials development, on-line planning, and staff training). These factors and their implications are discussed. P/D.

Michman, Ronald D. and Lynn Harris. "The Development of Marketing Channel Communication Models," *The Journal of Business Communication*, Vol. 14, No. 1, Fall 1977, pp. 28-41.

Several models are used to explain how a communications network among marketing channel members might work. They are used to pinpoint the advantages of marketing coordination. T/C.

Nielsen, Warren R. and John R. Kimberly. "Designing Assessment Strategies for Organization Development," *Human Resources Management*, Vol. 15, No. 1, Spring 1976, pp. 32-39.

Argues that systematic empirical assessment of organizational development interventions is important and benefits both organizations and researchers. Discusses suggested criteria for effective assessment of OD interventions. P/D.

Patten, Thomas H. "Time for Organization Development?" *Personnel,* March-April 1977, pp. 26-33.

Author identifies the various ways in which time influences OD's success of failure. Does the organization and the consultant have enough time? Is the organization ready and the political climate right? These questions and others are discussed. P/D.

Post, James E. Marc J. Epstein. "Information Systems for Social Reporting," *Academy of Management Review,* Vol. 2, No. 1, 1977, pp. 81-87.

Social accounting currently involves developing information about the organization's economic and social consequences. Case studies are used to describe two basic scanning approaches. T/C.

Reid, Douglas M. "Human Resource Planning: A Total for People Development," *Personnel,* Vol. 54, No. 2, March-April 1977, pp. 15-25.

A vice-president of one of Xerox's personnel departments describes the objectives, procedures, problems, and successes of their human resource planning system. Copies of forms, grids, and criteria used are included. P/D.

Roberts, Karlene H. and Charles A. O'Reilly. "Interpersonal, Work Group, and Organizational Communication: A Systemic Approach to Understanding Organizations," Califorina University, Berkeley Institute of Industrial Relations, August 1976, 58 p. Report No. TR-13 Contract N00014-69-A-0200-1054.

Discusses the various aspects of the research conducted by the Office of Naval Research. Using the concept of communication, as a unifying variable across individuals, the overall purpose of the research program was to assess organizations as social-psychological systems. Presents some possible applications of the results. T/C.

Schaub, Alfred R. "The Power of Poor Communications," *Journal of Educational Communication,* Vol. 1, No. 2, September-October 1975, pp. 4-5.

Presents a case that most breakdowns in communications result from a bid for power by organizational members, not the result of poor communication training. Organizational power may be accrued by withholding information, sabotaging communications, refusing to communicate bad news to superiors, and avoiding confrontations by not communicating at all. P/D.

Schermerhorn, John R. "Information Sharing As An Interorganizational Activity," *Academy of Management Journal,* Vol. 20, No. 1, 1977, pp. 148-153.

Data from 76 hospital administrators were examined in terms of the Path model, and it was found that information sharing is positively related to hospital size. FS.

Schuelke, L. David. "The Processes and Effects of an Internal Technology Discovery Program Upon Management, Minnesota University, St. Paul," paper presented at the International Meeting of the Forest Products Research Society, Toronto, Canada, July 1976, 10 p. ERIC ED 130 344.

Summarizes a field study concerned with the effects of a technology-monitoring program on communication activities, behaviors, and attitudes of employees. Twenty company managers who participated reported more frequent communications, concerning innovation, with supervisors, co-workers, people in different units within the company, and individuals not employed in the company. FS.

Schwartz, D. F. and E. Jacobson. "Organizational Communication Network Analysis: The Liaison Communication Role," *Organizational Behavior and Human Performance*, Vol. 18, No. 1, February 1977, pp. 158-174.

Evidence is presented supporting the validity of employing a sociometric procedure for identifying liaison persons as individuals who perform linking functions among primary groups in a complex organization. FS.

Shapero, Albert. "The Effective Use of Scientific and Technical Information in Industrial and Non-Profit Settings: Explorations Through Experimental Interventions in On-Going R&D Activities. Progress Report No. 2," Texas University—Austin, College of Business Administration, 1976, 54 p. ERIC ED 121 269.

Focuses on mapping the information-communication behavior of the engineering division of the Southwest Research Institute. Data include questionnaires, library records, travel records, telephone records, and contractual information. Findings show the need for better description and differentiation of different kinds of high-value information-communication behavior. FS.

Spector, Bertram I., Richard E. Hayes, and Mary Jane Crain. "The Impact of Computer-Based Decision Aids on Organization Structure in the Task Force Staff," Caci Inc.-Federal, Arlington, VA, Policy Sciences Division, September 1976, 260 p. Report No. CAC210 Contract N00014-76-C-0072.

Develops a set of operational hypotheses concerning the potential impact of computer-based tactical decision aids on task force command organization structure. A descriptive and prescriptive contingency model of organization structure is developed to project organization structures that maximize decision aids exploitation. The model is applied to task force decision environments and effective organization structures are derived. T/C.

Taylor, Richard L. "Communication Network Efficiency and Efficiency Stability in Four Urban Secondary Schools," 1974, 12 p. ERIC ED 123 743.

Describes the communication network efficiency and network efficiency stability of four urban high schools. Data was collected by using a sociometric questionnaire and a computer-developed communication matrix. Analysis of the data indicate that neither communication network efficiency nor network stability was significantly related to school size. FS.

Tichy, N. M. and H. A. Hornstein. "Stand When Your Number is Called: An Empirical Attempt to Classify Types of Social Change Agents," *Human Relations*, Vol. 29, No. 10, October 1976, pp. 945-967.

Four types of change agents are identified (Outside Pressure Type, Analysis for the Top Type, Organizational Development Type and People Change Technology type). FS.

Wergin, Jon F. *et al.* "The Practice of Faculty Development," *Journal of Higher Education*, Vol. 47, No. 3, May-June 1976, pp. 389-408.

Based on a 2-year-old faculty development program at an urban university, a model is derived that describes faculty development as an evolving process beginning with low mutual knowledge and trust and an "expert" consulting role, developing into greater mutual knowledge and trust, and a more "collaborative" consulting role. P/D.

Wheeler, Daniel W. and Thomas A. Petrie. "Decision-Making in a Teaching Center," *Clearing House*, Vol. 49, No. 5, January 1976, pp. 233-236.

Discusses ways to share, understand, and contribute to proper courses in colleges and to practice new ideas in the public schools. Decision making, as a result, will have to adjust to a more collaborative mode. Describes a decision making process which has been utilized in the Fredonia-Hamburg Teacher Education Center for the past three years. P/D.

Wigand, Rolf T. "Communication and Interorganizational Relationships Among Complex Organizations in Social Service Settings," 1976, 81 p. ERIC ED 122 313.

Explores communication and information flow in relation to organizational concepts. Ninety-one representatives of social service agencies at each hierarchical level were interviewed. Four communication networks were generated from the responses allowing for the construction of communication maps on the following topic areas: client referrals, direct treatment/service delivery, planning/innovation, and interpersonal relations. Consolidation and application of technology and use of checks on communication flow is recommended. FS.

Wiio, Osmo A. "Organizational Communication Studies: The LTT and OCD Procedures," paper presented at the Annual Meeting of the International Communication Association, Chicago, IL, April 1978.

Presents a summary of the communication audit studies (1970-1977) at the Helsinki Research Institute for Business Economics in Helsinki, Finland. Provides a definition of organizational communication; reviews methodological problems in applying a 75 question instrument measuring communication climate; and derives the following conclusions from audits of 22 organizations involving 5,578 persons in a total population of 30,000: 1) Organizational communication is situational; 2) Dissatisfaction with organizational communication increases with organizational distance between the source of information and the receiver; and 3) Direction of communication flow has an effect on organizational communication satisfaction with receivers being less satisfied than senders of information. FS.

(No author; alphabetized by title)

"AIPRC—BIA Management Study: Management Information," *American Indian Journal*, Vol. 2, No. 12, December 1976, pp. 7-12.

Provides some significant management observations on the content, flow, timeliness, and usefulness of management information as it is generated and communicated throughout the Bureau of Indian Affairs. FS.

"Information Transfer with the Ohio College Library Center Program as a Model. Paper No. 4," Michigan Library Consortium, Detroit, May 1975, 11 p. ERIC ED 111 378.

Discusses the possibility of the Michigan Library Consortium networking with the Ohio College Library Center as a data base. Recognizes the need for developing an international scale, for improving technology, and for creating administrative and communication structures to provide interface between network components. P/D.

"Management Information Study of Nursing Education, Santa Clara County, California," Allied Health Manpower Council of Santa Clara, CA, June 1972, 57 p. Grant PHS-NU-09521-01.

Discusses a study conducted to determine whether there existed a lack of coordination in utilization of health care facilities for nursing schools, deficient articulation between various nursing programs, and a shortage of nursing personnel in the organization. Analyzes the county programs' effectiveness. FS.

"Manual for Applying Management by Objectives to Human Services Programs," North Carolina Department of Human Resources, Raleigh, June 1973, 22 p.

Presents a manual for the use of management by objectives to human service programs. Basic concepts of management by objectives are formulated for each department, division, and employee within an organization. Goals, service objectives, constraints, strategies are discussed. P/D.

"Social Planning and Decision Making in Washoe County, Nevada, Volume 1," Community Services Agency of Washoe County, Reno, NV, December 1974, 73 p.

Describes a research project, proposing a decision-making mode to increase the information available in allocating resources and setting priorities. The decisionmaker's model is a four step process: Needs assessment, policy conference, priority setting, and resource allocation. Implementation of this model is recommended. FS.

SEE ALSO

Intragroup Variables: Taylor
Intergroup Variables: "Assessing and Improving Communications about School Programs & Services. A Handbook for the Professional Staff"
Communication Factors & Organizational Goals: Balk, Franklin, Hackman & Pearce & Caminis, Hackman, Hazelwood *et al*, Katerburg & Herman & Hulin, Lauderdale, Lederman & Costigan & Rogers, Pennings & Goodman, Peterson & Vogt, J. W., Seeborg, Smith, Strauss, Vogt, M. T., Wilde, Wergin
Software & Hardware: Alter, Flory, Lunine, McGough, "Social Services Information System: Management Overview Manual," "Study of the Quality and Organizational Structure of Information & Referral Services Presently Operating. Aggregate Report," Sylvia, Wuiff & Baker
Research Methodology: Langdale, Sussman & Krivonos
Texts, Anthologies, Reviews, and General Bibliographies: Bard & Zacker, Evan & Hamish, Farace & Monge, Galbraith, Hawley & Rogers, Hopper, James & Jones, Jaques, Lusato, Melcher, Pugh & Hining, Zaltman

RESEARCH METHODOLOGY IN
ORGANIZATIONAL COMMUNICATION

BOOKS AND DISSERTATIONS

Aghamirmohamadali, Alinaghi S. *A Study of the Relationships of Achievement Tendency of Secondary School Principals and Teachers with the
Principals' Leadership Behavior as Rated by Their Superiors and Subordinates.* Ed.D. Dissertation, University of Houston, 1976. DAI, Vol.
38, No. 1, p. 33-A.

Questions the sensitivity of the Profile of Organizational Characteristics
(Likert) to discriminate between different operational styles of management in education. Indicates that the Likert Profile was developed for
industry and business, and a new instrument should be developed for
education. FS.

Armstrong, Michael E. *A Study of the Organizational Climate Within a
Selected School District and Its Relationship to Social Character Structure of the District Leaders.* Ed.D. Dissertation, University of Houston,
1976. DAI, Vol. 38, No. 1, p. 33-A.

Reports that the *Survey of Organizations Questionnaire,* originally designed for industrial organizations, is applicable in an educational setting. FS.

Cole, Frank W. *The Relationship Between Teacher Openness and the
Rokeach Dogmatism Scale, the Education Scale VII, the Walberg-
Thomas, and the FIRO-F.* Ed.D. Dissertation, Northern Illinois Univer-
sity, 1976. DAI, Vol. 36, No. 4, p. 1972-A.

Studies principals' and students' perceptions of teacher openness and
concludes that of the four instruments used, Kerlinger's Education
Scale VII is the most accurate predictor of teacher openness when correlated with children's ratings, and when used to predict the composite
of principals' and children's ratings. FS.

Elbert, Norbert F. *An Examination of the Influence of Method Variance
on Climate-Satisfaction Measurements.* DBA Dissertation, University of
Kentucky, 1976. DAI, Vol. 37, No. 9, p. 5924-A.

Concludes that the three measures studied (Organizational Practices
Questionnaire—House and Rizzo; Organizational Climate Questionnaire
—Campbell and Pritchard; and Job Description Index—Smith, Kendall
and Hulen—are sufficiently different in structure and content to refute the argument that climate and satisfaction are redundant. T/C.

Ellsworth, John R. *An Investigation of the Relationship Between a Communication Skills Scale, A Dogmatism Scale, and a Behavioral Assessment of a Counseling Simulation.* Ph.D. Dissertation, University of
South Carolina, 1976. DAI, Vol. 37, No. 10, p. 6271-A.

Tests the relationships among the Carkhuff Communication Index Scale, the Dogmatism Scale, and a behavioral assessment of a counseling simulation, finding that the three measures do not correlate with each other regardless of the level of significance. LS.

Fields, Joseph C. *The Identification of a Humanistic Administrative Style.* Ed.D. Dissertation, Michigan State University, 1976. DAI, Vol. 37, No. 12, p. 7433.

Determines that an instrument designed to identify the characteristics of a humanistic administrative style did not yield sufficient data to draw conclusions about leadership style. FS.

Flanders, James N. *A Model for Organizational Behavior and Decision Making in Higher Education: A Methodological Study.* Ed.D. Dissertation, University of South Dakota, 1976. DAI, Vol. 37, No. 10, p. 6298-A.

Constructs an instrument to measure organizational behavior and decision making in a university, concluding that the use of daily logs was an effective technique. FS.

Green, Charles H. *The Organizational Climate Description Questionnaire: A Review and Synthesis of Research Conducted in Elementary Schools, 1963-1972.* Ed.D. Dissertation, University of Georgia, 1976. DAI, Vol. 37, No. 12, p. 7437.

Surveys research employing the Organizational Climate Description Questionnaire in studies of elementary schools, concluding that little attention has been given to the reliability and validity of the instrument. T/C.

Hatfield, John D. *The Development of a Category System for Analyzing Superior-Subordinate Communication Behavior.* Ph.D. Dissertation, Purdue University, 1976. DAI, Vol. 38, No. 2, p. 546-A.

Constructs two interaction category sets (Superior-Subordinate Interaction Analysis System—Form A and Form B) designed to record and analyze the oral message content of superior-subordinate communications. Form A is appropriate only for analyzing transcripts of interactions and Form B is appropriate only for analyzing live interactions or tape recordings. FS.

Isaacson, Randall M. *Development of the Interpersonal Skills Interaction Analysis: An Interaction Analysis Technique to Measure Interpersonal Communication Skills in Small Group Settings.* Ph.D. Dissertation, Michigan State University, 1976. DAI, Vol. 37, No. 9, p. 5702-A.

Concludes that the Interpersonal Skills Interaction Analysis instrument was a valid and reliable method of measuring interpersonal communication skills in small group settings. LS.

Kelliher, Raymond A. *Innovative Leadership Behavior—A Questionnaire for Elementary School Principals.* Ph.D. Dissertation, Boston College, 1977. DAI, Vol. 37, No. 9, p. 5492-A.

Develops a new instrument, the Principal Leadership Behavior Monitoring Questionnaire, as an effective device for determining the potential for curriculum innovation. FS.

Linstone, Harold and Murray Turoff. *The Delphi Method: Techniques and Applications.* Reading, MA: Addison-Wesley, 1975.

Compiles 26 papers primarily concerned with the application of the Delphi technique. The technique is a system for group problem solving which minimizes the problems with communication. Includes articles on the computerization of this method. T/C.

Lynch, Steven B. *Content Validation of the PEEL (Performance Evaluation of the Education Leader) Instrument.* Ph.D. Dissertation, Arizona State University, 1977. DAI, Vol. 38, No. 3, p. 1155-A.

Concludes that the Performance Evaluation of the Educational Leader (PEEL) Instrument is a valid and reliable indication of administrative competence. Further testing was recommended for some of the specific subscales. FS.

McGill, Mary E. *Observation of Communication Behavior: The Development of a Research Method for Use in Health Care Organizations.* Ph.D. Dissertation, The University of British Columbia (Canada), 1976. DAI, Vol. 38, No. 1, p. 371-A.

Tests the applicability of Bales' Interaction Process Analysis to health-care organizations, concluding that it significantly aids the study of communication behavior. FS.

Morrison, Frank E. *Use of the Delphi Technique in Day-to-Day Operrational Decision-Making in a Selected High School.* Ed.D. Dissertation, The University of Tulsa, 1976. DAI, Vol. 37, No. 9, p. 5502-A.

Reports that the Delphi Technique provides opportunity for subordinate input into decision-making. Recommendations for the more effective use of the technique are examined. FS.

Mullins, James W. *Analysis and Synthesis of Research Using the Organizational Climate Description Questionnaire: Organizations Other Than Elementary Schools, 1963-1972.* Ed.D. Dissertation, University of Georgia, 1976. DAI, Vol. 37, No. 12, p. 7452-A.

Summarizes research using the Organizational Climate Description Questionnaire, reporting that the instrument is both reliable and valid. Although a majority of the studies examined were not replicable due to inadequate information provided by researchers, more than fifty percent of the studies were found to have significant results. T/C.

Munzenrider. Robert F. *Organization Climate: Toward a Clarification of the Construct.* Ph.D. Dissertation, University of Georgia, 1976. DAI, Vol. 37, No. 12, p. 7956-A.

Investigates three organizational climate instruments (Likert's *Profile of Organizational Characteristics*, Litwin, Stringer, and Meyer's *Organizational Climate Survey*, and Halpin and Croft's *Organization Climate Description Questionnaire*), and finds considerable commonalities among them. T/C.

Neal, Michael M. *The Development and Validation of a Structured Interview to Identify Potentially Effective Teachers*. Ph.D. Dissertation, Georgia State University—School of Education, 1976. DAI, Vol. 37, No. 10, p. 6191-A.

Tests the comparability of the Purdue Teacher Observation Rating Scale and a structured interview process (CSII-4). Finds that the structured interview may be used in the identification of more effective teachers. FS.

Niehoff, Marilee S. *A Study of Comparative Strategies for Goal Attainment at a Midwest University*. Ph.D. Dissertation, Illinois State University, 1976. DAI, Vol. 37, No. 10, p. 6191-A.

Uses a modified Delphi Technique, and shows that statements on goal attainment strategies on which there was strong agreement on the first of three consensus rounds tended to produce final consensus. Of the four groups (faculty, students, administrators, and recent alumni), faculty members had the lowest rate of consensus. FS.

Rahim, M. Afzalur. *Managing Conflict Through Effective Organization Design Technology*. Ph.D. Dissertation, University of Pittsburgh, 1976. DAI, Vol. 37, No. 7, p. 4477-A.

Reports that organizational designs using MAPS (Multivariate Analysis, Participation, and Structure) to achieve congruent peoples clusters generated less intragoup and intergroup conflict. The output of the MAPS design was significantly greater than the output of designs containing incongruent peoples clusters. LS.

Robinson, William L. *Lines of Communication Within the University of Kansas Described by the System-Semantics Methodology*. Ph.D. Dissertation, University of Kansas, 1976. DAI, Vol. 38, No. 2, p. 548-A.

Demonstrates utility of the Systems Semantics Profile, a semantic differential instrument, in a study of organizational communication. FS.

Rollins, Kenneth M. *Relative Importance of Three Channels of Face-to-Face Communication in the Inference of Attitude by Educational Administrators*. Ph.D. Dissertation, Georgia State University—School of Education, 1976. DAI, Vol. 37, No. 7, p. 4044-A.

Concludes that the Mehrabian formula, which assigns various weights to communications content, vocal expressions and facial expression, is functional for educational administrators. LS.

Rooney, John F. *The Relationship Between the Measure of Organizational Climate and the Pennsylvania Educational Quality Assessment Inventory*.

Ed.D. Dissertation, Lehigh University, 1976. DAI, Vol. 36, No. 4, p. 1925-A.

Reports that there are significant correlations between some aspects of teacher perception of organizational climate as measured by the Organizational Climate Description Questionnaire and the condition variables of the Pennsylvania Educational Quality Assessment Inventory in thirty-two elementary schools. FS.

Sellick, Jay P. *A Procedural Model for the In-Process Assessment of an Ongoing Management-By-Objectives System of Administration.* Ph.D. Dissertation, George Peabody College for Teachers, 1976. DAI, Vol. 37, No. 8, p. 4766-A.

Develops an assessment model designed to identify the strengths and weaknesses of ongoing management-by-objectives programs. The instrument was found to be applicable to any organization. FS.

Seltzer, Joseph J. *The Organizational Implication of Group Composition as Related to the MAPS Design Technology.* Ph.D. Dissertation, University of Pittsburgh, 1976. DAI, Vol. 37, No. 7, p. 4479-A.

Finds that MAPS (Multivariate Analyses, Participation, and Structure) Design Technology, the system of clustering congruent people in groups, could be altered so that operational (routine) work is differentiated from strategic (planning) work. LS.

Smith, Carol A. Z. *The Development of a Measurement Instrument to Test the Application of the Differentiation-Integration Theory Concepts to Boston College.* Ph.D. Dissertation, Boston College, 1977. DAI, Vol. 38, No. 3, p. 1169-A.

Concludes that the measurement instruments designed by Lawrence and Lorsch to test the relationship of an industrial organization to its environment, were appropriate for higher education. FS.

Tomlinson, William E. *An Educational Planning Model to Facilitate the Systematic Interaction of Educational Decision Information.* Ed.D. Dissertation, The University of Tennessee, 1976. DAI, Vol. 37, No. 11, p. 6892-A.

Develops an educational planning model designed to use educational decision information. The model was found to be generalizeable to various school settings. FS.

Vadhanapanich, Saisawan. *Cost and Effectiveness Functions of Instructional Technology Systems: A Mathematical Model.* Ph.D. Dissertation, The Florida State University, 1976. DAI, Vol. 37, No. 6, p. 3330-A.

Develops a cost model and an effectiveness model to assist in the analysis of instructional technology. Provides cost categories (research and development costs, investment costs, and annual operating costs) and effectiveness criteria (student achievement, student attitude, system availability, downtime, system capability, and system simplicity). T/C.

Veal, Benjamin L. *A Study of the Relationship Among Teacher Philosophy, Teacher Behavior, and Organizational Climate in Developing Open Educational Practices.* Ed.D. Dissertation, Rutgers University, The State University of New Jersey, 1976. DAI, Vol. 37, No. 6, p. 3545-A.

Concludes that the abbreviated scores for openness on the Organizational Climate Description Questionnaire, as suggested by Croft, differs significantly from the total scores. There is inconclusive evidence to support a stronger relationship between organizational climate and teachers' philosophy. FS.

Wesolowsky, G. O. *Multiple Regression and Analysis of Variance. An Introduction for Computer Users in Management and Economics.* New York: Wiley and Sons, 1976.

Explains multicolinearity and focuses on errors in interpreting various coefficients and tests. Presents guidelines for selecting or excluding variables for regression, for interpreting multiple linear regression, and for extrapolation for purposes of prediction. Includes the advantages of the regression approach over analysis of variance. T/C.

Wilson, Sherwood A. *A Description of the Intercultural Communication Workshop Using Content Analysis.* Ph.D. Dissertation, University of Minnesota, 1975. DAI, Vol. 37, No. 6, p. 3434-A.

Finds that CONTENT (a computerized form of communications content analysis) was a reliable form of interaction analysis in an intercultural communication workshop setting. FS.

ARTICLES, PAPERS, AND U.S. GOVERNMENT REPORTS

Alexander, Ralph A. *et al.* "The Relationships Among Measures of Work Orientation, Job Attribute Preferences, Personality Measures, and Abilities, Akron University, OH, Department of Psychology, August 1975, 36 p. Report No. TR-7 Contract N00014-74-A-0202-0001.

Indicates that different measures of intrinsic and extrinsic orientation are neither operationally nor conceptually equivalent. Low relationships were found to exist among different measures of preference for job structural attributes. Individual preferences for job attributes were found to be significantly and differentially related to individual job related abilities, interests, and value orientations. FS.

Alley, William E., James W. Wilbourn, and George L. Berberich. "Relationships Between Performance on the Vocational Interest-Career Examination and Reported Job Satisfaction," Air Force Human Resources Lab, Brooks AFB, TX, December 1976, 32 p. Rerport No. AFHRL-TR-76-89.

Describes validation of an Air Force vocational interest inventory in the enlisted force. The Vocational Interest-Career Examination (VOICE) was administered to 18,000 recruits during basic training. After one year they were surveyed to determine job satisfaction. The Armed Services Vocational Aptitude Battery (ASVAB) served as control measures. Multiple regression analyses were used to characterize relationships between entry-level interests and eventual job satisfaction. Results of analyses indicated that VOICE provided reliable and significant prediction of job satisfaction for both males and females. FS.

Bolyard, William T. "Job Satisfaction: A Comparison of the Job Descriptive Index and Hoppock Measures," Air Force Institute of Technology, Wright-Patterson AFB, OH, School of Engineering, December 1976, 71 p. Report No. GOR/SM/76D-2.

Compares various measurements for job satisfaction including the measure of satisfaction with various aspects of the job and the measure of overall satisfaction. Using Hoppock's measurement of satisfaction and Smith, Hulin, Kendall's Job Descriptive Index, analysis of the data showed that Hoppock's measure includes several aspects studied by the JDI with the exception of pay levels and satisfaction. FS.

Buck, Ross. "A Test of Nonverbal Receiving Ability: Preliminary Studies," *Human Communication Research*, Vol. 2, No. 2, Winter 1976, pp. 162-171.

Develops a test of the ability to decode affect in others through the use of videotaped sequences of facial expressions and gestures. FS.

Caron, Paul F. "What is a Management Audit. How and Why it Should be Applied to Project Management in the Navy," Defense Systems Management College, Ft. Belvoir, VA, May 1974, 47 p.

Defines management auditing and the resulting benefits, explaining why a management audit should be applied to project management in the Navy, and how a management audit could be conducted. P/D.

Chase, L. J. and R. B. Chase. "A Statistical Power Analysis of Applied Psychological Research," *Journal of Applied Psychology*, Vol. 61, No. 2, April 1976, pp. 234-237.

Compared to fields such as social psychology, education, and communication the field of applied psychology is relatively strong in terms of average statistical power. T/C.

Crecine, John P. "Report of the Study Group on Organizational Change and Adaptation to the National Institute of Education, Washington, DC: HEW," 1974, 98 p. ERIC ED 131 548.

Discusses ways to conduct research on educational institutions and their development and adaptation to the environment. The three major sections of the report focus on a different method of organizing and structuring research on the adaptiveness of educational systems. T/C.

Duffy, Paul J. "Development of a Performance Appraisal Method Based on the Duty Module Concept," Army Research Institute for the Behavioral and Social Sciences, Arlington, VA, Agusut 1976, 45 p.

Analyzes duty modules as applied to the 30 entry-level specialty fields of the Officer Personnel Management System (OPMS) to determine job performance dimensions. Defines eight performance dimensions which are incorporated in the Job Proficiency Appraisal Form (JPAF). Allows ratings to be made by the immediate supervisor, another supervisor familiar with the ratee's work and one or more of the ratee's associates. FS.

Dunham, Randall B., Frank J. Smith, and Richard Blackburn. "Validation of the Index of Organizational Reactions With the JDI, the MSQ, and Faces Scales," *Academy of Management Journal*, Vol. 20, No. 3, September 1977, pp. 420-432.

A factor analytic analysis of the Index of Organizational Reactions confirm the satisfaction scales in a study involving more than 1000 employees of Sears. The comparisons with the JDI and MSQ make this an important study of job satisfaction. FS.

Ellison, Robert L. *et al*. "Validation of the Management Audit Survey Against Employment Service Criteria," Institute for Behavior Research in Creativity, Salt Lake City, UT, November 1976, 95 p. Contract DL-20-11-75-39.

Discusses the effects of management practices on productivity of employment service offices by examining employee responses to a 100-item questionnaire—The Management Audit Survey (MAS). The MAS scores with the most significant validities in predicting ES performance criteria were: operational efficiency, performance feedback, work satisfaction, morale, and satisfaction with pay. FS.

Ettlie, J. E. "Time Series Evaluation of the Critical Incidents Technique," *Perceptual and Motor Skills*, Vol. 42, No. 3, June 1976, pp. 875-878.

Critical incident techniques were found to have low convergent validity even when attempts are made to remove selective retention bias. LS.

Felsinger, Richard C. "Productivity Measurement and Enhancement on U.S. Navy Ships," Naval Postgraduate School, Monterey, CA, September 1976, 188 p.

Examines the problem of how to measure and enhance productivity on U.S. Navy Ships. Results showed that the level of productivity was related to four factors: adequacy of supplies, extent of team work, adequacy of planning, and adequacy of tools. A shipboard productivity improvement program was recommended. FS.

Fiks, A. I. *et al.* "Public Assistance Worker Job Trial," Job Trials Research Center, Philadelphia, PA, July 1976, 165 p. Contract No. DL-82-42-72-08.

Discusses the use of the Public Assistance Worker Job Trial which was developed as a personnel selection tool for the position of Income Maintenance Worker Trainee within the Pennsylvania Department of Public Welfare. Methodology used to validate the Job Trail is included. FS.

Goetzman, Gary R. and Wendell B. Wood. "Survey Response Bias: Effects of Introductory Approaches and Feedback on Honesty of Response," Air Force Institute of Technology, Wright-Patterson AFB, OH, School of Systems and Logistics, September 1976, 73 p. Report No. SLSR-19-76B.

Examines the concept of response bias of survey data which render survey findings suspects. It was hypothesized that approaching respondents humanistically and promising feedback in the form of results would reduce response bias. Support for the hypothesis was not achieved. FS.

Goldhaber, Gerald M. "The ICA Communication Audit: Rationale and Development," 1976, 78 p. ERIC ED 127 637.

Discusses the development of the ICA measurement system for analysis of communication in organizations. Includes pilot testing, comparisons between organizations, and development of auditing procedures. T/C.

Herold, David and Martin Greller. "Feedback: The Definition of a Construct," *Academy of Management Journal*, Vol. 20, No. 1, 1977, pp. 142-147.

A factor analysis of 58 Likert items yielded five factors grouped into positive and negative catagories. FS.

Hopp, Michael A. "The Development of Rating Scales to Measure Behaviors Associated with Worker Alienation and Their Perceived Causes," Minnesota University, St. Paul, MN, December 1976, 319 p. Contract DL-91-27-74-08.

Describes the construction and trial of two sets of behaviorally-oriented rating scales to measure worker attitudes. The first scale measures the amount of alienation in individual worker behaviors, while the second scale measures the perceived amount of alienation. A conceptual discussion of the work alienation concept is included. FS.

Howe, John G. "Group Climate: an Exploratory Analysis of Construct Validity," *Organizational Behavior and Human Performance*, Vol. 19, No. 1, 1977, pp. 106-125.

Two formal groups within one organization responded to 16 one-item climate measures in the "in-now," "should-be," and "would-like" frames of reference. Results were favorable for the group climate construct. FS.

Hurt, H. Thomas and C. Ward Teigen, "The Development of a Measure of Perceived Organizational Innovativeness," in *Communication Yearbook I*, Brent D. Rubin, ed., Austin, TX: International Communication Association, pp. 377-385.

A 25-item self-report measure (PORGI) was found to have excellent reliability, constructive, and predictive validity. The measure was found to be a significant predictor of our dimensions of job satisfaction. Employees' satisfaction with their own work was best predicted by individual innovativeness. FS.

Jones, Allan P. and Lawrence R. James. "Psychological and Organizational Climate: Dimensions and Relationships," Texas Christian University, Ft. Worth, Institute of Behavioral Research, March 1977, 75 p. Report No. IBR-77-5 Contract N00014-76-C-0008.

Reviews the basic theories related to the use of aggregating psychological climate scores to describe organizational climate. Results showed that aggregating psychological climate scores to describe organizational climate was useful for homogeneous subunits. FS.

Kirchoff, Bruce A. "Organizational Effectiveness Measurement and Policy Research," *Academy of Management Review*, Vol. 2, No. 3, 1977, pp. 347-355.

Empirical methodologies have not expressed the complexity of effectiveness which is multi-dimensional. A more accurate methodology is presented. T/C.

Kirton, M. "Adapters and Innovators: A Description and Measure," *Journal of Applied Psychology*, Vol. 61, No. 5, October 1976, pp. 622-629.

Describes the development and validation of a measure which distinguishes adaptors from innovators. FS.

Langdale, J. A. "Toward A Contingency Theory for Designing Work Organizations," *Journal of Applied Behavioral Science*, Vol. 12, No. 2, 1975, pp. 199-214.

A measure of bureaucratic-to-human relations organizational design was created. Analysis of responses to the measure indicated that neither bureaucratic nor human relations design strategies are universally appropriate across all organizational settings. FS.

Levine, Donald M. "Management Systems and Organizational Analysis: Part II," *IAR Research Bulletin*, Vol. 16, No. 3, March 1976, pp. 1-7.

Reviews the contributions of several psychological researchers whose work represents four major approaches to organizational research, focusing primarily on the organizational theories of Bion, Miller and Rice, and Levinson. T/C.

Meyer, Marshall W. and Robert O. Williams, III. "A Comparison of Innovation in Public and Private Sectors: An Exploratory Study," California University, Riverside, 1977, 105 p. Grant NSF-PRA75-19967.

Examines the techniques to be used in designing empirical studies comparing innovation processes in private and public sector organizations. T/C.

Mitchell, V. F. and P. Moudgill. "Measurement of Maslow's Need Hierarchy," *Organizational Behavior and Human Performance*, Vol. 16, No. 2, August 1976, pp. 334-349.

Describes a 10-item instrument for the measurement of Maslow's need hierarchy. A factor analysis found five corresponding to security, social, esteem, autonomy, and self fulfillment categories. FS.

Newman, John E. "Development of a Measure of Perceived Work Environment," *Academy of Management Journal*, Vol. 20, No. 4, 1977, pp.
520-534.

The PWE scales provide measures of 11 empirically-desired dimensions
of the perceived work environment. It was developed from data collected
from 1,200 employees in 4 organizations. One part of the study relates
the PWE to job facet satisfaction. FS.

Organ, Dennis. "A Reappraisal and Reinterpretation of the Satisfaction
Causes—Performance Hypothesis," *Academy of Management Review*,
Vol. 2, No. 1, 1977, pp. 46-53.

The hypothesis is reinterpreted in terms of current conceptual approaches, particularly theories of equity and social exchange. The
author argues that more judicious consideration should be given the hypothesis. T/C.

Pfeffer, Jeffrey. "The Ambiguity of Leadership," *Academy of Management Review*, Vol. 2, No. 1, 1977, pp. 104-111.

The analysis of leadership must be contigent on the intent of the researcher, and various conceptual problems are addressed. T/C.

Pierce, Jon L. and Andre L. Delbecq. "Organizational Structure, Individual
Attitudes and Innovation," *Academy of Management Review*, Vol. 2,
No. 1, 1977, pp. 27-37.

A series of propositions are set forth as directions for future research.
T/C.

Pressemier, Edgar A. "Identifying and Testing Communication Opportunities," *Communication Research—An International Quarterly*, Vol. 3,
No. 1, January 1976, pp. 63-75.

Presents a model designed to allow communication analysts to predict
the most promising approach to improving acceptance of a competitive
service or idea. T/C.

Raloff, Michael E. "An Empirical Investigation of a Belief Comparison
Change Model," paper presented at the Annual Meeting of the Speech
Communication Association, Houston, TX, December 1975, 56 pp.
ERIC ED 117 760.

Presents a model to clarify the relationship between persuasive messages
and attitudes. Presents six hypotheses to establish the validity of the
model. Three hypotheses out of the six are confirmed, providing support for the research utility of the model. LS.

Rush, Michael, Jay Thomas, and Robert Lord. "Implicit Leadership Theory:
A Potential Threat to the Internal Validity of Leader Behavior Questionnaires," *Organizational Behavior and Human Performance*, Vol. 20, No.
1, 1977, pp. 93-110.

This study explores two effects of implicit leadership theories on leadership ratings and raises questions about the validity of the Leader Behavior Description Questionnaire. P/D.

Sackman, H. "Toward More Effective Use of Expert Opinion: Preliminary Investigation of Participating Polling for Long-Range Planning," Rand Corporation, Santa Monica, CA, October 1976, 86 p. Report No. P-5570.

Discusses a participating polling technique and its key features: iterative polling, participant interpreted reasons for responses, evaluation, group feedback, and questionnaire design, and analysis. Explains why other techniques, such as Delphi, impose severe limitations which must be overcome. FS.

Schwartz, Donald F. and Eugene Jacobson. "Organizational Communication Network Analysis: The Liaison Communication Role," *Organizational Behavior and Human Performance*, Vol. 18, No. 1, 1977, pp. 158-174.

The utility of a procedure for describing and analyzing communication networks was tested on 142 college faculty. Differences were found that lead to a systematic understanding of liaison roles. FS.

Selvidge, Judith. "Methodology for the Retrospective Evaluation of Decision Analysis," Decisions and Designs Inc., Mclean, VA, September 1976, 42 p. Report No. TR-76-13 Contract N00014-76-C-0074.

Discusses the effectiveness of formal techniques of decision analysis. Users of decision analysis are encouraged to evaluate their experience after every analysis and to produce general statistics concerning the strengths and weaknesses of decision analysis as it is used. T/C.

Steers, R. M. and D. N. Braunstein. "A Behaviorally Based Measure of Manifest Needs in Work Settings," *Journal of Vocational Behavior*, Vol. 9, No. 2, October 1976, pp. 251-266.

Describes the development and validation of an instrument measuring the four needs of achievement, affiliation, autonomy, and dominance. FS.

Stumpff, John F. and Roger Douglas, "An Analysis and Proposal for Revision of the Coast Guard Enlisted Performance Evaluation System," Naval Postgraduate School, Monterey, CA, December 1976, 121 p.

Analyzes the Coast Guard enlisted performance evaluation system which requires a semiannual evaluation of all enlisted personnel in the areas of proficiency, leadership, and conduct. A format and methodology was designed for development of a new performance evaluation system that will differentiate individual performance as well as aid in individual career development through counseling. P/D.

Sussman, Lyle and Paul Krivonos. "Reducing the Distortion in Upward Distortion Data," paper presented at the Annual Meeting of the Western

Speech Communication Association, San Francisco, CA, November 1976, 21 p. ERIC ED 132 619.

Reviews the various approaches to operationalizing "Upward distortion," and emphasizes those which are misleading, and suggests operational procedures which will improve measurement of upward distortion. Four categories of operational definitions are reviewed: disparity scores, questionnaire—interview data, actual encoding of messages, and selection-transmission of messages. T/C.

Sykes, Richard E. "A Design for Observer Sampling of Member Interaction in a Large, Spontaneous Group," Minnesota System Research Inc., Minneapolis, February 1977, 38 p. Report No. TR-3 Contract N00014-75-C-0075.

Describes a technique for studying the frequency of interaction by observers of large, spontaneous groups. The technique employed was based on estimates made of size of the counts necessary to infer the existence of informal groups from a large matrix of such counts. T/C.

————. "Development of Measures of Attitudinal and Structural Similarity," Minnesota Systems Research Inc., Minneapolis, February 1977, 68 p. Report No. TR-4 Contract N00014-75-C-0075.

Compares various scales for measuring the effects of structural and attitudinal similarity, proximity on interaction, and attraction. Results of the scaling test are included as well as simple descriptive statistics on the responses. FS.

Terborg, James R. *et al.* "Organizational and Personal Correlates of Attitudes Toward Women as Managers," *Academy of Management Journal*, Vol. 20, No. 1, 1977, pp. 89-100.

The validity of the Women as Managers Scale (WAMS) is discussed, and attitudes were regressed on the variables of sex, age, education, and marital status. T/C.

Weick, Karl E. "Laboratory Experimentation with Organizations: A Reappraisal," *Academy of Management Review*, Vol. 2, No. 1, 1977, pp. 123-138.

Laboratory experiments are either sensible or senseless. There are no independent variables in nature. Laboratory studies have often been criticized legitimately, but the criticized studies probably represent a restricted sample of what can be done with laboratory techniques. T/C.

Wilborne, James M., Nancy Quinn, and Sandra A. Leisey. "Validation of Non-Verbal Measures for Selection and Classification of Enlisted Personnel," Air Force Human Resources Lab, Brooks AFB, TX, December 1976, 24 p. Report No. AFHRL-TR-76-72.

Discusses the potential usefulness of nonverbal measures in future operational test batteries of enlisted military personnel. Findings substantiate validity and utility of these measures. FS.

Young, George C. "An Empirically Testable Model of Maslow's Theory of Human Motivation: Specification and Analysis," Air Force Institute of Technology, Wright-Patterson AFB, OH, May 1976, 231 p. Report No. AFIT-TR-76-11.

Reviews the basic concepts related to Maslow's theory. This experimental study designed nine hypotheses testing the validity of the underlying theory, against data on Air Force officer and enlisted personnel. Results indicated no evidence supporting the hypotheses derived directly from Maslow's theory. FS.

Yelland, Robert C. "Better Tests," *Training and Development Journal*, Vol. 30, No. 5, May 1976, pp. 42-44.

Discusses the feasibility of using multiple choice questions as a reliable procedure in testing trainees. Suggestions for test construction are offered. T/C.

Zytowski, Donald G. "Predictive Validity of the Kuder Occupational Interest Survey: A 12- to 19-Year Follow-Up," *Journal of Counseling Psychology*, Vol. 23, No. 3, May 1976, pp. 221-232.

Presents a study of more than 1000 persons who were located more than 12 years after taking the Kuder Occupational Survey. Fifty-one percent were employed in occupations consistent with their early interest profiles. These people did not report greater job satisfaction or success but did show greater continuance in their occupational career. FS.

(No author; alphabetized by title)

"Occupational Employment in Manufacturing Industries, Florida, 1974," Florida Department of Commerce, Tallahassee, Office of Research and Statistics, October 1975, 95 p.

Discusses the development of the Occupational Employment Statistics program as a major tool in meeting educational and training objectives. This system collects data on recurring basis and in a manner that will permit estimates by industry at the national, state and area levels. P/D.

"SESA Productivity Measurement System: Measuring the Productivity of the State Employment Service Agencies," Analytic Systems Inc., Vienna, VA, September 1976, 234 p. Contract DL-20-11-75-47.

Reviews a procedure for measuring the productivity of state employment service agencies. The purpose of the research was to identify outputs resulting from Employment Services treatment, to develop quantification procedures and means to combine and weigh all quantifiable outputs. FS.

"System Operator's Manual: Management and Social Services Information System," Wyoming Department of Health and Social Services, Cheyenne, Division of Public Assistance and Social Services, 1973, 59 p.

Presents a supporting documentation for a profile of the Management and Social Services Information System (MSSIS) in Laramie, Wyoming (SHR-0001107). A guide to methods of data accumulation, information processing, and preparation of management and statistical reports is described. P/D.

SEE ALSO

Interpersonal Variables: Cahn, Landy

Communication Factors & Organizational Goals: Carrell & Dittrich, Krivonos, Reely, Wergin

Communication System Analysis: Bass, Hanson, Kilmann, Schwart & Jacobsen

Texts, Anthologies, Reviews, and General Bibliographies: Shonyo

COMMUNICATION YEARBOOK 3

Editor: DAN NIMMO
   (Dept. of Political Science, University of Tennessee, Knoxville)

What is the Communication Yearbook?

Over the past quarter of a century the study of communication has emerged as one of the fastest growing, most topically diverse, richly multi-disciplinary and international in scope of scholarly enterprises. Each year witnesses a vast increase in the number of reported new research techniques, methodologies, perspectives, findings and controversies. Until recently an up-to-date view of what was taking place in the burgeoning communication sciences could be obtained only by tediously following developments in innumerable books, monographs, journals and conference papers appearing throughout the world.

Now, however, the International Communication Association has undertaken the publication of a series of annual volumes affording scholars easy access to reviews, syntheses and critiques of developments in key substantive areas of communication theory and research. Under the editorship of Brent D. Ruben, the first volume, *Communication Yearbook 1,* appeared in 1977 and *Communication Yearbook 2* was published the following year. Each volume provided reviews and commentaries, state-of-the-art overviews covering various dimensions of communication, representative studies and an extensive index.

What about Communication Yearbook 3?

The third volume in the *Yearbook* series builds upon its predecessors, yet offers attractive innovations. Retaining the basic *Yearbook* format COMMUNICA-TION YEARBOOK 3 contains the following variety of selections:

a. **Review and Commentary** articles provide critical and informative syntheses in areas of generic relevance to all communication scholars no matter what their particular specialization.

b. **Theory and Research Overviews** provide opportunities for reviewing current trends in the diverse substantive domains within communication, sometimes updating and integrating theory and research in an entire area or at others reviewing developments in a subarea of particular importance.

c. **Selected Studies** are edited versions of reports of current research that have been competitively chosen for special recognition at the annual conference of the International Communication Association.

d. **The Index** facilitates continuity of COMMUNICATION YEARBOOK 3 with earlier volumes in the series. Author and concept indices provide ready access to key topics, ideas and methodological dimensions.

To order, write: International Communication Association
   Balcones Research Center, 10,100 Burnet Road
   Austin, Texas 78758
   AC 512 836-0440, ext. 3061

TEXTS, ANTHOLOGIES, REVIEWS, AND GENERAL BIBLIOGRAPHIES

TEXTS

Allen, Richard K. *Organizational Management Through Communication*, New York and London: Harper & Row Publishers, 1977.

Reviews and integrates the two disciplines of management and communication. Includes such topics as organizational structure and management, the role of communication in management, management control of information flow, and the manager as change agent, interpersonal motivator, and small group leader. T/C.

Baird, John E. *The Dynamics of Organizational Communication*. New York: Harper & Row, 1977.

Provides an introduction to theories of communication and organizations. Covers motivation, interviews, group dynamics, leadership, and communication channels and networks. Each chapter is followed by a series of brief case histories illustrating the material covered. Takes a systems perspective in studying communication in the organizational context. T/C.

Bard, Morton and Joseph Zacker. *The Police and Interpersonal Conflict: Third Party Intervention Approaches*. Norwalk, CT: Police Foundation, 1976.

Examines third party intervention strategies employed by police officers and whether such approaches could systematically be taught to police officers. Concludes that "policing as a discipline contains a vast body of untapped knowledge about conflict management." P/D.

Behling, Orland and Chester Schrieheim. *Organizational Behavior*. Boston, MA: Allyn and Bacon, 1976.

This text is divided into two units: Theory and research, and application. Each section discusses individual, group, and structural variables. T/C.

Bernstein, Paul. *Workplace Democratization*. Kent, OH: Kent State University Press, 1977.

Discusses the changing nature of authority in the working environment. Includes a study which supports the notion that organizations are changing toward greater worker participation in decision making. P/D.

Bowen, Peter. *Social Control in Industrial Organizations, Industrial Relations and Industrial Sociology*. London: Routledge and Kegan Paul, 1976.

Emphasizes the sociological aspects of organizational theory. Also discusses social change and conflict. T/C.

Bowers, David G. *Systems of Organization: Management of the Human Resource.* Ann Arbor: Michigan Press, 1976.

Summarizes the theory and research of Rensis Likert. Includes such topics as motivation, group psychology, and leadership. T/C.

Bowman, J. D. and B. D. Branchaw. *Understanding and Using Communication in Business.* San Francisco, CA: Canfield Press, 1977.

Covers such topics as writing skills, reports, letters, reading, listening, nonverbal communication, interpersonal communication, oral communication, small groups, organizational communication, formal presentations, and job applications. P/D.

Brennan, John. *The Conscious Communicator: Making Communication Work in the Work Place,* Addison-Wesley Publishing Co., Reading, 1974.

Directed towards persons interested in understanding and improving communication in professional relationships. Reflects on the nature of communication and provides guidelines for better communication. Also provides models for evaluating individual and organizational behaviors, plotting career progress, and improving the communication climate. Can be used in training activities. T/C.

Castetter, W. B. *The Personnel Function in Education,* 2nd edition. New York: Macmillan Publishing Company, Inc., 1976.

Discusses the thesis that "individuals are the most important of organizational components." Focuses on manpower planning, compensation, collective negotiations, personnel information, and continuity of personnel service. Perceives personnel administration as achieving organizational purposes by strengthening the individual in his relationship with the system. T/C.

Cohen, Allan R. *et al. Effective Behavior in Organizations: Learning from the Interplay of Cases, Concepts, and Student Experiences.* Homewood, IL: Richard D. Irwin, 1976.

Adopts a social-psychological perspective in discussing such topics as interpersonal relations, leadership, and group dynamics. Includes a series of case studies chosen to illustrate the topics discussed in the text. T/C.

Davis, Keith. *Human Behavior at Work: Organizational Behavior,* 5th edition. New York: McGraw-Hill, 1977.

Discusses such topics as social environment, group processes, communication networks, as well as other traditional topics. T/C.

DiSalvo, Vincent C. *Business and Professional Communication: Basic Skills and Principles.* Columbus, OH: Charles E. Merrill Publishing Co., 1977.

Covers such topics as interviewing, oral reports, and small group interaction in addition to general introductions to organizations and communication. P/D.

Duncan, W. Jack. *Essentials of Management.* Hinsdale, IL: The Dryden
Press, 1975.

Summarizes the theory and research on such topics as communication,
motivation, leadership, decision making, and group processes. Primarily
an introductory management text. P/D.

Dyer, William G. *Insight to Impact Strategies for Interpersonal and Organizational Change.* Provo, UT: Brigham Young University Press, 1976.

Discusses general communication concepts and techniques useful for
"anyone who finds his interaction with others does not have the results he intends." P/D.

Evan, William M. *Organization Theory: Structures, Systems and Environments.* New York: John Wiley and Sons, 1976.

Presents outlines of the general theory of organization based on three
models: structural, systematic, and environmental. Examines these
models in four parts: assumptions underlying hierarchical designs, problems of role strains and interpersonal conflicts, complex boundary relations among organizations, and trans-organizational environments. T/C.

Farace, Richard V., Peter R. Monge, and Hamish M. Russell. *Communicating and Organizing.* Reading, MA: Addison-Wesley, 1977.

Views organizational communication from a system perspective. Focuses
on communication variables and includes sections on communication
networks, information load, and coping with overload. T/C.

Faules, Don F. and Dennis C. Alexander. *Communication and Social Behavior: A Symbolic Interactionist Perspective.* Reading, MA: Addison-
Wesley, 1977.

Takes a symbolic interaction perspective. Focuses on the interdependence between communication and social behavior emphasizing the use
of symbols. Part IV is devoted to organizational communication. T/C.

Finch, Frederic, Halsey R. Jones, and Joseph A. Litterer. *Managing for Organizational Effectiveness: An Experimental Approach.* New York:
McGraw-Hill Book Company, 1976.

Presents theory, demonstrations, and simulations for leader-subordinate
relations. Can be used in training. T/C.

Galbraith, Jay R. *Organization Design.* Reading, MS: Addison-Wesley Publishing Company, 1977.

Utilizes an information processing model to explain organization design.
Presents more traditional perspectives on the topic along with case
studies. T/C.

Hall, Douglas T. *Careers in Organizations.* Palisades, CA: Goodyear Publishing Company, 1976.

Includes discussions of communication related topics such as job training, job reviews, and occupation information planning. Primarily an introductory textbook. P/D.

Hall, Richard H. *Organizations: Structure and Process,* 2nd edition. Englewood Cliffs, NJ: Prentice-Hall, Inc., 1977.

Emphasizes the role of organizations in society and the importance of the political processes within organizations as crucial decisions are made regarding the directions organizations will take. Also includes discussions of leadership, decision making, organizational change, and communication. T/C.

Hargreaves, J. *Good Communications: What Every Manager Needs to Know.* Wiley & Sons, 1977.

Examines the structure of communication and its flow vertically and horizontally. Gives some checkpoints for success, and deals briefly with some of the techniques. Geared to practicing managers. P/D.

Harlem, Ole K. *Communication in Medicine: A Challenge to the Profession.* Basel, Switzerland: S. Karger, 1977.

Covers the broad topics of the relationship between communication and medicine, the process of communication, and communication in practice. Topics include doctor-patient relationships and communication, writing, interpersonal communication, medical instruction, and models of communication. Designed for members of the health professions. T/C.

Harris, Morgan and Patti Karp. *How to Make News and Influence People.* Blue Ridge Summit, PA: Tab Books, 1976.

Outlines steps to follow in developing publicity or in public relations work for organizations from the local to national levels. Topics include "how to write a news story," "how to use photographs," and "how to get your stories published." P/D.

Hatch, Richard. *Communication in Business.* Chicago, IL: Science Research Association, 1977.

Integrates theory and practice in its discussion of business communications. Emphasizes the psychological basis of communication. Discusses why messages should be constructed in certain ways. The topics covered include communication processes, messages drafting, media selection, communication preparation, job application, report writing, and memos. T/C.

Heirs, Ben and Gordon Pehrson. *The Mind of the Organization.* New York: Harper & Row, 1977.

Emphasizes creative thinking as a way of improving organizational productivity. Organizational problems are attributed to faulty thinking. T/C.

Hopper, Robert. *Human Message Systems.* New York: Harper & Row Publishers, Inc., 1976.

Presents the two major methods of teaching communication: through practice-performance and through theories and principles. In addition, the book presents sections relevant to organizations: communication concepts including listening; human communication codes including nonverbal systems; levels of predictions including relationship development and organizational systems; and public communication including coping with messages. T/C.

Huse, Edgar F. and James L. Bowditch. *Behavior in Organizations: A Systems Approach to Management,* 2nd edition. Reading, MS: Addison-Wesley, 1977.

Covers such topics as: "The Organization as a System"; "The Individual in the Organization"; "Interpersonal Perception and Communication"; "Groups in Interaction"; "Influence, Power, and Leadership"; and "Toward an Integrated Systems Theory of Organizational Development." T/C.

Ingalls, John D. *Human Energy: The Critical Factor for Individuals and Organizations.* Reading, MA: Addison-Wesley Publishing Company, 1976.

Formulates a theory of human motivation based on group dynamics, psychoanalysis, and Eastern religion. Other topics discussed include problem definition and solution, organizational development, experimental learning, and organizational dysfunctions. T/C.

Jaques, Eliott. *A General Theory of Bureaucracy.* London: Heinemann, 1976.

Argues for formalization of authority in bureaucracies, and emphasizes the necessity of distributive justice systems. Argues that such changes make organizations compatible with principles of democratic theory. T/C.

Johnson, Bonnie McDaniel. *Communication: The Process of Organizing.* Boston, MA: Allyn and Bacon, 1977.

Integrates communication theory with research on organizational behavior. The introductory section is based on theoretical concepts such as meaning, organizational intelligence, and organizational integration. Also covers implications for persons working in organizations. The second section discusses the types of communication situations found in organizations. The third section deals with the implications of organizational structure for communication. T/C.

Klein, Howard J. *Other People's Business: A Primer on Management Consultants,* New York: Meson/Charter, 1977.

Reviews many examples to show how and why consultants influence corporate decisions as much as they do. Provides covert pointers about how to be a successful consultant. P/D.

Landy, Frank J. and Don A. Trumbo. *Psychology of Work Behavior.* Homewood, IL: The Dorsey Press, 1976.

Focuses on the individual worker as the unit of analysis. Treats industrial and organizational psychology as the application of psychological principles and methods to problems in the work content. Includes sections on personnel decisions, interviews, and other nontest predictors, motivation, leadership, job satisfaction, and role of the organization in behavior, designing machines for people, and performance abilities, and limitations. T/C.

Levinson, Harry. *Psychological Man.* Cambridge, MA: The Levinson Institute, 1976.

Explicates a Freudian perspective of man in the work environment. Includes a theoretical discussion of personality and emotional stress, and specifically addresses the problem of applying these theories to managerial situations. T/C.

Lillico, Michael. *Managerial Communication.* New York: Pergamon Press, 1977.

Includes extensive reference to data collected by the author, and emphasizes the pragmatic aspects of communication in organizations. Integrates recent research with the traditional research on organizational communication, e.g. communication networks, managerial styles, interpersonal communication, norms. Also contains a chapter on improving organizational communication. Appendixes include the instruments used by the author in his study of 7 electronics companies. T/C.

London, Keith. *The People Side of Systems.* Berkshire, England: McGraw-Hill, 1976.

Provides a useful guide for designing and implementing information systems. Particular emphasis is placed on dealing with humans in this process. Topics discussed include communicating to systems users, motivaton, interviewing techniques, and management decision making. Primarily designed for practitioners. P/D.

Lussato, Bruno (translated by Alison R. Julien). *A Critical Introduction to Organizational Theory.* New York: Holms and Meier Publishing Company, Inc., 1976.

Views the history and development of organization theories and establishes a new theoretical approach using concepts borrowed from linguistics and psychoanalysis. T/C.

Macoby, Michael. *The Gamesman: The New Corporate Leader.* New York: Simon and Schuster, 1976.

Explicates an ideal typology of managers based on personality attributes. Adopts a humanistic perspective reminiscent of Freud and Marx. Criticism is given to the work of Maslow and McGregor. T/C.

Melcher, Arlyn. *Structures and Process of Organizations: A Systems Approach.* Englewood Cliffs, NJ: Prentice-Hall, 1976.

Develops a model of intra-organizational behavior. Structural variables such as size, task, work flow, control systems, departmentalization, and sanctions are considered primary determinants of organizational behavior while leadership styles and personality variables are considered mediating factors. T/C.

Oaks, L. Robert. *Communication by Objective.* South Plainfield, NJ: Groupwork Today, Inc., 1977.

Discusses functional aspects of communication. Covers external communication topics such as public relations, telephone solicitations, speaker bureaus, etc. and internal communication topics such as staff motivation, annual reports, and writing. Primarily for practitioners in voluntary organizations. P/D.

Pugh, D. S. and C. R. Hining (editors). *Organizational Structure: Extensions and Applications.* Hants, England: Saxon House, 1976.

Discusses several experiments and theoretical perspectives relevant to organizational structure. Includes section headings of: Structure in Context; Extensions to Other Forms of Organization; and Relationship to Performance. T/C.

Reitz, H. Joseph. *Behavior in Organizations.* Homewood, IL: Richard D. Irwin, 1977.

Includes comprehensive coverage of contemporary research in communication. Includes specific chapters on interpersonal attraction, group formation, communication networks, group decision making, conflict, influence and power, and leadership behavior. T/C.

Richardson, Ivan L. and Sidney Baldwin. *Public Administration: Government in Action.* Columbus, OH: Charles E. Merrill, 1976.

Presents a text in public administration which includes chapters on communication, decision making, and leadership. P/D.

Rosenblatt, S. Bernard, Richard T. Chetham, and James T. Watt. *Communication in Business.* Englewood Cliffs, NJ: Prentice-Hall, 1977.

Covers both theory and application of communication concepts. Theory topics include communication and management, business communication systems, persuasion, nonverbal communication, and visual communication. Application topics include interviewing, report writing, and mass media selection. The appendix includes examples of many types of written communication used in business organizations. P/D.

Roskey, Edward H. *Communicating in Organizations.* Cambridge, MA: Winthrop Publishers, 1977.

Designed for practitioners, this book is application oriented. Includes communication models, listening, managerial style, communication planning, and media utilization. Each chapter includes a statement of objectives, skill development exercise, and the transcript of a panel discussion between managers and scholars concerning the chapter's topic. P/D.

Rothman, Jack, John L. Erlich, and Joseph G. Teresa. *Promoting Innovation and Change in Organizations and Communities: A Planning Manual.* New York: John Wiley and Sons, 1976.

Designed primarily for students. Discusses strategies for promoting innovation, organizational change, increasing participation, and promoting effective role performance. P/D.

Scott, William G. and Terrence R. Mitchell. *Organization Theory: A Structural and Behavioral Analysis* 3rd edition. Homewood, IL: Richard D. Irwin, Inc., 1976.

Covers classical, neoclassical, and systems theory; management of individuals and groups; various organizational processes; and concepts and technologies of organizational change. T/C.

Simon, Herbert A. *The New Science of Management Decision.* Revised edition. Englewood Cliffs, NJ: Prentice-Hall, 1977.

Discusses the future of management, particularly as it is affected by automation. Emphasizes the importance of authority and structure for organizational decision making, worker satisfaction, and even creativity. T/C.

Steers, Richard M. *Organizational Effectiveness.* Santa Monica, CA: Goodyear Publishing Company, 1977.

Summarizes the literature on employee performance, technology, and environment. Offers guidelines for improving an organization's effectiveness. Includes suggestions in the areas of communication, personnel training, job design, organizational change, and goal setting. T/C.

Steiner, Richard. *Managing the Human Service Organization.* Beverly Hills, CA: Sage Publications, 1977.

Adopts a problem-solving method in discussing problems relative to service organizations such as communication, conflict, motivation, management training, and evaluation. T/C.

Sutermeister, Robert. *People and Productivity.* New York: McGraw-Hill, 1976.

Covers both human and mechanical factors which affect worker productivity. Offers extensive discussion of the literature on job satisfaction and motivation. Includes a series of articles on theory, research, and criticism. T/C.

Vogel, Robert A. and William D. Brooks. *Business Communication.* Menlo Park, CA: Cummings, 1977.

Deals with importance of communication on the job, employment interviews, business conferences, and preparation and presentation of formal business speaking. P/D.

Wofford, Jerry C., Edwin A. Gerloff, and Robert C. Cummins. *Organizational Communication: The Keystone to Managerial Effectiveness.* New York: McGraw-Hill, 1977.

Takes an interdisciplinary perspective. Provides a textbook intended for both undergraduate and graduate students. Discusses many issues and terms that have arisen in organizational communication during the last 20 years. T/C.

Zaltman, Gerald and Robert Duncan. *Strategies for Planning Change.* 1977.

Discusses various tactics available for creating social change through: bringing together current literature on innovation and organizational change; identifying the experiences of change agents; and pinpointing various considerations that change agents must be sensitive to and stating numerous principles as guidelines. T/C.

ANTHOLOGIES

Ansoff, F. H., R. P. Declerck, and R. L. Hayes, eds. *From Strategic Planning to Strategic Management.* New York: Wiley & Sons, 1976.

Twenty contributors concentrate on interaction between firm's capabilities and strategy. Views problem from an economic, psychological, sociological, informational, and political perspective. T/C.

Arnold, William E. and Robert O. Hirsch. *Communicating Through Behavior.* St. Paul: West, 1977.

Presents readings that are divided into two major sections: elements of communication and communication settings. Includes an essay on legal communication which has implications for organizational settings. T/C.

Craig, Robert L. editor. *Training Development Handbook.* 2nd edition. Madison, WI: McGraw-Hill, 1976.

Includes a collection of articles in the areas of training purposes, program development, training applications, media and methods, and training resources. Articles discuss communication training, group methods, programmed instruction, instructional systems, organizational development, etc. P/D.

Eakins, Barbara, editor. "SISCOM '75 Women's (and Men's) Communication Proceedings of the SCA's Summer Conference," avail. Speech

Communication Association, Falls Church, VA, 1975, 214 pp. ERIC ED 127 643.

Consists of papers dealing with: interpersonal communication between the sexes; current research in the field; sex differences in language, speech, and nonverbal communication; stereotyping in both sexes' speech; and the use, evaluation, and generation of nonprint media on the subject of communication. Particularly applicable in the training environment. T/C.

Gilmer, B. von Haller and Edward L. Deci. (Eds.) *Industrial and Organizational Psychology.* 4th edition. New York: McGraw-Hill, 1977.

Provides a current reader in industrial psychology which includes new studies on nonverbal communication (environmental psychology), leadership, and motivation. Includes traditional studies as well as the new. T/C.

Gruneberg, Michael. *Job Satisfaction: A Reader.* New York: Halsted Press, 1976.

Includes several readings on the Herzberg theory of satisfaction as well as readings on the effects on job satisfaction of participative decision making, job design, reference groups, organizational structure, age, sex, and education. The last part of the book covers the relationship between satisfaction and turnover, absenteeism, and work performance. T/C.

Hackman, I. Richard and Loyd Suttle (Eds.) *Improving Life at Work: Behavioral Science Approaches to Organizational Change.* Santa Monica, CA: Goodyear Publishing Co., 1977.

Covers traditional topics of career development, work design, and rewards systems with chapters on group and intergroup relations as well as managerial style. T/C.

Hawley, Willis D. and David Rogers. *Improving Urban Management.* Beverly Hills, CA: Sage Publications, 1976.

Includes several articles on organizational change and innovation in public administration. P/D.

Huseman, Richard C., Cal M. Logue, and Dwight L. Freshley. *Readings in Interpersonal and Organizational Communication.* Third edition. Boston, MA: Holbrook, 1977.

Presents articles relative to the nature of communication, organizational structure, upward and downward communication, conflict, motivation, interviewing, small groups, listening, etc. P/D.

Ruben, Brent D. (Ed.) *Communication Yearbook I.* New Brunswick, NJ: Transaction Books, 1977.

Compiles the first annual publication of the "divisional top three" papers presented at the International Communication Association each year. Pages 331-385 are devoted to organizational communication. FS, T/C.

GENERAL BIBLIOGRAPHIES

Balachandran, Sarojini. *Employee Communication: A Bibliography*, American Business Communication Association, Urbana, IL, 1976, 55 p.

Includes annotated bibliography of several hundred items published since 1965. The categories included are: communication in management, communication in personnel management, reports to employees, attitude surveys, employee publications, bulletin boards, employee evaluation and ratings, and employeee motivation and training. P/D.

Bolch, Eleanor, *et al.* "Information and Referral Services: An Annotated Bibliography," Institute for Interdisciplinary Studies, Minneapolis, MN, June 1972, 254 p. Grant SRS-93-75051.

Presents a collection of abstracts in the field of information and referral services that were prepared by the staff of the Information and Referral Center Study at the Institute for Interdisciplinary Studies (IIS). Intended for those providing information and referral services and for those with a general interest in the coordination of human services. P/D.

Earles, James A. and William R. Winn. "Assessment Centers: An Annotated Bibliography," Air Force Human Resources Lab., Brooks AFB, TX, May 1977, 26 p. Report No. AFHRL-TR-77-15.

Includes research studies to determine best methods for arriving at a single evaluation of managerial potential from assessment center data, and reports on validities of assessment center evaluations. The general finding is that assessment center evaluations are more predictive of future management success than traditional evaluations. P/D.

Falcione, Raymond L. and Howard H. Greenbaum. *Organizational Communication 1976: Abstracts, Analysis, and Overview.* A joint publication of the American Business Communication Association, Urbana, IL, and the International Communication Association, Austin, TX. December, 1977.

Provides over 1,000 abstracts of the literature for the year 1976 in the form of a classified and annotated bibliography. Abstracts are divided into classifications of the organizational communication discipline, including books and dissertations, articles, papers, and government publications. An overview of the literature and two indexes are also provided in this volume.

Grooms, David W. "Decision Making in Management (A Bibliography with Abstracts)," National Technical Information Service, Springfield, VA, July 1977, 249 p.

Reviews decision making research on Federal, state, and local government. Discusses various decision making aids and evaluations of objectives used in decision making. This bibliography contains 244 abstracts. P/D.

Shonyo, Carolyn. "Human Work Measurements (A Bibliography with Abstracts)," National Technical Information Service, Springfield, VA, December 1976, 96 p.

Summarizes measurement techniques of human work at jobs and tasks. Included are topics on work analysis and evaluation, workload management, operations analysis, task complexity, and performance measurement. T/C.

————. "Industrial Psychology (A Bibliography with Abstracts)," National Technical Information Service, Springfield, VA, December 1976, 196 p.

Reviews the theoretical and applied aspects of the physical work environment, attitudes, and personnel relations. T/C.

————. "Job Satisfaction. Volume 2. 1975-October, 1976 (A Bibliography with Abstracts)," National Technical Information Service, Springfield, VA, October 1976, 158 p.

Reviews selected abstracts of studies on specific and generalized areas of civilian and military job satisfaction. Attention focuses on improvement of management techniques and personnel development. P/D.

Young, Mary E. "Labor Relations. Volume 2, 1975-April 1977 (A Bibliography with Abstracts)," National Technical Information Service, Springfield, VA, May 1977, 130 p.

Contains an updated bibliography discussing labor management relationships, labor problems, effects of labor unions and labor attitudes. P/D.

————. "Mathematical Models of Manpower and Personnel Management. Volume 2. 1974-July 1977 (A Bibliography with Abstracts)," National Technical Information Service, Springfield, VA, July 1977, 207 p.

Cites reports dealing with models of manpower allocation, systems, and requirements, as well as specific task systems, forecasting and evaluation. Both military and civilian requirements are covered. T/C.

REVIEWS

Chapanis, Alphonse. "Interactive Human Communication: Some Lessons Learned From Laboratory Experiments," John Hopkins University, Baltimore, MD, Department of Psychology, September 1976, 55 p. Report No. TR-5 Contract N00014-75-C-0131.

Discusses 11 experiments on interactive communication. Some of the findings are: 1) face-to-face communication is generally wordier than communication by voice alone; 2) communicators are much more likely to take control of a communication system if the system has a voice channel; 3) natural human communication is extremely unruly; 4) oral communication is highly redundant. T/C.

James, L. R. and A. P. Jones. "Organizational Structure: A Review of Structural Dimensions and Their Conceptual Relationships with Individual Attitudes and Behavior," *Organizational Behavior and Human Performance*, Vol. 16, No. 1, June 1976, pp. 94-113.

Reviews and synthesizes research on organizational structure. T/C.

Kirschenbaum, Howard. "Clarifying Values Clarification: Some Theoretical Issues and a Review of Research," *Group and Organization Studies*, Vol. 1, No. 1, March 1976, pp. 99-116.

Explores some of the major components of the values clarification theory and discusses some of the most frequent criticisms which have been made of the theory. A major part of the paper summarizes the early research on values clarification and reviews nineteen more recent studies. T/C.

Lau, A. W. "Organizational Climate: A Review of Recent Literature," paper presented at the Annual Meeting of the Western Speech Communication Association, San Francisco, CA, November 1976, 30 p. ERIC ED 130 359.

Reviews literature on organizational climate with emphasis on conceptual issues. Communication is briefly reviewed as an important component of organizational climate. T/C.

Rabinowitz, S. and D. T. Hall. "Organizational Research on Job Involvement," *Psychological Bulletin*, Vol. 84, No. 2, March 1977, pp. 265-288.

Reviews the literature on job involvement via definitions, theoretical perspectives, correlates, and profiles. T/C.

Schroeder, Roger G. and Carl R. Adams. "The Effective Use of a Management Science in University Administration," *Review of Educational Research*, Vol. 46, No. 1, Winter 1976, pp. 117-131.

Provides academic administrators and researchers with a critical review of available tools in management techniques; a structure for considering possible analytical projects to undertake and the steps that should be taken by administrators to ensure proper organization, planning, and control of management science efforts. P/D.

SEE ALSO

Interpersonal Variables: Metzler, Roloff, Sykes
Intragroup Variables: Cooper, Gulley & Leathers, Schlenker, Taylor
Intergroup Communication: Newsom & Scott
Communication Factors and Organizational Goals: Bowers, Clegg, Cummings & Berger, "Decision Making in Educational Organizations," Goodman & Pennings, Hargreaves, Metowidlo *et al.*, Schafer, Steele & Jenks, Weinberg, Young
Skill Improvement and Training: Stenzel & Feeney
System Analysis: Alan & Rowe
Research Methodology: Wesolowsky

appendix 1

Research methods and limitations

Literature Sources

The following literature sources were utilized for this year's volume:

Books: *Subject Guide to Forthcoming Books;* book reviews in leading periodicals; copies of books sent by the major publishers; *Communicontents,* a monthly publication containing abstracts of books in the field of communication published at Arizona State University, Tempe, Arizona.

Dissertations: *Dissertation Abstracts International, Humanities, and Social Sciences,* October 1976-September 1977. Each monthly issue was examined for dissertations relative to organizational communication sponsored by the following disciplines: Business Administration, Economics, Education Administration, Public Administration, Sociology, and Speech; *Dissertation Abstracts International, Sciences,* October 1976-September 1977. Each monthly issue was examined for dissertations relative to organizational communication sponsored by the following disciplines: Industrial Psychology and Social Psychology.

Published Articles: *Applied Science and Technology Index, Business Periodicals Index, Current Index to Journals in Education, Engineering Index, Personnel Management Abstracts, Public Affairs Information Service Bulletins,* and *Psychological Abstracts;* other journals not abstracted in the above indexes were also included. In these cases, the actual articles were abstracted.

Unpublished Papers: *Research in Education.* Unpublished papers were selected from this monthly volume, which is sponsored by the Educational Resources Information Center (ERIC). Full texts of the documents indexed are available on microfiche in research libraries or directly on order from EDRS, P.O. Box 190, Arlington, VA 22210.

U.S. Government Publications: National Technical Information Service (NTIS) of the U.S. Department of Commerce, Washington D.C.

Research Limitations

Time Period Covered: Following the practice of the preceding three volumes of abstracts, the literature appearing in the year 1977 was liberally interpreted as encompassing the period October 1, 1976 through September 30, 1977 in order that the editing and publication might be completed by midyear 1978.

It is important to emphasize the unique problems encountered by generally depending on abstract services, including book reviews. Due to the sheer mass of work involved in reviewing all periodicals, books, dissertations, and unpublished papers, it was decided that maximum use should be made of existing abstract services, but where deficiencies were realized, individual periodicals would be reviewed and abstracted. Thus, where the original publication is not the source of the abstract, and where an abstract service is being used (e.g., Dissertation Abstracts International), the October 1, 1976 through September 30, 1977 dates refer to the dates of publication of the particular abstract service. Consequently, this means that our abstracts for the year 1977 have many 1976 and some 1975 and 1974 dates because these items of literature were first abstracted by the service consulted during the months of October 1976 through September 1977. Hence, the research method results in providing abstracts for some writings published prior to 1977, and does not provide abstracts for many writings published in 1977 because such writings have not as yet been abstracted. In the case of books, a book review appearing in a journal fulfills the same function as an abstract and is subject to the same time limitatations noted above.

Contents of Bibliography: There are inherent reasons why many published and unpublished writings have not come to our attention. *Unpublished* papers may not appear here because they were not processed by the ERIC organization and published in abstract form during the period October 1976 through September 1977. In some cases, the papers may not have been presented to ERIC, and if presented, not accepted. In other cases, the papers may have been accepted but are scheduled to appear in a monthly issue of *Research in Education* subsequent to September 1977. Assuming future annual issues of this publication, these latter abstracts will be encountered and included.

In the area of *published* writings, our general procedure of using existing abstract services (including book reviews) results in our not reporting certain works published in 1977 since they have not yet been abstracted or reviewed by the reference employed, and reporting other works finished in 1976, 1975, and even 1974, where the authors delayed submitting abstracts, or the book review publication was considerably later than the publication of the book. This kind of limitation can be minimized by the consistent use of specified abstract services and keeping abreast of the book reviews in the leading periodicals.

We are acutely aware of the limitations placed on us by following the above methods. There may be many important papers and articles missed by us in this publication. To those authors who feel they should have been included please write and inform us of our oversight, and we will include you in the next volume.

Even though this document may not be fully representative of the literature relevant to organizational communication, it is our feeling that it can make a significant contribution to those students, researchers, teachers, and practitioners interested in a fascinating and rapidly expanding field of study.

Publications available from aBCa:

	Member	Nonmember

Organizational Communication Abstracts—1976

Raymond Falcione and Howard Greenbaum. — $10.00 — $12.00
Over 1,000 abstracts, covering nine categories
of organizational communication, of publications
published in 1976.

Organizational Communication Abstracts—1975

Howard Greenbaum and Raymond Falcione. 700 — $6.00 — $7.00
abstracts of books, dissertations, articles, papers,
and government publications published in 1975.

Organizational Communication Abstracts—1974

Howard Greenbaum and Raymond Falcione. — $4.00 — $5.00
Contains 400 descriptive abstracts.

Guidelines for Research in Business Communication

Prepared for ABCA by the 1976 Research — $5.00 — $6.00
Committee. Part I: Planning and Conducting
Research; Part II: Analyzing Research Data; Part
III: Reporting Research Findings. 96 pages.

Business Communication Casebook Two

Contains 68 problems and cases. An invaluable — $5.00 — $6.00
aid for classroom teachers of business communication. Prepared by the ABCA Committee of
Letters, Reports, and Cases. 1977.

Employee Communication

A partially annotated, ten-year bibliography, — $4.00 — $5.00
1965-1975. Subject headings are: communication
in management, communication in personnel
management, reports to employees, attitude
surveys, employee publications, bulletin boards,
employee evaluation and rating, and employee
motivation and training. 55 pages.

Index to The Journal of Business Communication, Volumes 1-10

In *The Journal of Business Communication*, Vol. — $5.00 — $5.00
13, No. 4, Summer 1976.

Index to The ABCA Bulletin, Volumes 23-38 (October 1958 to December 1975)

In *The ABCA Bulletin*. Vol. XXXIX, No. 4, — $2.50 — $2.50
December, 1976.

Send your order and check to:

American Business Communication Association
911 S. Sixth St.
University of Illinois
Champaign, IL 61820

A $2 fee will be added if we have to invoice you.

appendix 2

Author index

appendix 3

Index of organizational types in field studies of organizational communication

This index is limited to those abstracts describing field studies; and indicates the type of organization furnishing data for each field researcher. The types of organizations are classified as follows:

—Industrial organizations
—Governmental organizations
—Educational organizations
—Health-care organizations
—Other service organizations

In the event that a study analyzed more than one type of organization, that study was indexed under each of the types of organization.

Statistically, of the 343 field studies indexed here, 238 (70%) are contained in books and dissertations and 105 (30%) are contained in articles, papers, and government reports. The distinction between the two formats is maintained because books and dissertations generally contain more data than articles, papers and government reports. Space limitations in articles and papers preclude extensive documentation, exhibits, and bibliography.

The index should be used as follows: Assume that one wishes to read book abstracts relative to field studies of educational organizations. The initial step would be to investigate the category "Educational Organizations" under the section for Books and Dissertations in this index. Authors are arranged alphabetically within each category. Then, reference to the Author Index in Appendix II will provide the page numbers on which abstracts of various studies are located.

For example, *Kay, N.* is found in this index under "Educational Organizations" in the section for Books and Dissertations. Reference to Appendix II (Author Index) indicates that the classified abstract for this field study by Kaye is located on page 226.

BOOKS AND DISSERTATIONS

INDUSTRIAL	GOVERNMENTAL	EDUCATIONAL
Alessandra, A.	Bhandari, L.	Absher, H.
	Bonett, H.	Acton, M.
Barker, R.	Broom, G.	Aghamirmohamadali, A.
Barnett, A.		Allman, J.
Brandt, F.	Caine, B.	Anglin, R.
Brannen, D.	Carrell, M.	Apter, R.
	Cureton, R.	Aragona, L.
Eich, R.		Armstrong, M.
	Dodge, C.	
Farrow, D.	Dunning, C.	Bandy, L.
Fatehi-Sedeh, K.		Barbanell, L.
Fenley, L.	Ezell, A.	Barber, J.
		Bartley, M.
Gaymon, D.	Gaulfeldt, F.	Bateman, C.
Geary, W.		Behrman, E.
Gehrmann, P.	Hackathorn, R.	Berman, W.
	Hale, G.	Blue, T.
Hatfield, J.	Heim, J.	Blumstein, T.
Hoffman, D.		Bonen, R.
	Kilpatrick, S.	Bouch, R.
Jenks, C.	Koenig, R.	Brooks, C.
	Kroeber, D.	Burgett, K.
King, D.		Bunning, R.
Kusterer, K.	Lamoreaux, J.	Burke, B.
	Leenhouts, T.	Buxton, M.
Lyons, A.	Leonard, R.	
		Capie, R.
Mazzaroppi, L.	Marshak, R.	Carter, M.
		Cerullo, N.
Nykodym, G.	Nicholson, J.	Chaplain, O.
		Charlier, P.
Owen, B.	Pollak, P.	Childress, R.
		Chiosso, E.
Pasmore, W.	Ryan, E.	Cibotti, T.
Powell, G.		Coburn, D.
	Scaggs, E.	Cole, F.
Rings, R.	Spencer, W.	Cox, R.
Ryan, S.	Spurgat, F.	Craft, G.
	Stead, W.	Crosby, W.
Schou, A.	Steinhauer, M.	Curtis, G.
Stano, M.		
Streker, I.	Torres, S.	Dachanuluknukul, S.
		Davenport, I.
Vesgo, R.	Whiting, B.	Diran, K.
		Dobbins, J.
Waller, T.	Yeager, S.	Dunagan, F.
Wolfe, M.		Duncan, D.

Gorodezky, M.

Leszczynska, M.

McGill, M.
Mullinx, J.

Steinberg, M.

Wegner, M.

OTHER SERVICE
Lundy, S.
(Consumer Group)

Merton, K.
(Manpwr. Agncs.)

Smith, S.
(Social Welfare)

Thompson, C.
(Physicians)

Wigand, R.
(Social Services)
Wilson, S.
(Commun. Workshop)

ARTICLES, PAPERS, AND GOVERNMENT REPORTS

INDUSTRIAL
Adams, R.
Aranya, N.

Bolyard, W.
Brannen, P.

Cummings, T.

Emery, F.

Gemmill, G.
Grunig, J.

Hackman, J.
Hansen, G.
Hill, J.
Hill, R.
Horan, M.
Housel, T.

Jones, A.

Karasek, R.
Katerburg, R.
Kirten, M.
Klein, L.
Koch, J.
Krivonos, P.

Lillico, M.
London, M.

Martino, J.
Merryman, C.
Moller, I.

Nebeker, D.
Nichols, T.

Penrose, J.

Reinkober, T.
Retondi, J.
Roeber, J.

Schmitt, N.
Schuelke, L.
Schuler, R.
Shapero, A.

Umstet, D.

Warsylik, J.

GOVERNMENTAL
Adams, R.
Air Forces Ocp. Cntr.
Alexander, R.
Alley, W.
Analytic Systems
Applied Mngmt. Serv.
Asbaugh, D.

Baird, L.
Brief, A.
Brownlee, D.

CO Dept. of Soc. Serv.

Duffy, P.

Felsinger, R.
Fiks, A.
Flory, A.

Gould, B.
Grace, G.
Gunderson, E.

Hilgendorf, E.

Johnson, L.

Kennedy, T.

Lancaster County

Mansperger, T.
McGough, D.

Peterson, D.
Powers, T.
Puma, M.

Reeley, R.
Rizzo, W.
Rosenburg, B.

Schmid, J.
Schou, A.
Scoville, P.
Seyboh, J.
Silverman, G.
Spector, B.
Stahl, M.
Sykes, R.

✟✟✟

The
International Communication
Association
Is:

Professional Involvement

ICA was formed in 1950 to bring together academicians and other professionals whose research interests are focused on human communication. ICA has a world-wide active membership, most of which are teaching and conducting research in colleges and universities. Other members are in government, the media, communication technology, business, law, medicine and related professions. ICA Divisions include Information Systems, Interpersonal Communication, Mass Communication, Organizational Communication, Intercultural Communication, Political Communication, Instructional Communication and Health Communication.

Publications

ICA members receive HUMAN COMMUNICATION RESEARCH, THE JOURNAL OF COMMUNICATION and the ICA NEWSLETTER as part of their benefits. HCR features reports of empirical studies and reviews of current research. The JOC is concerned with the study of communication theory, practice and policy. The ICA NEWSLETTER contains news about ICA, its members and significant communication activities throughout the world.

International Conferences

Each year, ICA members have the opportunity to meet to exchange ideas and information about new frontiers and international communication research. ICA's annual conferences have for more than a quarter century been the sites where international leaders in communication research join in scholarly interaction. Occasionally, summer conferences are conducted primarily to permit selected students to interact with noted scholars.

On Membership

ICA has a variety of membership categories available to students and non-students. For additional membership information, please write:

ICA Headquarters
Balcones Research Center
10,100 Burnet Road
Austin, TX 78758

appendix 4

Index of data collection methods in field studies of organizational communication

This index is limited to those abstracts describing field studies, and indicates the data collection instruments utilized by the researchers in order to obtain raw data. The types of data collection instruments and codes adopted for this compilation are as follows:

I—Interview   OR—Organization Records
O—Observation   Q—Questionnaire
L—Log

The index consists of the author name followed by coding for the data collection instruments employed. Thus, for R. Barker (Q1, I, O, OR) listed under Books and Dissertations, the meaning intended to be conveyed by the codes is that Barker employed a self-designed questionnaire (Q1), interviews (I), observation (O), and organization records (OR) for the purpose of deriving data for that study.

In the instance of the questionnaire as a data collection instrument, it was considered valuable to indicate when a researcher employed a recognized instrument, e.g., Smith, Kendall, and Hulin's Job Description Index, as distinct from the researcher utilizing a self-developed instrument. Consequently, the coding of questionnaire instruments involves a numeric following the letter "Q". This numeric allows the reader to refer to Table 11 in order to determine the recognized questionnaire instrument employed or to know if there has been developed a specific questionnaire instrument for the study involved. The questionnaire types are listed in Table 11 with related coding, author of instrument, and frequency of use in the year 1977.

Table 11

QUESTIONNAIRES USED IN 1977 FIELD STUDIES
CODES, AUTHORS, AND FREQUENCY OF USE

Code	Name of Instrument	Author	Frequency of use
1	Self-Designed Questionnaire	Author of Study	137
2	Achieving Tendency Scales	Mehrabian	1
3	Affective Measures of Class Climate	Newberg & Borton	1
4	Air University Faculty Motivation Survey	N/A	2
5	Armed Services Vocational Aptitude Battery	N/A	2
6	Assumption Inventory	N/A	1
7	Behavior Rating Scale	N/A	1
8	Berger Instrument of Acceptance of Self and Others	Berger	1
9	CFK Ltd. Climate Profile	N/A	2
10	Change Agent Questionnaire	N/A	1
11	Change Scale	Trumbo	1
12	Checklist of Trait Names	N/A	1
13	Classroom Observer Rating Scale	Ed. Devel. Center	1
14	Classroom Organizational Climate Questionnaire	Thayer	1
15	Cognitive Style Interest Inventory	N/A	1
16	College and University Environmental Scales	Pace	2
17	Conceptual System Test	N/A	1
18	C S Communication Audit	Koswitz	1
19	CST Agenda Questionnaire	N/A	1
20	CST Group Effectiveness Measure	N/A	1
21	Decision Locator Questionnaire	N/A	1
22	Defining Issues Test	Rest	1
23	Diagnostic Survey for Leadership Improvement	N/A	1
24	Differentiation-Integration Survey	Lawrence & Lorsch	1
25	Dogmatism Scale	Rokeach	3
26	Education Demographic Data Form	N/A	1
27	Education Scale VII	Kerlinger	1
28	Educational Administrative Style Diagnosis Test	N/A	1
29	Educational Beliefs Questionnaire	Walberg-Thomas	1
30	Empathy Scale	Hogam	1
31	Executive Professional Leadership Scale	Gross & Herriott	4
32	Flanders Interaction Analysis Categories	Flanders	1
33	Fundamental Interpersonal Relations Orientation-Behavior	Schutz & Wood	2
34	Fundamental Interpersonal Relations Orientation-Feelings	Schutz	1
35	General Information Questionnaire	N/A	1
36	Gordon Personal Profile	Gordon	1
37	Grapevine Profile	N/A	1
38	Group Climate Questionnaire	Johnson	1
39	Guidance Services Rating Scale	N/A	1
40	Guttman Scales	Guttman	1
41	Hahnemann High School Behavior Rating Scale	N/A	1
42	Illinois Rating of Teacher Effectiveness	N/A	1
43	Index of Adjustment and Values	N/A	6
44	Inner-Other Social Preference Scale	Kassarjian	1
45	Interaction Test (HE-ME)	N/A	1
46	Interpersonal Orientation Scale	Alcorn, Erb, & Davis	1

TABLE 11, CONTINUED

Code	Name of Instrument	Author	Frequency of use
47	Interpersonal Rating Form.	Bales	1
48	Iowa Test of Basic Skills .	Lindquist, Hieronymous, et al.	2
49	Job Description Index	Smith, Kendall, & Hulin.	5
50	Job Functions Inventory for School Principals .	Univ. of Chicago	1
51	Job Proficiency Appraisal Form.	N/A.	1
52	Job Satisfaction Questionnaire	N/A.	1
53	Johari Awareness Model	Luft & Ingham	1
54	Leader Behavior Description Questionnaire	Stogdill.	18
55	Leadership Opinion Questionnaire	Fleishmann	1
56	Leadership Behavior Description Questionnaire	Halpin & Winer	7
57	Least Preferred Co-Worker Scale	Fiedler	4
58	Mach V Attitude Inventory Scale.	N/A.	1
59	Management Audit Survey.	N/A.	1
60	Managerial Grid	Blake & Mouton.	1
61	Managerial Philosophies Scale	Jacoby & Terborg.	1
62	Measurement of Satisfaction.	Hoppock.	1
63	Minnesota Satisfaction Questionnaire	Dawes, Lofquist, & Weiss.	3
64	Network Questionnaire.	N/A.	1
65	Organizational Climate Description Questionnaire	Halpin & Croft	22
66	Organizational Climate Description Questionnaire (1965 Margulies revision).	Halpin & Croft	1
67	Organizational Climate Index 375-SF	Stern & Steinhoff.	1
68	Organizational Development Inventory	Owen.	1
69	Organizational Fairness Questionnaire	N/A.	1
70	Participative Policy Determinator.	Niles	1
71	Pennsylvania Educational Quality Assessment Inventory	State of Penn.	1
72	Personnel and School Data Index.	N/A.	1
73	Personal and Situational Data Form	Bailey.	1
74	Productivity Instrument .	N/A.	1
75	Profile of a School Questionnaire.	Likert.	1
76	Profile of Organizational Characteristics .	Likert.	4
77	Prototypic Profiles	N/A.	1
78	Psychological Participation Index.	Vroom & Mann	1
79	Pupil Control Ideology Form	Hoy et al.	1
80	Purdue Teacher Evaluation Scale	N/A.	1
81	Purdue Teacher Observation Rating Scale	N/A.	1
82	Purdue Teacher Opinionnaire	Bentley & Rempel .	13
83	Quality of Air Force Life Survey	N/A.	1
84	Relationship Inventory.	Barrett & Leonard .	3
85	Risk-Taking Questionnaire.	N/A.	1
86	Role-Taking Test	Feffer.	1
87	Satisfaction with Negotiations Questionnaire	N/A.	1
88	School Administrator Morale Measure	N/A.	1
89	School Management Questionnaire	N/A.	1
90	Selector Aptitude Index	N/A.	1
91	Sentence Completion Test.	Loevinger	1
92	Sociometric Questionnaire.	N/A.	1
93	Status Perception Questionnaire	N/A.	1
94	STS Youth Inventory.	N/A.	1
95	Student Assessment of Teacher Affect.	N/A.	1

TABLE 11, CONTINUED

Code	Name of Instrument	Author	Frequency of use
96	Student-Teacher Interactive Incident Form	N/A	1
97	Styles of Management Inventory	Teleometric International, Inc.	1
98	Supervisor Behavior Style Scale	Blumberg & Amidon	1
99	Supervisory Behavior Questionnaire	N/A	1
100	Survey of Organizations Questionnaire	Univ. of MI	1
101	System-Semantics Profile	N/A	1
102	Teacher Philosophy Questionnaire	Ed. Devel. Cntr.	1
103	Teacher Problems Q-Sort	Bills	1
104	Teacher Response Patterns Inventory	N/A	1
105	Tennessee Self-Concept Scale	Fitts	5
106	University Faculty Questionnaire	N/A	1
107	University of Maryland Attitude Scale	N/A	1
108	University of Maryland Information Questionnaire	N/A	1
109	Value Survey	Rokeach	1
110	Vocational Interest-Career Examination	N/A	1
111	XYZ Test	Reddin	1
112	Homophily-Heterophily Measure	McCrosky, Richmond, & Daly	1
113	Interpersonal Attraction Measure	McCrosky & McCain	1
114	Perceived Supervisory Credibility Measure	Falcione	1
115	Personal Report Communication Apprehension	McCrosky	1
116	Self-Esteem Index	McCrosky & Richmond	1
117	WAT	Daly & Miller	1
118	26 Item Communication Scale	House	1
119	Role Conflict and Ambiguity Scale	Rizzo, House, & Lirtzman	1
120	Job Involvement Scale	Lodahl & Kejner	1

NOTES:

1. N/A: Authorship of instruments employed in field study not available from source of abstract information or from library resources to this date.

2. Techniques as Ecco Analysis, Delphi Technique, and Critical Incident Technique have not been treated as recognized instruments for reason that researchers employ the basic technique in self-designed approaches.

The index below treats books and dissertations separately from articles, papers, and government reports for reasons stated earlier in Appendix III relative to the organization-type index.

Use of this index may be motivated by various circumstances. If the reader is interested in a certain abstract involving field research, this index will provide information as to the research techniques; if the reader is contemplating the use of a certain recognized instrument, this index may provide a lead as to others who have recently employed the same recognized instrument; if the reader is considering empirical research in a type of organization, this index, together with the organizational type index may be able to give some insight as to the instruments heretofore employed.

Examples:

—Reference *H. Absher* (Q21, 73, 82). This should be interpreted as meaning that researcher Absher utilized the Decision Locator Questionnaire (Q21), Bailey's Personal and Situational Data Form (Q73), and Bentley & Rempel's Purdue Teacher Opinionnaire (Q82).

—Reference *R. Bouch* (Q1). This indicates that Bouch employed a self-developed questionnaire (Q1), and that no other data collection methods were noted in the sources furnishing information on this study.

BOOKS AND DISSERTATIONS

Whiting, B. (Q1)
Wigand, R. (O)
Wilson, S. (O)
Wolfe, M. (O)
Wood, D. (O)
Wortman, R. (Q54)

Yeager, S. (O)

Zerla, A. (Q10, 65)
Zibilich, F. (Q82)

ARTICLES, PAPERS, AND GOVERNMENT REPORTS

Adams, R. (Q1)
Air Force Occupational Measure-
    ment Center (Q1)
Alexander, R. (Q1)
Alley, W. (Q5, 110)
Allied Health Manpower Center
    of Santa Clara (Q1)
Analytic Systems (Q1)
Applied Management Services (OR)
Aranya, N. (O)

Baird, L. (Q1, O)
Baker, H. (O)
Bolyard, W. (Q49, 62)
Brief, A. (Q1)
Brownlee, D. (Q40)
Buck, R. (O)

Carrell, M. (Q63, 69)
Clegg, S. (O)
Cummings, T. (Q1)

Danish, S. (O)
Duffy, P. (Q51)

Ellison, R. (Q59)

Falcione, R. L. (Q112, 113, 114,
    115, 116, 117)
Felsinger, R. (Q1)
Fiks, A. (O)

Gemmell, G. (O)
Gould, B. (Q1)
Gunderson, E. (Q1)

Hackman, J. (Q1)
Hansen, G. (O)
Hilgendorf, E. (Q1)
Hill, J. (OR)

Hopp, M. (Q1)
Horan, M. (Q1)
Hurt, H. T. (Q1, 49)

Johnson, L. (O)
Jones, A. (Q1)

Katerburg, R. (Q1)
Kaufman, H. (O)
Kavanagh, M. (Q1)
Kennedy, T. (Q53, 60, 97)
Kirten, M. (Q1)
Kreck, L. (Q1, I)
Krivonos, P. (O)
Krivonos, P. (Q1)

Lancaster County (OR)
London, M. (Q1)
Longest, B. (Q1)

Mansperger, T. (Q1)
March, J. (O)
Martino, J. (O)
McElreath, M. (O)
McGough, P. (O)

Nebeker, D. (Q1)

Penrose, J. (Q1)
Perry, H. (Q1)
Peterson, D. (Q1)
Powers, T. (Q1)

Reeley, R. (Q4)
Retondi, J. (Q1, I)
Roeber, J. (O)

Sackman, H. (Q1)
Schmid, J. (Q1)
Schmitt, N. (Q1)

✝✝✝